PRENTICE-HALL SERIES IN WORLD RELIGIONS

ROBERT S. ELLWOOD, JR., EDITOR

Richard C. Martin

Arizona State University

ISLAM
a cultural perspective

Prentice-Hall, Inc., Englewood Cliffs, New Jersey 07632

Library of Congress Cataloging in Publication Data

Martin, Richard C.
Islam, a cultural perspective.

(Prentice-Hall series in world religions)
Bibliography:
Includes index.
1. Islam. I. Title. II. Series.
BP161.2.M34 297 81-8526
ISBN 0-13-506345-0 AACR2

Interior/cover design by Maureen Olsen
Editorial production/supervision by Frank Hubert
Manufacturing buyer: Harry P. Baisley

For Mother, Father, Eric,
Don, and Roberta—in memory

Printed in the United States of America

10 9 8 7

ISBN 0-13-506345-0

Prentice-Hall International, Inc., *London*
Prentice-Hall of Australia Pty. Limited, *Sydney*
Prentice-Hall of Canada, Ltd., *Toronto*
Prentice-Hall of India Private Limited, *New Delhi*
Prentice-Hall of Japan, Inc., *Tokyo*
Prentice-Hall of Southeast Asia Pte. Ltd., *Singapore*
Whitehall Books Limited, *Wellington, New Zealand*

Contents

3 boundaries of community, faith, and practice 54

4 islamic expressions of form and beauty 69

part 2

FAITH, WORSHIP, AND COMMUNITY

5 belief and thought in islam 88

6 *worship and ritual in islam 113*

7 *community and society in islam 136*

Foreword

The Prentice-Hall Series in World Religions is a new set of introductions to the major religious traditions of the world, which intends to be distinctive in two ways: (1) Each book follows the same outline, allowing a high level of consistency in content and approach. (2) Each book is oriented toward viewing religious traditions as "religious cultures" in which history, ideologies, practices, and sociologies all contribute toward constructing "deep structures" that govern peoples' world view and life-style. In order to achieve this level of communication about religion, these books are not chiefly devoted to dry recitations of chronological history or systematic exposition of ideology, though they present overviews of these topics. Instead the books give considerable space to "cameo" insights into particular personalities, movements, and historical moments that encourage an understanding of the world view, life-style, and deep dynamics of religious cultures in practice as they affect real people.

Religion is an important element within nearly all cultures, and itself has all the hallmarks of a full cultural system. "Religious culture" as an integrated complex includes features ranging from ideas and organization to dress and diet. Each of these details offers some insight into the meaning of the whole as a total experience and construction of a total "reality." To look at the religious life of a particular country or tradition in this way, then, is to give proportionate attention to all aspects of its manifestation: to thought, worship, and social organization; to philosophy and folk beliefs; to liturgy and pilgrimage; to family life, dress, diet, and the role of religious specialists like monks and shamans. This series hopes to instill in the minds of readers the ability to view religion in this way.

I hope you enjoy the journeys offered by these books to the great heartlands of the human spirit.

ROBERT S. ELLWOOD, JR., editor
University of Southern California

Preface

During the time of my undergraduate studies, the late 1950's, most of my generation knew very little about the people and cultures of the Islamic world. Gasoline was cheap and plentiful. The realities and potentialities of conflict in the Middle East were there, but for the most part far from our minds. The media, too, were not much drawn to report on that part of the world. Foreign students from Islamic countries were few and not very visible in our everyday social experiences. Hardly any courses on Islam were taught except at a few universities with graduate centers for specialized research on the Middle East. There were few Departments of Religious Studies, and their curricula seldom encompassed Islam. The world of Islam was barely noticed in the West in those days.

Much has changed since then. The names of Muslim sects and religious leaders have become household words in America. Middle Eastern students, travelers, and businesspeople are now present everywhere in the West. Courses on Islam are in much greater demand and growing supply at many universities. The media consult with ''experts'' in packaging an increasing number of special programs on the Islamic world. In commerce, on campus, and through the communications media we are beginning to learn more about Islam.

This remarkable change seems welcome, but not without some personal misgivings. Western awareness of Islam, as in the days of the Crusades, still seems to run in waves of emotion that threaten to crest in high tides of conflict. In spite of the changes in the media and academia, knowledge and understanding are still in short supply. What is it that impels us to read (and write) about Islam? Is it intellectual curiosity or emotional unrest? Are our reasons selfless, or are they selfish in ways we can't fully comprehend? How much and how well are we prepared to bridge the yawning gap that separates our own experience of the world from the experience of those who see the world as Muslims do?

This book presents an interpretation of Islam as religion. Much that is incontrovertible about Islam—names, dates, places, articulated beliefs, and practices—is to be found in these pages. But the living religious tradition of the more than 700 million Muslims is not just a set of facts to be enumerated and learned, as though Islam could be presented in the style of an almanac. Therefore, I have also attempted to *explain* and *interpret* the information Islam presents about itself. Explanation and interpretation are necessary because we need to understand much that is not merely factual—symbols, myths, rituals, unarticulated beliefs, and values—in short, human cognitive and behavioral patterns that are quite different from those that underpin life in the West.

Offering interpretations, like offering opinions, carries a responsibility.

Although we may mean well, harm is easily done. Here we may be able to learn something from the Islamic impulse toward learned consensus. What we venture to say about other peoples and cultures requires communication and dialogue with the people of those cultures, and furthermore requires meaningful modes of discourse and valid approaches of study within our own intellectual environment.

This book does not follow the usual historical and thematic treatments of Islam found in most works already available. Two reasons can be given for the departures I have taken. First, the present volume is part of a series and so it conforms to a common format. Second, the format of the series allows for the historian of religions to give greater visibility to aspects of the subject that are often overlooked, such as minority and opposition movements, the arts, ritual and worship, and social patterns and structures. Although the use of Arabic and other special ''Islamic'' terms should be kept to a minimum in an introductory textbook, I have nonetheless found it necessary to use some. I have attempted to define and illustrate the meaning of such terms, especially for students who may wish to consult more advanced works, where knowledge of these terms is often assumed. Like the Koran, Islamic culture cannot be satisfactorily translated into completely familiar terms without losing a great deal in the process.

In this regard I should like to mention that the sources available in the preparation of this work have been generally adequate for such an undertaking, even if I have not always understood them as well as I should have liked. Texts and materials from the earliest days of Islam down to the present articulate exceedingly well the various ways in which Muslims have understood their own religious tradition at various times and places. In the course of my studies in America, Europe, and the Middle East, I have enjoyed numerous friendships with Muslim students, professors, and the uneducated as well; their kind handling of my many questions and misunderstandings has made learning about Islam pleasurable and rewarding. Colleagues in the Department of Religious Studies at Arizona State University have helped me to identify viable approaches to the study of Islam as religion. Students in my classes have pushed for understanding when I would have otherwise been content to merely present them with facts. The editors at Prentice-Hall have provided the resources and expertise for making a book out of an author's attempt to write a draft.

I should particularly like to thank Professor Robert S. Ellwood, Jr., of the University of Southern California, who, as General Editor of the Prentice-Hall Series in World Religions, has offered encouragement and useful criticism throughout the project. Professor Richard Eaton of the University of Arizona and Dr. Muhammad Abdul-Rauf, professor at al-Azhar University in Cairo have also read portions of the first draft. Their suggestions and criticisms have been received with appreciation and generally followed. Elizabeth Gottschalk served as my research assistant during the preparation of the first draft when library legwork, typing, and a mountain of details required her competent assistance. Emily Khalid Lovell, a Muslim and student of Islam for many years, helped me immeasurably with the tasks of correcting copy and galley proofs. Holly, my wife and gentle critic, helped me say better in my own native language—English—what I wanted to say, chapter by chapter. Chapter 4 on Islamic art would have been impossible for me to write but for her knowledge of writing about the arts. The shortcomings that remain are a product of my own judgment despite the much appreciated help of friends and colleagues.

RICHARD C. MARTIN

part 1

THE OVERALL PERSPECTIVE

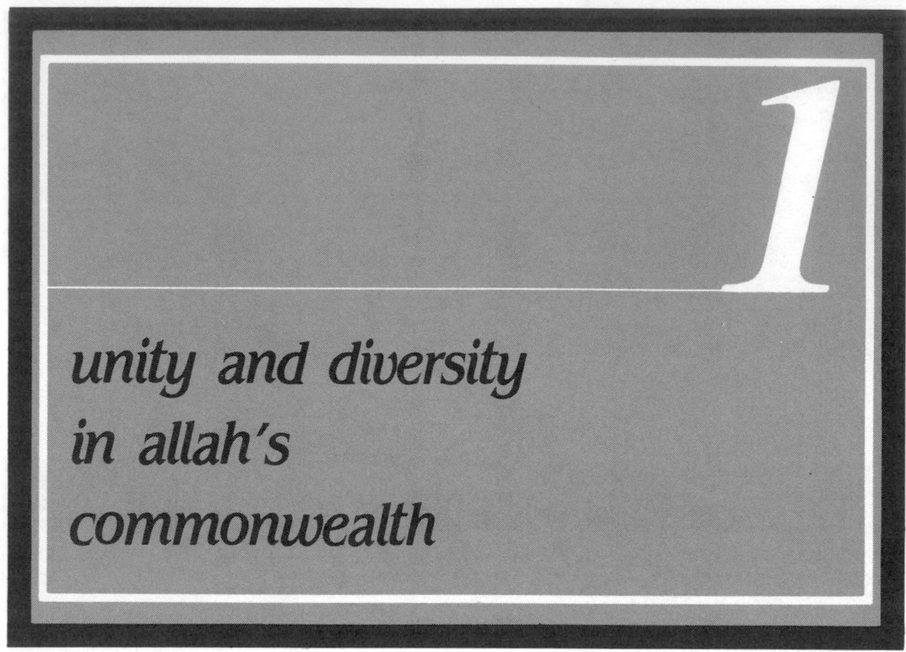

GOD IS THE GREATEST

Being in Cairo should have carried no surprises, but it did. I had taken several courses in Arabic and on Islamic topics, and I had enjoyed numerous friendships with Muslim students as well as many happy moments of sharing food and customs. But all of this had happened in America and Europe. Living in Cairo brought a whole new experience of Islamic culture.

The Western visitor to Cairo is impressed with the great diversity of strange sights, sounds, and smells that greet the senses. Garlic peddlars and tea confectioners call out their wares in musical tones. Bicyclists balance broad trays of flatbread on their heads as they ride through streets snarled with the traffic of man, beast, and machine. Buses are stuffed with Cairo's multitudes, jostling each other frantically for the right of passage to bureaus and bazaars. But above the clamor and din, five times each day there reverberates the central and unifying summons of Muslims to prayer. *Allāhu akbar,* "God is the greatest," it begins.

God is the greatest, God is the greatest,
God is the greatest. I witness that
There is no God but Allah; I witness that
There is no God but Allah. I witness that
Muhammad is His Apostle; I witness that
Muhammad is His Apostle.
Come to the prayer! Come to the prayer!
Come to the betterment! Come to the betterment!
God is the greatest. God is the greatest.
There is no God but Allah.

Allāhu akbar! For more than thirteen centuries this Arabic phrase has sounded from the highest place that the muezzin, the person charged with sounding the call, could climb. From minarets of mosques, piercing upward through cluttered urban skylines, or lacking mosques, from rooftops of houses, the call has been heard throughout the Muslim world. Five times each day this simple statement summons the faithful to prayer. It means God is infinitely greater and more majestic than His entire creation. Sung out in stylized chant, its first utterance announcing, it reaches a high note, a sensation uplifting, above the petty and mundane. In response to this declaration of divine majesty, the prayer is ''performed'' on artfully woven rugs or simple towels spread out in mosques, homes, and sidewalks—anywhere; it is an act that achieves its highest significance in touching the forehead to the ground as an expression of total submission to Allah.

Declaring boldly the greatness of Allah and submitting ritually to His will are central to Islam. The Arabic word *islām* means ''submission'' and ''peace.'' A Muslim is one who submits to Allah and finds therein peace. Tradition teaches that Bilāl, a black slave freed by companions of the Prophet Muhammad, was the first Muslim to chant the summons to prayer. The year was 622 A.D., year one of the Islamic calendar. In the Arabian city of Medina, from the roof of the newly built house which served as the Prophet's home and first mosque, in tones loud and clear, the call sounded. *Allāhu akbar.* Each day since 622 that phrase has continued to rise above the more familiar sounds of this world, declaring divine majesty, summoning the faithful to prayer.

FIGURE 1.1. Muslims performing the Salat, Iran. (Photo by J. Isaac. Courtesy of the United Nations.)

The Witness

The *shahāda* or witness that "there is no God but Allah" and that "Muhammad is His Apostle" is the first of five "Pillars" of Muslim faith and practice. All five Pillars—the witness, the prayer, the giving of alms, fasting, and the pilgrimage to Mecca—play important roles in the intellectual and social dimensions of Islamic life. We will have more to say about the Pillars in this and other chapters. First, the two themes of the witness or Shahada are worthy of attention.

"THERE IS NO GOD BUT ALLAH . . . " Islam is one of the three great monotheistic religions to arise in the Middle East; along with the other two—Judaism and Christianity—it stresses the oneness and unity of God. The word *Allāh* means "the God," the same God confessed and worshipped in the other monotheistic traditions. In the call to prayer, in the Shahada, and in everyday discourse, the name Allah is constantly heard. The name also appears in Arabic writing and calligraphy in books, on mosques and public buildings, and on wall hangings in homes and offices. Allah is the central focus of Islamic religion and culture.

The affirmation of God's oneness and unity is comprehended in the important Arabic religious term *tawḥīd.* The early Muslim community in Arabia, where pagan polytheism had been widely practiced, regarded the *association (shirk)* of other gods with Allah as a serious threat to God's unity. Shirk was the earliest and most repugnant form of heresy. Pagan gods were familiar and pliable beings, made of stone and easily "possessed." The concept of Allah stood above such associations. As Islam spread to lands and cultures outside of Arabia, the Christian doctrine of the Trinity and the Zoroastrian dualistic conceptions of good and evil divine powers were also seen by Muslims as aberrations of God's unity or Tawhid. Muslim theologians sought arguments, both from scripture and through reason, to make persuasive the fundamental oneness and unity of Allah, to the exclusion of other "lesser" gods or plural implications of a "godhead" that threatened that unity. Muslim mystics practiced special meditations or modes of remembrance *(dhikr)* that focused the consciousness upon God, for in their view God was the only Reality. The average Muslim, even without

FIGURE 1.2. "Allah" in Arabic calligraphy.

special theological knowledge or spiritual techniques, nonetheless thinks of God in the way of Tawhid.

". . . MUHAMMAD IS HIS APOSTLE." The second phrase of the Shahada declares that Muhammad is God's chosen messenger to humankind, sent to his own people in seventh-century Arabia. Accepting the Judaeo-Christian Biblical tradition in large part, Muslims believe that God had sent prophets and messengers to other nations in the past with the same revealed message Muhammad was to recite to the Arabs. Muhammad's mission brought the final positing of divine Truth, and thus Muhammad is regarded as the "Seal of the Prophets."

Muslims look to the person and example of the Prophet Muhammad as important spriritual resources. Like the other prophets recognized in the Muslim religion, including Moses, Jesus, and several other Biblical and non-Biblical figures, Muhammad was thought to be an ordinary mortal, a prophet raised from the midst of his own people. Far from having any notion of a divine "nature" or of divine qualities, Muslims remember Muhammad as one of the common people of his time, without formal education or literacy. The contrast between the Prophet's humble circumstances and the reverence in which he is held is truly remarkable. A visit to Muslim homes and places of business is instructive. Pictures and representations of the Prophet and his family are frowned upon and seldom seen, for reasons we will discuss in Chapter 4. Yet ask Muslims about the Prophet, and the response is always enthusiastic and respectful. Queries about Islam are often greeted with responses such as "the Prophet used to say . . . " or "Once while addressing a group of companions the Prophet did such and such."

Both the historical and the religious dimensions of Muhammad's life in seventh-century Arabia are important ingredients of any understanding of Islamic civilization. Along with the *Koran,* God's Word recited by the Arabian prophet, Muslims have looked for guidance in the *Sunna,* Muhammad's example as recorded in his deeds, sayings, and silent approval. His closest companions and those whom they taught during the next two generations carefully transmitted the Prophet's sayings *(ḥadīth)* until the need was felt to write them down and test them for authenticity. In matters of personal piety, public conduct, and legal transactions Muslims often cite both the Koran and the Sunna of the Prophet as authorities.

The proper context for understanding both Koran and Sunna is the life of the Prophet, a story that we shall consider in more detail when we look at the overall history of Islam in the next chapter. We may anticipate the main features of that story by noting the following. Muhammad was born of humble circumstances, as already noted, to a clan belonging to the powerful tribe of Quraysh in Mecca. Raised as an orphan by his uncle, Muhammad had no wealth or education until he was about twenty-five. His marriage to an older widow gained him an important personal relationship as well as some means and experience with the caravan trade that dominated the Meccan economy. His call to be a prophet came when he was about forty, although the message he delivered directly challenged the religious and social values of the time. Thus, he was not immediately well-received and very few people chose to follow him at first. Eventually, he and his followers emigrated from Mecca to Yathrib (later called Medina), an Arabian city that proved to be more hospitable to his leadership. The date of the emigration (Hijra) was 622. During the final ten years of his life, Muhammad completed delivering God's message, and with the help of his growing number of followers, much of Arabia, including Mecca, accepted the religion he preached. The story of his life is dramatic and arresting. It is filled with tensions and conflict—with communities of Jews and Christians but primarily with the tribal paganism that isolated Arabia from the world it was soon to conquer. During Muhammad's lifetime a new civilization was born that radically changed the history of the world.

Koran: The Word of God

Our initial encounter with Islam must include a grasp of the importance of the Koran to Muslims. The Koran is the book that records in beautiful Arabic style, thought to be inimitable by ordinary mortals, the divine message of Allah as it was recited by the Prophet on various occasions during his mission in Mecca and Medina. In literary form the Koran comprises 114 *sūras* (chapters), which vary in length from a few to over two hundred *āyas* (verses). Whereas terms such as "Bible" and "scripture" are derived from words meaning "writing," Koran (Arabic, *qur'ān*) probably comes from a verb which means "to recite." Like other scriptures, the Koran is a book. It contains a message that is comprehensible and meaningful. More than that, however, the Koran is an oral phenomenon. Its distinctive and proper recitation is essential to the total impact it has upon Islamic culture.

A visit to a Muslim town or village will quickly confirm these remarks about Muslim scripture. In both its literary and oral forms the Koran is a constant in Muslim life. Everyday speech is often punctuated by phrases *(āyas)* from the Koran. Muslim children begin their earliest education learning to recite it in the proper manner of enunciation and intonation. An important milestone in life is reached when a Muslim is able to recite the Koran entirely from memory. Koranic calligraphy graces many public buildings and shrines. The Koran dominates Muslim culture as an ever-present symbol and reminder of the communication of God to humankind through His Messenger, Muhammad.

For Muslims the Koran is a divine miracle, recited to the Arabs by specially trained reciters in their own tongue in speech that even the greatest of poets are said to be incapable of imitating. Understood within the Muslim world view, it is the record of God's, not Muhammad's, communication to humankind. Muslims believe the Koran was written on a Heavenly Tablet that was the same source of revelation as that received by earlier prophets. It was delivered to Muhammad by God's angel, Gabriel. The divine nature of the Koran is often compared to the divine nature of Christ as conceived by most Christians. The Koran, not the Prophet, is the word of God.

The message of the various *āyas* and *sūras* is for the most part *plain* and direct, although some passages are recognized to be *obscure* and difficult to understand. Muslims strive constantly to internalize the Koran through memorization and thoughtful reflection on its meanings, yet it is generally acknowledged that the complete meaning is known only to God. Nonetheless, both the plain and the obscure passages are constant subjects of devoted reflection and meditation. The classical commentaries on the Koran continue to be published and studied even as contemporary scholars offer new interpretations appropriate to the changing times.

The oral form of the Koran, the original mode of its deliverance by the Prophet, is still maintained by schools of reciters who take many years of training to perfect their art. Their performance is in constant demand, especially during Muslim festivals and holidays, when the beautiful and distinctive tones of Koranic chanting may be heard throughout Muslim neighborhoods and villages. Even on more personal occasions, such as marriages and deaths, Muslim families often employ the services of a Koran reciter to enunciate properly God's Word to the joy and comfort of those present. Muslims also personally recite brief passages of the Koran on other occasions, particularly during the daily prayers. The more devout may undertake to recite the entire Koran at regular intervals.

FIGURE 1.3. Muslim reciting the Koran.

The Koran is authentic only in its original Arabic form, even for those Muslims who speak little or no Arabic. Thus, the attempt to know and understand its meaning through translations has never been encouraged. For many persons, of course, both non-Muslims and those Muslims who do not speak and understand much Arabic, translations may provide the only access to its meanings. A word of caution is necessary in this regard. Grasping approximate meanings of Koranic sentences, even when they are carefully translated, is not enough. From what we have just learned, it should be clear that the total effect of the Koran in Muslim life cannot be grasped without confronting its Arabic oral and written forms. The non-Muslim student is urged to listen to authentic recordings of Koranic recitation and to gaze upon the pages of graceful calligraphy in which Muslim scripture is recorded, in order to grasp its total import.

THE ABODE OF ISLAM

Who are the Muslims? This question is commonly answered, "the Arabs." This is a mistaken impression that is true only insofar as Islam arose among the Arabs, its Prophet and many of its adherents were and are Arabs, and its scripture, the Koran, when used in worship, must be recited in its original Arabic form. The majority of the world's Arab population, living primarily in the Middle East and North Africa, is Muslim. The Arabs comprise only 25 percent of the present population of Islam, however. In the Middle Ages the Islamic Empire stretched from Spain in the West to India in the East, from Turkey in the North to Yemen in the South—the largest empire of adjoining lands the world has ever known. Many ethnic groups became Muslim along with the Arabs.

Beyond those distant borders of the *Abode of Islam*—the part of the world under Muslim political control—at different times Muslims penetrated into Russia, China, Southeast Asia, Sub-Saharan Africa, and Europe. More recently Islam has taken firm root in North America. Muslims are found in almost every country of the world. They form a majority of the population in thirty-six countries, and nearly half of the population in five others. In 1978 the strength of Islam was estimated at 720 million people, almost one-seventh of the world's population. Islam is the world's third largest religion, behind Christianity and Buddhism, and its present rate of growth and vitality rivals both traditions.

In an important sense the Abode of Islam knows no boundaries. In the Middle Ages boundaries between Muslim and non-Muslim peoples were occasional lines of conflict. Caliphs, the rulers of the Islamic Empire, were responsible for maintaining the peace and defending the faith and the faithful from enemy attack. Beyond the Abode of Islam was the *Abode of War*—often more a geographical concept in a religious than in a military sense. Today Islam no longer forms a single political entity. Vast in size and appeal to all races of mankind, the Islamic world is situated mainly in a broad belt of nonindustrial nations stretching across Africa, the Middle East, South Asia, and Southeast Asia. Some

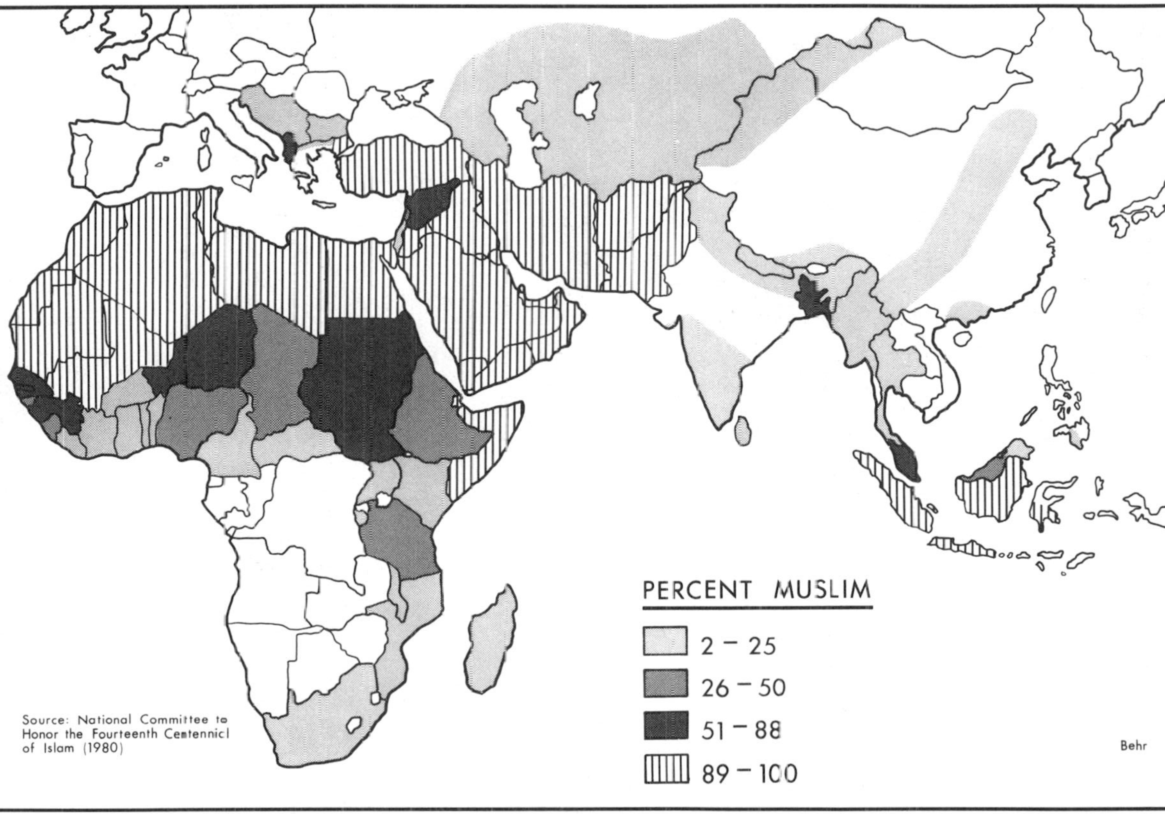

FIGURE 1.4. Distribution of Muslim populations. (Map by Michelle Behr, adapted by permission from "Islam: An Introduction," prepared for a conference in Washington, June, 1980, jointly sponsored by the National Committee to Honor the Fourteenth Centennial of Islam, the Washington Center of the Asia Society, and The Johns Hopkins University School of Advanced International Studies. © 1980.)

Islamic countries, rich in natural resources, especially petroleum, have begun to acquire considerable economic and political power. One consequence has been a much greater visibility of Islamic religion and culture in the Western world.

Islam is often treated as an urban religion by academia, and as a religion of camel-driving nomads by Hollywood. There is much truth in the former image; the latter is partly true, no doubt because the religion originated in a land known for nomads and camels. Great cities such as Cairo, Damascus, Baghdad, and Isfahan, however, have been important centers of Islamic culture for centuries. Achievements in art and architecture are associated with mosques and royal buildings which are urban phenomena. It is also important to realize, however, that Islam has been the faith of peasants as well as princes and Bedouin *shaykhs* (Arabian nomadic chiefs). Today the vast majority of Muslims are sedentary rural dwellers, living primarily in agricultural communities where family units usually extend to include large numbers of kin. Another significant segment of Islamic population continues to live in nomadic tribal structures. Both village and nomadic life sustain cultural systems that have remained relatively isolated from the impact of the modern world. The less modern areas have traditionally retained elements of local folk customs although the main tenets and practices of Islam are firmly held by tribesmen and peasants.

By contrast less than 30 percent of the world's Muslim population lives in cities.[1] There kinship ties are qualified by much greater opportunities for education, social and economic mobility, and alternate lifestyles. Between nomadic and rural Islam on the one hand, and urban Islam on the other, there are many important cultural differences. For Islam the challenge of the twentieth century to religion is occurring chiefly in urban areas.

Sunni Islam

One's first acquaintance with another religious tradition often brings the impression that it forms an undifferentiated whole. This is never the case. Not only do Muslims represent many races and socioeconomic settings, but from a very early time there were significant divisions of opinion within the commonwealth or *umma* of Islam on *how* to be Muslim. The unity of Islam cannot be appreciated fully without a consideration of its diversity and its ability to incorporate divergent interpretations of basic beliefs.

The main body of Muslims is known by the term *Sunni.* The recorded practice and teachings of the Prophet Muhammad were early regarded as his Sunna, an Arabic term meaning "path" or "way." These traditions, as we have seen, became powerful symbols for the Islamic religion, models of right belief and practice. Like all religious symbols, the collection of the Prophet's

[1] On the demography and ethnography of Islam today, see Richard V. Weekes, ed., *Muslim Peoples* (Westport, Conn.: Greenwood Press, 1978).

Hadith or "sayings" comprising his Sunna or "authoritative example" required interpretation and application to a variety of situations in everyday life.

Majority or "Sunni" Islam developed four schools of interpretation whose functions were to decide upon the proper application of the Koran and Sunna to virtually all aspects of the life of the community. Each of the four schools takes its name from a famous early jurist to whom later followers trace many of the school's distinctive opinions: *Hanifites* (after Abū Ḥanīfa, d. 767), *Malikites* (after Mālik ibn Anas, d. 795), *Shafi^c^ites* (after Muhammad al-Shāfi^c^ī, d. 819), and *Hanbalites* (after Aḥmad ibn Ḥanbal, d. 855). Acceptable differences of interpretation exist among the four schools, and a Sunni Muslim may seek to conform his or her practice of Islam to any one of them. Beyond theoretical differences, geographic differences account for the preponderance of one or more schools over the others in given regions of the world of Islam.

What sorts of questions are decided by the jurists of these schools? The answers to many kinds of questions are sought in the Koran and Sunna, and some of the most important are those pertaining to religious duties. For example, every Muslim must perform the daily prayers in a state of ritual purity. Conditions of purity are usually met by prescribed acts of hygiene (which may vary in their particulars from school to school). But what if bathing facilities are not available when the call to prayer sounds? Or what would constitute defilement of ritual purity between the moment of washing and the moment of prayer? Answers to such questions are not arbitrary but must be sought from the traditional bodies of opinion of the Hanifite, Malikite, Shafi^c^ite, and Hanbalite schools. Nor is the extent of religion in Islam determined by ritual alone. Matters pertaining to marriage, divorce, inheritance, and even proper government also come under the jurisdiction of Islamic law.

The learned doctors of law belong to a class of leaders in Islamic society known as the *Ulema*. They are highly respected for their learning in the religious sciences. Islam has no clergy or priesthood as such. Members of the Ulema in every village and city attain such status through their own personal piety and devoted study of the roots of right belief and practice. With respect to Islamic law, by common agreement these roots are (1) the *Koran,* (2) the Prophet's *Sunna,* (3) the learned *consensus* of the Ulema, and (4) reasoning by *analogy* from accepted interpretations of the first two roots to new problems not directly addressed therein.

These four roots had been established as fundamental principles of Islamic law by the ninth century. Late in the seventh century, after the deaths of the four "rightly guided" caliphs (see Chapter 2) who had been living companions of the Prophet, differences of opinion about the meaning of Koran and Sunna began to increase, as we might expect. Some jurists preferred to rely upon the Koran and Sunna entirely. Others felt that even with such awesome bodies of authority as scripture and tradition at hand, an individual's exercise of reason (related to number 4 above) was necessary, especially in those cases where Koran and Sunna seemed to be silent. By the tenth century most jurists maintained the theory that independent reasoning was ended, other than restricted uses of analogy to Koran and Sunna. Arriving at legal opinions through the consensus of learned scholars (number 3 above) was another important principle under considerable discussion. It was based on a Hadith attributed to the Prophet: My Umma (community) will never agree upon an error. In the strict sense this has been taken to mean legal judgments. In practice, however, as we shall see more clearly, consensus is an important social ingredient of Islamic culture. Perhaps this is another way of saying that traditional modes of thought and behavior, though these may differ from place to place, retain a sense of constancy. Even changes in custom require broad consensus based upon interpretations of Koran and Sunna.

All four roots form a concept of the revelation of God's will to the historic community of Islam. The term for this concept is *sharī^{c}a.* Like the notion of Torah in Judaism, Shari^{c}a is more than scripture. It implies a composite source of teaching and practice that presumes the interrelation of divine and human activity. It involves the Koran and the Sunna of the Prophet, and it requires authoritative human interpretation and application. Sunni Islam, comprising the majority of Muslims, has tended to place little social or religious distance between the Ulema and the common people. Understanding and living by the Shari^{c}a with the help of the Ulema have played and continue to play important roles in the social and religious affairs of Sunni Muslims.

Shi^{c}i Islam

A significant minority of Muslims, known as *Shi^{c}i's* or Shi^{c}ites, have differed from the Sunni majority on certain religious and political matters almost since the beginning of Islam. Today about 10 percent of the Islamic population of the world is Shi^{c}ite, living mostly in Iran and Iraq. Shi^{c}ite communities also exist in many other Muslim countries, including such Sunni strongholds as Saudi Arabia. The differences between these two branches of Islam will be discussed by topic throughout this book. Such historical and religious differences as do occur should not obscure the broad lines of agreement between the two branches. It is no longer desirable, as scholars in the past have tended to do, to tell the story of Islam solely or primarily from a Sunni point of view, as if Shi^{c}ite Islam were a heterodox sect or an aberration of the "true" Islam.

Shi^{c}ites differ little from Sunnis in belief and practice. Their few points of difference, mainly in modes of leadership and piety, are nonetheless significant. During the first centuries of Islam, the majority of Muslims accepted the caliphs, or successors of Muhammad, as the legitimate political leaders of Islam. Many, however, sought guidance in both political and religious matters from spiritual leaders descended from Ali, Muhammad's cousin and son-in-law and the fourth caliph of Islam. Ali was assassinated in 661. The civil strife that resulted in his assassination left an indelible mark upon the Islamic Umma. The partisans (singular, *shī^{c}a*) of Ali accepted his sons and their descendants as their spiritual leaders or *Imams.* For the Shi^cites, allegiance to *Alid* Imams tended to replace loyalty to the figure of the reigning caliph, and at times even to the Sunni Ulema. Shi[c]ites believe that Muhammad had passed on a significant part of his teaching directly to Ali, and hence to subsequent Imams. Although the twelfth and last Imam disappeared late in the ninth century (expected some day to return), the Shi[c]ite Ulema carry on the distinctive teachings and interpretations they trace back through the Imam lineage to the Prophet. The teachings of the sixth Imam especially, Ja[c]far al-Ṣādiq (d. 765), became the basis of the *Ja[c]fari* school of law, which serves the same function in Shi[c]ite Islam as do the four schools in Sunni Islam. Like their Sunni counterparts, the Shi[c]ite Ulema of the Ja[c]fari school are concerned to keep Islam on the track of Shari[c]a according to the four roots mentioned previously. In addition to their pious learning in these roots and in the teachings of their Imams, however, the Shi[c]ite Ulema have often assumed a stronger role of leadership and charisma, able from time to time to rally great masses of people under their persuasion.

The emotional intensity that characterizes Shi[c]ite Islam culminates on the tenth day of Muharram (the first month of the Islamic calendar). On this date in Karbala, Iraq, in 680, Husayn, son of Ali and grandson of Muhammad, was brutally murdered by troops of the Umayyad Caliph, Yazid. On each anniversary of this event, Shi[c]ites reenact the events of Karbala during the first ten days of the month. The scene is one of emotional bereavement. Black tents are set up and the attire and gestures of mourning are assumed. For nine days, representing the days of siege by Yazid against Husayn and his family, those who have gathered hear the story of Husayn's demise dramatically retold.

On the tenth of Muharram emotions reach a crescendo in the staging of the Karbala tragedy. Actors representing both sides in this sacred drama—the forces of Yazid and the Alid family of Husayn—recreate the religious Passion of Islamic, particularly Shi[c]ite, history. Other protagonists on stage include the Angel Gabriel, the slain Husayn, and the deceased Prophet Muhammad. Toward the end of the Passion, the central theme has become clear: suffering and martyrdom are exalted virtues, the way to salvation. Through the ultimate vicarious suffering and martyrdom of Husayn, sinners are released from the flames of hell. The Shi[c]ites who witness the drama are also participants, for the plot of the story is ingrained in their shared consciousness of this event. It is a moment of catharsis, indicated by the final line of one version of the Passion, uttered by a chorus: "God be praised! By [Husayn's] grace we are made happy, and by his favor we are delivered from destruction. . . . We were thorns and thistles, but now are made cedars owing to his merciful intercession."[2]

Remembering the tragedy of Husayn on the tenth of Muharram is a recommended religious act for Sunnis as well as for Shi[c]ites. The dramatic reenactment of these events and the emotional identification with their mean-

---

[2] G. E. von Grunebaum, *Muhammedan Festivals* (Atlantic Highlands, N.J.: Humanities Press, Inc., 1976), p. 94. Used by permission of Humanities Press, Inc. New Jersey 07716.

ings, however, is a special characteristic of Shi^cite Islam. The history of Shi^cism has included periods of political protest and uprisings, and consequent repressions. During such periods the Imams and the Ulema who have since represented them have often served as leaders of spiritual and political resistance. In this context the Passion of Husayn has served as a symbol of the ultimate promise of salvation. Participation in the Passion is participation in a salvation history that has distinct tones in Shi^cite Islam. In the pages ahead it will be important to distinguish the differences of tone without losing sight of the essential agreement of faith and practice between the two branches, Sunni and Shi^cite Islam.

The Common Denominator

Let us return, then, to consider in brief the Five Pillars of Islam. They are (1) the witness, (2) the prayer, (3) the alms, (4) the fasting, and (5) the pilgrimage. We have already seen how the witness or Shahada contains two essential themes in Islam when a Muslim declares: "I witness that there is no God but Allah; I witness that Muhammad is His Messenger." The other four Pillars are known as the "Acts of Worship" (Arabic, *^cibādāt*). The rules governing these acts of worship in particular have been carefully argued and expounded by each of the Sunni and Shi^cite schools of law with slight variations among them. This is because the Pillars are considered "obligatory" for all Muslims whereas other Acts of Worship are "recommended." Without going into the complexity of Muslim worship at this point, let us nonetheless consider the main features of worship.

PRAYER (ṢALĀT). Performing the daily prayers is the second Pillar of Islam. As in other religions, prayer is an act of communication between human beings and God, and Muslims may choose to pray at many times and for a variety of reasons. Five daily prayers are considered a duty for all Muslims, and on these occasions preparations in ritual purity are required. The prayer must be said and performed while facing in the direction of Mecca. It may be performed virtually anywhere except on Fridays, when at the midday call to prayer Muslims should gather at a nearby mosque. There a sermon is heard and then the prayer is performed in uniform rows of worshippers.

ALMS (ZAKĀT). The mission of the Prophet Muhammad was directed in part against the injustices that the tribal Meccan economy imposed upon widows, orphans, and others without means. The Zakat is a form of giving to those who are less fortunate, and, as the third Pillar, it is obligatory upon all Muslims who have the means to do so. The schools of law have interpreted this Pillar in general to mean that one should give a certain amount from that part of one's wealth and assets each year in excess of what is required for a respectable standard of living. Normally this should be done before the beginning of the month of Muharram, the first of the new year. Each Muslim may choose the

FIGURE 1.5. Muslims performing Salat in mosque, Pakistan. (Photo by J. Powell, Rome.)

form and the recipient of his Zakat. Giving the Zakat is considered an Act of Worship because it is a form of offering thanks to God for the means of material well-being one has acquired.

FASTING (ṢAWM OR ṢIYĀM). Another expression of thanksgiving is the fourth Pillar, fasting. Like the Zakat, Sawm is considered meritorious whenever it is performed (without detriment to one's health), but it falls as a duty to all Muslims to fast in particular during the ninth month, the month of *Ramaḍān.* During Ramadan refraining from food, drink, and sexual activity during daylight is enjoined upon all Muslims except those who are in ill health. This restriction also applies to pregnant and menstruating women and to those engaged in strenuous work or demanding travel. One's duty then is to make up lost days of fasting at a later time. Each day of Ramadan the time of fasting is from just before sunrise to just after sunset. Breaking the fast is otherwise permitted, and often evenings during Ramadan are joyous and sumptuous occasions in Muslim homes. It is reported that the Prophet often fasted, particularly when he was directing his attention toward God in meditation. Sawm during Ramadan or any time is recognized as physically demanding but spiritually rewarding.

PILGRIMAGE (ḤAJJ). The pilgrimage season begins in the tenth month, the month following Ramadan, and lasts through the middle of the twelfth month, Dhu al-Hijja. The fifth Pillar requires all Muslims who are physically and financially capable of it to make the Hajj to Mecca once during their lives.

The actual rites and prayers take place at the sacred Ka^{c}ba in Mecca and at other locations nearby. The rite of pilgrimage is very old, having existed in pagan forms long before Muhammad. Muslims associate the origin of the Hajj and the founding of the Ka^{c}ba with the prophet Abraham. Today the Hajj is a spectacular gathering of Muslims at Mecca from all over the world, numbering about two million people each year.

STRIVING (JIHĀD). Although it is not universally recognized as a Pillar of Islam, the Jihad is a duty in one form or another. The general meaning of the term is "striving for moral and religious perfection." Jihad is the form that patriotism and citizenship take within the Islamic Umma. Because Islam regards itself as a universal religion, Jihad can be in the service of the spread or defense of Islam. This sense of Jihad is often translated as "holy war." In the event of attack from outside forces, Jihad calls for fighting, and, if necessary, dying, for the sake of Islam. In this case it is a duty that falls to all able-bodied male Muslims. It is true that the cry for "Jihad!" has been raised from time to time in Islamic history, but it is the broader meaning of striving within the context of one's life and community for moral and religious perfection that is the main sense of this duty in Islam. One who so strives is known as a *mujtahid.* Every Muslim can and should be a Mujtahid.

Being a Mujtahid, a striver for moral and religious perfection, involves numerous forms of public and private devotion that characterize the "practice" of Islam generally. We will encounter some of these in greater detail in Chapters 6 and 7. Among the most important dietary laws are the Koranic injunctions against eating pork and drinking alcohol. Muslims are also enjoined to respect their parents and elders, to help provide for close relatives and kin, and to give to the poor and disadvantaged when at all possible. On the other side, murder, theft, fornication, adultery, lying, cheating and wrongly accusing or testifying against someone are all strictly forbidden by the Shari^{c}a, the sacred law.

The term *islām* in a technical sense means "the practice of the religious and social duties" outlined above. There is another term, *īmān,* which means "faith," and like the Five Pillars, Iman can be divided into parts or categories. In Chapter 5 we will consider the content of Muslim faith and thought in more depth. As we proceed to learn about Islamic history and culture generally in the next few chapters, it will be useful to bear in mind the six parts of Iman or "faith."

1. *God and His Attributes.* Belief in Allah and His unity (Tawhid) entails belief in His attributes such as knowledge and speech. God's attributes are inherent in His being and not apart from Him. In popular piety it is believed that God has ninety-nine beautiful names or attributes, and rosaries of thirty-three beads are used to conduct private devotions that consist in remembering God by naming his attributes.
2. *Prophets.* The Muslim belief that Muhammad is the Messenger of Allah is grounded in the belief that many prophets preceded Muhammad. Selected from

among ordinary mortals to bring the divine message to humankind for their guidance, prophets and messengers were necessary for salvation. From Adam (the first) to Muhammad (the final "Seal"), prophets have taught humankind about matters of faith and practice necessary to salvation.

3. *Angels.* In addition to the earthly messengers of God's will, Muslims believe there are numerous invisible beings who execute the commands of God in the invisible, supramundane sphere. The most important of these are *Gabriel,* the messenger of God's will to His prophets; *Michael,* in charge of the natural world; *Israfil,* who trumpets in the Last Judgment; and *Azrael,* the angel of death.
4. *Sacred Books.* Belief in sacred books or scriptures sent to confessional communities, particularly to the Jews and Christians, is the fourth category of Iman. It follows from the aspects of faith just mentioned, for God's communication to His prophets through His angels has resulted in other sacred books. In addition to the Koran, Muslims acknowledge the Torah of Moses, the Psalms of David and the Gospel of Jesus as previously sent scriptures.
5. *The Last Day.* Muslims believe that the world as we know it will end in divine destruction followed by a Day of Resurrection at which all of humankind, past and present, will be brought to strict account for the degree to which they kept the faith and practice enjoined upon them by their prophets. Those who obeyed God and His messengers will henceforth enjoy Paradise; those who did not will suffer in Hell. Those who had Iman 'faith' but who nonetheless sinned in significant ways will suffer temporarily before attaining Paradise.
6. *Predestination.* The sixth part of faith is the omnipotence of God, that is, belief in His total power *(qadar)* as Creator to shape and determine the course of His creation. The paradox of divine power and agency in all events versus human responsibility for moral and immoral acts indicates that the frequent charge of fatalism against Islam is no more true than in any religious tradition that believes in divine predestination. Belief in predestination or *qadar* is a positive affirmation of God's power and majesty for most Muslims, and not an excuse to become resigned to the way things are in the world.

These general descriptions of Iman and Islam, that is, of faith and practice, apply throughout the tradition. Like believers of other religious traditions, Muslims vary in the intensity of their faith and the diligence of their practice. Some are very pious, however, and one important form of pious devotion throughout the centuries has been Islamic mysticism.

Mystical Islam

From the interior of a compound in North Africa the name of Allah may also be heard—as it frequently is throughout the Muslim world—but not from a muezzin, nor at intervals prescribed by the Shari^{c}a. Those who utter it call themselves Sufis. They are Islamic mystics gathered in a community around a spiritual master or Shaykh. Such communities have existed for a long time in Islam, and those who have chosen the path of mysticism have been Sunnis in some cases, Shi^{c}ites in others.

In Sufi gatherings the two syllables *Al-lah* dominate the atmosphere. In quiet moments in his or her own cell, each adept softly murmurs the divine name repeatedly. "Allah." One is conscious of nothing else. At other times the divine name is more audible, more disturbing. A French physician attending to the health of a Sufi Shaykh reported the following experience:

> Fairly often . . . while I was talking directly with the Shaikh, the Name "Allāh" had come to us from some remote corner of the zāwiyah [Sufi convent], uttered on one long drawn out, vibrant note:
>
> "A. . .l. . .lā. . .h!"
>
> It was like a cry of despair, a distraught supplication, and it came from some solitary cell-bound disciple, bent on meditation. The cry was usually repeated several times, and then all was silence once more.
>
> "Out of the depths I have cried unto Thee, O Lord."
>
> "From the end of the earth will I cry unto Thee, when my heart is overwhelmed: lead me to the rock that is higher than I."
>
> These verses from the Psalms came to my mind. The supplication was really just the same, the supreme cry to God of a soul in distress.
>
> I was not wrong, for later, when I asked the Shaikh what was the meaning of the cry which we had just heard, he answered:
>
> "It is a disciple asking God to help him in his meditation."
>
> "May I ask what is the purpose of his meditation?"
>
> "To achieve self-realization in God."
>
> "Do all disciples succeed in doing this?"
>
> "No, it is seldom that anyone does. It is only possible for a very few."
>
> "Then what happens to those who do not? Are they not desperate?"
>
> "No: they always rise high enough to have at least inward Peace." Inward Peace. That was the point he came back to most often, and there lay, no doubt, the reason for his great influence. For what man does not aspire, in some way or other, to inward Peace?[3]

Peace. Submission. Two sets of notions—one a state of mind and a social ideal, the other a conscious attitude and a physical posture—all comprehended in the notion, *Islam.* But beyond the religious notions of peace and submission, the word Islam and its adjective "Islamic" connote many things: the Arabesque style of art, the exquisite Persian miniature paintings, the architecture of magnificent mosques, the literature of the *Thousand and One Nights,* the poetry of Omar Khayyam, the philosophy of Averroës, and much more. These more familiar hallmarks of Islamic civilization are but the tip of the iceberg. Islam means religion. It also means a great civilization that has subsumed many cultures, achieving a remarkable unity. The next task in this study of Islam is briefly and selectively to consider its history.

---

[3] Martin Lings, *A Sufi Saint of the Twentieth Century: Shaikh Ahmad al-ᶜAlawi; His Spiritual Heritage and Legacy,* 2nd ed., rev. and enl. (Berkeley, Calif.: University of California Press, 1971), p. 22. Used by permission of University of California Press and George Allen & Unwin Ltd.

Celebration of the fourteenth centennial of the Prophet's Hijra from Mecca to Medina began in November 1979.[1] It may serve as a useful orientation to survey briefly the main events of those 1,400 years and then to focus on select personalities and moments within that span.

The historian's task of reconstructing what "happened" during the many centuries since the Hijra has been facilitated by the preserved writings of Muslim scholars and travelers throughout the centuries. Islamic documents and records are plentiful and diversified. Regarding the earliest centuries, however, the task is somewhat difficult. There are hardly any records or statements from non-Islamic sources about Islam during the first two centuries after the Hijra. Furthermore, to a large extent Islamic traditions about those first two centuries have survived mainly in texts that date from the third century after the Hijra onward. This gap is not unique to Islamic history. Historical analysis of the founding periods of all the major religious traditions is similarly qualified. Scriptures and pious recollections appearing in later texts characterize the main sources of our information about the founding years of Christianity, Judaism, Buddhism, and several other traditions.

---

[1] Islamic years are reckoned on a lunar calendar of about 354 days. Each century of our Western solar calendar is equivalent to about 103 lunar years. Writers on Islamic topics usually list together the A.H. and A.D. dates of events. For example, "al-Ghazzali (d. 505/1111)" means that the Muslim theologian al-Ghazzali died in the year 505 after the Hijra, which corresponds to A.D. 1111. To make things simpler, only the A.D. dates will be cited in these pages.

Thus historians are faced with a dilemma. It would be a mistake to throw out all "religious" literature as unreliable statements of what actually happened and why. It would also serve no useful purpose to accept religious texts uncritically in the search for verifiable historical information. Ambiguities, contradictions, and anachronisms regularly appear that beg to be explained. Scholars of religions, in their investigations of the formative years of a given religion, and in the absence of independently reliable historical documents, have used such terms as "tradition" and "sacred history" to designate a religion's view of its own unique history.

It is usually held that history began when humankind learned to write and keep records. In the Middle East writing dates from ca. 3000 B.C. Yet until much more recently only an elite few could read and write. Information was gained and passed on orally—a method of learning and shaping one's world view that has transpired in human civilization sometimes independently of literary traditions. It is partly in this sense that we will speak about the Islamic religious *tradition.* Notwithstanding the absence of full and unambiguous documentary evidence dating from the time of the events themselves, the written texts from later centuries are obviously the result of a tradition in the making since the earliest times.

In the next few pages a brief overview of Islamic *history* will be sketched. We will then consider in more depth some aspects of the *tradition* or sacred view of history that gave Islamic history its shape as viewed within world history.

FOURTEEN CENTURIES OF ISLAM

Arabia dramatically entered the stage of world history in the seventh century, although it had been playing a regional role for several thousand years. South Arabia had once been well known as the Kingdom of Sheba, and it became a source of frankincense and myrrh and other spices and exotica from the East, destined for Mediterranean markets. Less important on the larger world scene was the nomadic population of central Arabia. Its main city, Mecca, was barely known to the rest of the world until just before the time of the Prophet. Yet it was from central and not South Arabia that the Islamic Empire was launched across North Africa and the Middle East.

The occasion for the early seventh-century outpouring of Arabs into Syria, Iraq, Persia, and later into Egypt and North Africa was a new vision of monotheistic religion inspired by the Prophet Muhammad. Born of humble circumstances in the city of Mecca late in the sixth century, in about A.D. 610 Muhammad began to preach a message that attacked the tribal provincialism, social injustice, and polytheistic paganism that had differentiated the Arabs from their more urbanized and cosmopolitan neighbors in Byzantium and Persia, and the settled peoples of Syria and Iraq. Although Muhammad died before the Arab armies were to expand their control significantly to lands outside of Arabia, the message he recited in the form of Revelation accompanied his most trusted companions and generals, thus taking root where they established political control throughout the Middle East. The history of Islam, then, begins properly with the Prophet Muhammad and the Revelation recited by him to the peoples of Mecca and Medina, about which we shall have more to say later in this chapter.

It may be useful to think of the outpouring of Arabs from the Arabian Peninsula in the seventh century as a *Völkerwanderung,* a mass migration of people not unlike earlier migrations in the Middle East. For example, late in the third millennium B.C. a migration of Semitic peoples had moved into Mesopotamia and had established the ancient Babylonian Empire. The Biblical story of Abraham's migration from Ur of the Chaldees (Babylonia) to Haran and then to Palestine corresponds to what we know of such a *Völkerwanderung* from Mesopotamia to Palestine ca. 2000 B.C. The conquest of Canaan (Palestine) by the Hebrew people several centuries later was part of a large pattern of migration which included the Philistines and other newcomers to that area. Migrations such as these inevitably involved wars and conquests. They also brought new ideas as Semites, Persians, and other peoples encountered one another and established new civilizations on top of older ones. The older civilizations were not always destroyed in the process; each new conquering people took command but absorbed much of the culture of the previous landlords, adding new ideas and developing distinctive forms. Thus, power in the Middle East had already changed hands many times prior to the Arab conquests in the seventh century. A successful economy of agriculture and trade had existed for nearly four millennia, and in this context cultural achievements in writing, literature, monumental architecture, and legal institutions had left a rich heritage on which the Arabs and the people they conquered could now build an Islamic Empire.

Two great empires gave way to the Arab conquests. The troops of Byzantium, the Orthodox Christian Empire with its capital in Constantinople, were pushed out of Syria and Iraq by Muslim armies. Centuries of Christian and Jewish presence in these lands was not greatly affected by the changing of the guard. Many became Muslim, but the existing culture was left more or less intact. Byzantium retained its strength in Anatolia (modern Turkey) until the fifteenth century, when the Ottoman Turkish Muslims successfully marched on Constantinople. During the eight centuries of coexistence between Islam and Byzantium, the occasional military clashes did not prevent important cultural exchanges.

The Sassanian Persian Empire fared less well when the Arab armies made their march across the Middle East. The Persians had already played out their resources after centuries of conflict with the Byzantine Empire. By the middle of the seventh century the last Persian king was assassinated, and the once great Persian Empire fell to the Arabs. The political and cultural implications of this change of balance in Middle Eastern powers was considerable. Henceforth the ethnic and cultural composition of the Abode of Islam was a mixture of Arab, Persian, Turkish, Armenian, and other Middle Eastern peoples.

FIGURE 2.1. Caliphate at its greatest extent. (Map by Michelle Behr.)

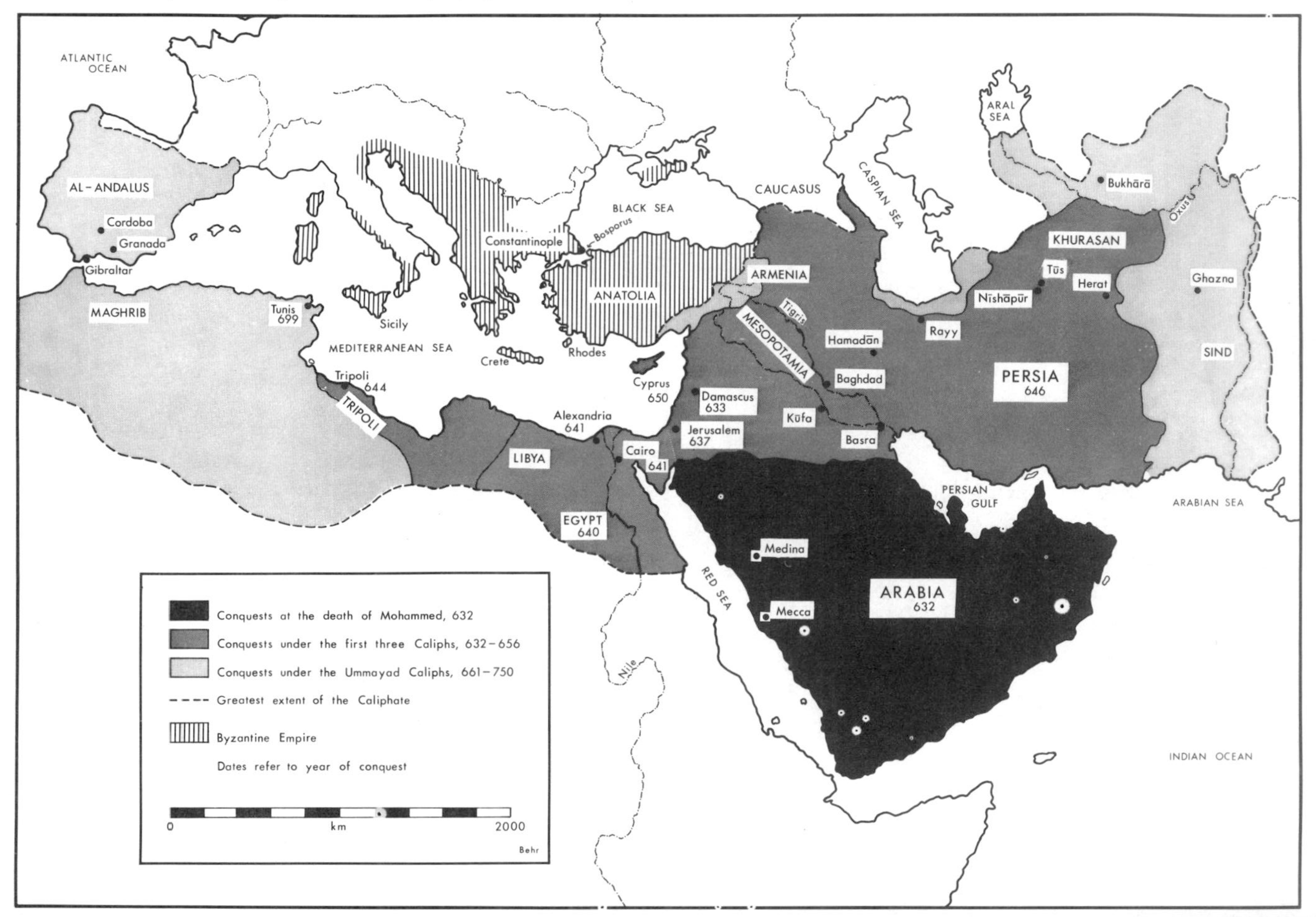

The Classical Age

From the seventh to the thirteenth centuries, Islam formed an empire dominated by the caliphate. We will pay closer attention to some of these caliphs or rulers of Islam later in this chapter.

THE RASHIDUN (632-661). Following Muhammad's demise, the first caliphs ruled from Medina in Arabia. They were known as the Rashidun or "rightly guided" caliphs because they had been companions of the Prophet. By the end of the Age of the Rashidun, Medina proved to be an impractical command post for the growing empire.

THE UMAYYADS (661-750). The next period of the caliphate was under an Arab dynasty that ruled in Damsacus, Syria. Known as the Umayyad caliphate, this was the period of the consolidation of Arab rule and gradual growth of Arabic and Arab influence over the still existing languages and institutions of previous civilizations. The religion of the Muslim conquerers was adopted by many of the conquered peoples, and a mode of coexistence was worked out with several of the religious communities that did not convert to Islam.

In culture, the Arabic language expanded beyond local Arabian *oral* traditions of poetry and Islamic worship to become an important *literary* language. The Arabic Koran played a key role in this development. Soon literature about the Prophet and various aspects of Islamic religion appeared. Muslim scholars sought to broaden the base of the language by consulting pure Bedouin usage and by writing grammars and dictionaries. The works of earlier Greek philologists appear to have been fundamental to this enterprise. In art, the field of architecture dominated as the Muslim conquerers continued the ancient Middle Eastern mode of cultural expression through monumental architecture. One of the signal achievements of the Umayyad Age was the Dome of the Rock mosque in Jerusalem, built by Caliph Abd al-Malik in 691.

SPAIN. In the year 711, Umayyad forces crossed the Straits of Gibraltar and established a branch of the Umayyad caliphate in Spain. Al-Andalus, as the Arabs called it (Andalusia in English) remained in Muslim hands until the Christian *Reconquista* in the thirteenth century. During five centuries of Islamic rule, culture flourished under the Spanish Muslims (Moors), and al-Andalus served as an important point of contact between Christendom and the Islamic world. In literature, philosophy, and architecture, the Spanish Muslims made several notable achievements that have survived to this day. An example is the richly decorative design of the Alhambra. The writings of the Moorish philosopher Averroës inspired considerable philosophical discussion in later Medieval Europe. The Spanish language itself bears witness to the Islamic heritage, for it has served as a conduit of many Arabic words into other Western languages.

FIGURE 2.2. Dome of the Rock, Jerusalem. (Courtesy of the Israel Government Tourist Office.)

THE ABBASIDS (750–1258). In 750 the Umayyad caliphate in Damascus fell to another Arab family, the Abbasids. The Abbasid caliphate established its own capital, Baghdad, along the banks of the Tigris River in Mesopotamia. Under Abbasid rule, Arab hegemony gave way to increasing influence from other elements within the Islamic population. At first the Abbasid caliphs were able to coordinate successfully and productively the tensions between Sunni and Shi^c^ite Muslims, Arabs, Persians, Turks, and other ethnic groups, and the various social and professional classes of the older civilizations still living in the Middle East. But such diversity within the vast Islamic Empire had a centrifugal effect, and the caliphate in Baghdad started losing control over people and lands that were distant from the capital.

Eventually the centrifugal effect also became centripetal. Turkish and Persian Muslim dynasties grew independently powerful enough to make demands upon Baghdad. A radical Shi^c^ite dynasty known as the Fatimids ruled first in North Africa, then Syria and Egypt from 909 to 1171. Under the Fatimids, Cairo became an important political capital; its institutions of learning and culture rivaled those of Baghdad. Today in Cairo, Muslim students from all over the world attend al-Azhar University, built by the Fatimids nearly a thousand years ago, two centuries before universities were established in Medieval Europe. Originally Shi^c^ite, al-Azhar is now a Sunni university.

Although the Abbasid caliphate remained the central symbol of political authority throughout these upheavals, first the Persian Shi^c^ite dynasty known as the Buyids (945–1055) and then the Turkish Sunni dynasty known as the Seljuqs (1055–1258) brought the Abbasid caliphate under their respective controls.

Throughout the Abbasid Age, regardless of these political shifts, the level of cultural achievement remained high. It was during this period that ancient Persian reemerged as a Middle Eastern vernacular language, using the Arabic script and absorbing many Arabic words. Persian became a potent medium not only of Islamic religious literature along with Arabic, but also of several distinctively Persian genres of *belles-lettres* and poetry. Chiefly in Baghdad, classic governmental, educational, and religious institutions such as hospitals, academies of science, schools called *madrasas,* and commercial ventures were established and thrived.

The Abbasid Age was also the period in which the classic schools of Islamic law and theology flourished. Disciplines that studied the four roots of the Shari^c^a (see Chapter 1) branched out into the four orthodox schools that are accepted in Sunni Islam. The Shi^c^ites formed schools or traditional interpretations of their own. The important oral tradition of sayings (*ḥadīth*) attributed to the Prophet Muhammad was written down and codified. Since the Abbasid Age there have been six orthodox collections, the best known of which is the *Authentic* by al-Bukhari (d. 870). Traditional religious disciplines such as law, Koranic studies, and studies of the prophetic traditions went on mainly in mosque schools. Late in the Abbasid Age enlightened patrons separately established academies known as *madrasas.* Well-known professors were appointed to the faculties of these institutions and were paid salaries, replacing the more informal arrangements of the earlier mosque schools.

Empire After the Caliphate

With the invasion of the central Islamic lands by Mongol warriors, the Classic Age of the caliphate came to an end. We can only imagine what those decades of invasion and destruction must have been like for the Persians, Turks, Arabs, and other Muslims who lived and died in the path of the Mongol hordes. Originating in Eastern Siberia, the Mongols swept through Russia, China, Central Asia, and finally to the Middle East under the brilliant command of Chingiz Khan. His son, Hūlāgu, captured Baghdad in 1258. The Abbasid caliphate and its Seljuq lords were destroyed. But ironically, in just a few decades the Mongol lords who occupied the Abode of Islam themselves became Muslims, and the general shape of Islamic civilization remained remarkably stable without the caliphate as its central political symbol.

THE MAMLUKS (1250–1517). Not all of the Abode of Islam fell to the Mongols. In Egypt and Syria an independent Islamic government had been set up that was able to resist Mongol pressures. The leaders of this regime were called the Mamluks. Originally Turkish slaves (*mamlūk* means "owned"), they were strict Sunni Muslims. In art and literary scholarship, the Mamluk period was productive. Culture was supported by royal patronage. The religious notables or Ulema were allowed complete authority over Islamic faith and practice.

To this end the Mamluks maintained the fiction of a caliphate by permitting figurehead caliphs to sit in Cairo for a while. The most impressive literary achievements were in historical writing. One scholar of the period, Jalal al-Din al-Suyuti (1445–1505), wrote histories of Islam and scholarly studies of the Koran that soon gained great prestige throughout the Islamic world. In less scholarly circles some of the popular romances and tales of *The Thousand and One Nights* were generated in the Mamluk period.

THE OTTOMAN TURKS (1412–1918). The Muslims known to most Europeans after the sixteenth century were called Saracens. In fact they were the Ottoman Turks, a Sunni Islamic empire that lasted until the beginning of the present century. At the height of their power, the Ottomans took possession of much of the western portions of the Abode of Islam and marched as far as Austria in Europe before they were repulsed. Alarm over the Saracen threat appears in the writings of such figures as Martin Luther, signaling the serious military and psychological threat posed by the Ottomans. Basing themselves mainly in Anatolia (modern Turkey), they took possession of Syria, Egypt, and North Africa. Through the use of a highly trained paramilitary force known as the Janissaries, and of hand guns and artillery, the Ottoman sultans were able to capture and control large territories with relatively small forces. Their greatest prize was Constantinople, captured from the ailing Byzantine Empire in 1453. Renaming it Istanbul, the Ottomans made it their capital, adding to its many architectural treasures splendid monuments of their own. During the latter period of Ottoman rule, the Islamic lands paying tribute to the sultans in Istanbul were rewarded with serious neglect, causing cultural stagnation in the eastern and southern Mediterranean regions. The present century has seen a remarkable reversal of this trend.

THE SAFAVIDS OF PERSIA (1500–1779). At the same time that the Ottomans were establishing hegemony in western Islam, a Shi^c^ite dynasty gained control of Persia. Known as the Safavids, they established their capital in Isfahan, making it one of the most beautiful cities in the Islamic world. They retained power until the mid-eighteenth century, when they were overthrown by Muslim warlords from Afghanistan. Mistrustful of Ottoman intentions with good reason, the Safavid kings or *shahs* established diplomatic and economic ties with European powers. In art and architecture a distinctively Persian expression of Islamic culture developed. An outstanding example may be seen in the magnificent buildings erected by Shah Abbas (1587–1628).

THE MUGHALS OF INDIA (1526–1730). While the Ottomans and Safavids were carving out their empires, Turkish and Afghani warlords moved into India to establish the Islamic empire of the Mughals (a form of the word *Mongol*). Sunni in religious persuasion, the Mughal rulers made Delhi their capital. There and elsewhere they built impressive royal palaces and mosques.

FIGURE 2.3. Taj Mahal, India. (Courtesy of Air India.)

The best known of these is the Taj Mahal (see illustration). The Mughal emperors ruled an Indian population of which the vast majority was Hindu, not Muslim. The remarkable growth of Islam within this context was due not so much to the Sunni religious commitments of the rulers but rather to the Sufis or mystics, whose modes of piety were particularly at home in the Indian environment. Later in this chapter we will take a closer look at one Mughal emperor in particular, the famous Akbar.

From India, Muslim missionaries went to Malaysia and Indonesia, where Islam has grown with amazing vitality. Today Islam is quite strong throughout Southeast Asia, a fact that Westerners often overlook, so strong is the association of Islam with the Middle East. Another area of vital growth for Islam is the continent of Africa. South of the Sahara, where Islam had not penetrated in the initial push across North Africa to Spain, Islam is now growing rapidly as black tribal groups confront the twentieth century.

Islamic World Since the Nineteenth Century

This brief historical sketch of the history of Islam concludes with a look at the past two centuries. Because of the impact the West has had upon the Islamic world during the nineteenth and twentieth centuries, and more recently with a counter-impact of Islamic nations upon the West, distortions are difficult to avoid. After the decline of Ottoman, Safavid, and Mughal power in the eighteenth century, European powers began to encroach upon Islamic lands, often in the form of economic and political meddling, buying influence by supporting the extravagant tastes of corrupt sultans and rulers. Fixing blame for the decline of Islamic governments during this period is dangerous and not essential to our purpose here. More broadly, Europe was gaining a position of superiority in the important spheres of the military, economics, and technology. Islam seemed on the decline. One important exception was Egypt. In 1805 a Turkish subject, Muhammad Ali, with nominal connections to the Ottomans in Istanbul, set himself up in Cairo as ruler of a state that included Egypt and Syria, and for a while Arabia. Not unaware of the European advantage, he sought to westernize the Egyptian economy and the traditional Islamic institutions. His successors were far less capable rulers, and from the mid-nineteenth century until 1956, Western powers, notably the British, were able to maintain a strong presence in Egypt.

With the collapse of the Ottoman Empire after World War I, the modern state of Turkey emerged under the brilliant leadership of Ataturk. More than Muhammad Ali, Ataturk believed the road to recovery would have to be paved by Western forms of modernization. He had the capital moved out of traditional Istanbul to Ankara. The Arabic script in which the Turkish language had been written since the time of the Ottomans was replaced by the Latin alphabet of European languages, and the Turkish language itself was modernized. Those religious practices regarded as excessively emotional, such as certain Sufi dances, were severely constrained by governmental decree. In many ways, Ataturk's reforms were successful. He and the "Young Turks" who aided his efforts rapidly formed a modern state—one in which the role of traditional Islam was much less in evidence than elsewhere in the Islamic world. More recently there have been signs of a resurgence of popular Islamic religious sentiments in the general population of Turkey. The Islamic world's most radical attempt to de-Islamize traditional culture in favor of Western modes may prove to be a pendulum that has started its swing back.

In Persia the Safavids were replaced by the Qajar dynasty. Internally, the nineteenth century was relatively peaceful under the Qajars except for some sectarian uprisings. Externally, the British and the Russians were mounting pressure on the borders of Qajar Iran. In 1925 the Qajars were overthrown by the Pahlavi shahs, who labored to turn Iran into a modern state under their tight control. The Pahlavi government was opposed by Muslim religious and nationalist groups that wanted reforms but not at the expense of their religious and national heritage. The second and most recent Pahlavi shah was overthrown in 1979. The popular religious uprising that helped to make this revolution possible is but another sign of the widespread longing for a return to more traditional forms of Islamic government and ways of life in the Middle East. These traditional forms will be discussed more in detail in Chapter 7.

We close this section, then, with an observation. Throughout the Islamic world during the past two centuries Muslims have been struggling to reform and redefine their faith over and against the challenges of modernization and internal corruptions. The average person in the West has been largely unaware of these developments until quite recently. Often described as a "militant revival" of Islam, the reforms that are going on in several parts of the Islamic world are part of a much longer and less ominous process when seen in perspective. It is hoped that this study of Islamic religion and culture will provide some insight into why hundreds of millions of Muslims struggle to preserve and live within their Islamic heritage. Islamic history is not concluded in these pages, but remains an ongoing process with an important future. Our next task is to examine the religious view of Islamic history.

SACRED TRADITION IN ISLAM

Islam stands in the light of history as the last of the three monotheistic religions to arise in the Middle East. Affinities among Judaism, Christianity, and Islam have been noted. The political and cultural symbiosis of these three religious communities in the Middle East during the past thirteen centuries, despite heavy polemics and occasional conflict, has been possible largely because of their compatible religious world views. In Western scholarship Islam is often seen as having originated as an Arabian expression of monotheism, the last in a long and dynamic succession of Middle Eastern empires and states in antiquity. Islamic sacred history takes account of this overall development of the three faiths that trace their origins to Abraham and Adam.

The early Islamic community was conscious of having roots in earlier civilizations, for it believed that monotheistic religion was older than either Christianity or Judaism. But, as has been noted, Muslim historians wrote about the ancient past with a much different sense of history than our own. The Jewish and Christian communities that fell under Muslim rule were able to enjoy special status as *People of the Book.* This term occurs in the Koran and it refers to those confessional religious communities to whom Muslims believed Allah had already sent prophets and scriptures. Many of the early Islamic historians began their works with the general Judaeo-Christian-Islamic notion of God's creation of the world. This was usually followed by stories of prophets, from Adam to Jesus, who were sent to various peoples prior to Islam. These stories formed a prologue to the sending of the Prophet Muhammad to the Arabs. As one scholar of Islam has said:

> The Qur'ān's [Koran's] own presentation of the pre-Islamic history of God's revelatory activity demonstrates how thoroughly the sending of Muḥammad and the revelations to him are felt as rooted in an earlier *Heilsgeschichte* [sacred history], the knowledge of which is essential to the Muslim. Nevertheless, the scholarly concern with the precise "origins" and "authenticity" of materials with a pre-Islamic background such as those found in the Ḥadīth is only one type of concern. Of potentially greater significance for the historian who is trying to

> understand early Islam is the more subtle question of the meaning and function of such materials in the individual and collective life of the early Muslims.[2]

Although some of the prophets of the Islamic tradition are foreign to the Bible, the classic concept of sacred history in Islam was much closer to the concepts of early Judaism and Christianity than any of these ideas are to modern ideas of history.

The Middle Eastern monotheistic traditions share a common lore about the past that includes creation myths, legendary patriarchs and prophets, divine acts of reward and punishment directed to nations, and manifestations of God in word (scripture) and deed (history). Sacred history locates the religious community within an overall divine plan. The very structure of the divinely created *cosmos* also provides proper orientations that place one in harmony with the divine will. For example, highly significant in the Islamic cosmology is the sacred Ka^c^ba in Mecca. A rectangular house that enshrines a black stone in one corner, the Ka^c^ba is the focal point of all Muslims in the rituals of prayer and of pilgrimage. Muslims believe that the Ka^c^ba achieved fundamental significance long prior to the sending of Muhammad, Jesus, and Moses as prophets. Tradition teaches that the sacred Ka^c^ba was founded by Abraham (Ibrahim in Arabic). The Prophet Muhammad, then, appeared in a moment of sacred history that had begun with Adam and the creation of the world, and the Ka^c^ba was seen as the center of a number of sacred sites and ritual orientations; indeed, the Ka^c^ba is the center of a cosmos religiously conceived by Muslims. Properly understanding Islam as religion begins with a knowledge of sacred history and of the cosmological views of the Islamic community.

Muhammad in the Prophetic Tradition

In Islamic sacred history, Muhammad ibn ^c^Abdallah, an orphan raised under the protection of the powerful Quraysh tribe of Mecca, was called at the age of forty by Allah to recite a message that was eternally inscribed in Heaven. That message directly challenged the tribal society into which he was born and whose protection he enjoyed less the more he spoke Allah's truth. That message was, in its essentials, similar to the divinely sent word borne by others, including Moses (Torah), David (Psalms), and Jesus (Gospel)—a message that Muslims believe the Jews and Christians had not only not heeded, but also altered to suit their own ends. The *sending* of the Prophet Muhammad is seen by Muslims as the final historical positing of the timeless scripture. Koran *(qur'ān)* is the Arabic word for the recitation of the message from Allah that Muhammad delivered during his lifetime. As *Seal* or last of all the prophets since Adam, the unlettered Muhammad had uttered the word of Allah in miraculously eloquent Arabic to a

---

[2] William A. Graham, *Divine Word and Prophetic Word in Early Islam* (The Hague: Mouton Publishers, 1977), p. 2.

people whose cultural pride lay in their oratory and poetic skills. Herein lay the chief sign of his prophetic calling.

The Koran clearly identifies Muhammad's prophetic mission to the Arabs in the context of previous divinely sent messengers to various peoples of the Earth. Both Muslim and non-Muslim scholars have frequently observed that the present collection of the Koran probably does not reflect the original order in which the verses were recited by the Prophet. The result is a text that often seems disjointed and difficult to comprehend in translation. Nonetheless, many of the 114 *sūras* of the Koran can be seen to form narrative wholes or structures with specific messages boldly stated. One such *sūra,* the twenty-sixth, is called the *sūra* of the Poets, and it carries the specific message of Muhammad's prophetic mission against the background of other prophets sent by Allah.

The *sūra* of the Poets begins (verses 1–9) with a general consolation from Allah to the Prophet concerning the Arabs' failure to heed the message of Allah through his messenger, Muhammad. In the opening verses we hear Allah saying (verses 2–9):

These are the signs of the Scripture that makes clear.
Perhaps you torment yourself [O Muhammad] because they believe not.
If We willed, We could send a sign down upon them that would force them to bow their necks [in acceptance];
No new remembrance is brought to them from the Merciful that they do not renounce.
They charge lies! So tidings of what they used to scoff at will be brought to them.
Don't they see the Earth, how we have produced in it every fruitful pair?
Truly in this is a sign, though most of them believe not.
Truly your Lord is the Mighty, the Beneficent!

In the next large section of the *sūra* (versus 10–191) we learn of seven other messengers who preceded Muhammad: Moses, Abraham, Noah, Hud, Salih, Lot, and Shu^{c}ayb. Notice that three of them—Hud, Salih, and Shu^{c}ayb—are not Biblical figures. There is some trace of these three in the folklore and records of Middle Eastern sources outside of the Bible and the Koran. What captures our attention, however, is that all seven forerunners of Muhammad are similarly presented in the narrative of the *sūra.* Each was sent by Allah to his own people with the message: "Won't you fear God? Truly I am a faithful messenger unto you. So fear God and obey me." (In the longer passages on Moses and Abraham this common formula is stated in different words.) Thereafter we find mention of the specific ways in which each people have transgressed Allah's will. For example, Moses charged Pharaoh with obstructing Allah's command to let the Israelites go free; Abraham condemned the idol worship of his clan; and

Shu^{c}ayb accused his people of dishonest business practices. In each case the people rejected the messengers raised from their midst, in some cases after first asking for a sign that would prove the messengers were sent from Allah. The subsequent refusal to accept these signs proved disbelief and rejection of Allah and His messenger. The seven passages end announcing divine retribution against the seven nations.

Recall that each of the seven passages ends with the phrase: "Truly herein is indeed a sign; yet most of them believe not. And truly your Lord! He is indeed the Mighty, the Merciful." By combining the names of both Biblical and local Arab figures of legendary times in similar prophetic roles, the Koran declares that the sacred history of Islam is comprehensive of not just the Arabs but all other Middle Eastern peoples. In this view, the Arabs had always been a part of the divine scheme of salvation about which both Jews and Christians had already had much to say!

The final passage of the *sūra* (verses 192–227) ties the examples of the seven prophets and nations to Muhammad as messenger to his own people (192–196):

> *Truly (the Koran) is sent down by the Lord of the Worlds,*
> *Brought down by the Faithful Spirit*
> *Upon your heart (O Muhammad), that you may be one of the warners in clear Arabic speech.*
> *Truly it is in the Scriptures of the Ancients.*

The divine commands and prohibitions—the *Guidance,* as these are often called—reflect the pure monotheistic religion of Abraham more uniquely than they do any other prophet. Like Muhammad, Abraham had discerned the impiety and wickedness of idol worship among his kin. But the banishment of Abraham's slave wife, Hagar, and their son, Ishmael (Isma^{c}il in Arabic), had an important consequence not told in Judaeo-Christian scripture. According to Islamic tradition (sacred history), when Hagar and Ishmael were banished, Abraham escorted them to Mecca, where he helped Ishmael construct the house for the sacred black stone, the Ka^{c}ba. Hence, the Ka^{c}ba is regarded by Muslims as the first house of worship. According to tradition, from that archaic moment the Ka^{c}ba remained a place of worship for Arabs, but by Muhammad's time it had degenerated into a shrine of pagan idols of the sort Abraham had renounced. One of Muhammad's last acts was to perform the pilgrimage to Mecca, where he asserted the Abrahamic meaning of that rite, of the Ka^{c}ba, and of the several other sacred sites in and near Mecca. Thereby the Prophet established, indeed reestablished, the annual pilgrimage of Muslims to the first house of worship. What had been a local pagan rite among the Arabs became a sacred duty for all Muslims throughout the Abode of Islam.

Islamic sacred history begins, then, with Allah and the creation of the world. Messengers/warners had already been sent to various communities of humankind by the time of Muhammad. In many ways Abraham, as presented in the Koran and Islamic tradition, became the most significant example for Muslims because of his pure monotheistic belief and his disavowal of the idol worship that corrupted his clan. Although the Koran was specifically an Arabic scripture, received in the time of the Prophet, it carefully weaves into the fabric of Muhammad's biography an overall sacred history of humankind. A consideration of that biography is next.

Muhammad in History

Information about Muhammad's life prior to his fortieth year is sparse. It is commonly agreed that he was born around A.D. 570 in Mecca and that he was left without parents at an early age. As he was an orphan, his economic fortunes were not promising. He received no formal education and, like so many people of the Bedouin tribal environment, he was illiterate. What he learned of the cosmopolitan culture streaming in and out of Mecca may have been enhanced by traveling with caravans to Syria. There the older manifestations of Judaism and Christianity would have appeared in sharp contrast to the pagan culture of Arabia. At age twenty-five he married Khadija, then a widow of forty, who entrusted to him the management of her family's caravan company.

It was fifteen years later that Muhammad first experienced in a traumatic way the voicing of the message for which he has been remembered. Muslim historians themselves have differed on whether or not the many stories about Muhammad's special gifts and powers—some of them quite fantastic—were actually true. Truth in Islam *is* the Koran. It is revered as the document of Allah's revelation conveyed through His Messenger, Muhammad. Both as revelation and as foundation for the Prophet's sacred biography, the Koran is the apogee of Islamic salvation history.

The moment that marks the irruption of sacred time into the life of the Prophet is usually held to be the *Night of Power,* a night late in the ninth Muslim month of Ramadan, during which Muhammad is said to have first experienced his call to prophethood. Tradition has elaborated the circumstances of this occasion. Muhammad often retreated to hills near Mecca to brood and meditate on the spiritual malaise of the Meccans. On one such occasion, at the age of forty, he was moved by a strange experience. A bright, blinding light appeared on the horizon; it was a manifestation of the Angel Gabriel. Here the Koran speaks for itself (in Arabic, the style is simple and direct): "Recite, in the name of the Lord who created, created man from a clot. Recite, and thy Lord is the most Bounteous, who teaches man what he does not know" (Koran 96: 1–5).

The Koran relates that when Allah required Moses to appear before the great Pharaoh and demand freedom for the Israelites, Moses was sore afraid. Allah assured him that divine signs would enable him to convince Pharaoh and his chiefs. So, too, later sacred biographies and commentaries explained that on the Night of Power Muhammad was filled with fear and awe, reluctant to go out and face the powerful Quraysh tribe of Mecca with Allah's message of judgment. But Muhammad was reassured that he would not be left to his own resources. As Muhammad had feared, the Quraysh did scoff, saying he was mad or infused with poetic enthusiasm. Like Pharaoh and the folk of earlier prophets, the Quraysh asked Muhammad for a sign of his prophethood. The Koran relates that Muhammad challenged them to "bring a *sūra*" as eloquent and beautiful as those of the Koran, which, in the irony of typical sacred biographies, was Allah's word recited on the lips of a common, illiterate man. Later Muslim theologians explained that the failure of the Quraysh to match Muhammad on these occasions was the sign of his prophethood, a sign the Quraysh significantly refused to acknowledge.

The Quraysh, Muhammad's tribe, had established supremacy in Mecca by virtue of its monopoly over the caravan trade; given the nature of the terrain of Arabia, it was convenient for such commerce to pass through the city. The Quraysh also controlled the pagan shrines around Mecca, including the Ka^{c}ba. Throngs of pilgrims streamed into Mecca during the sacred months each year. Huge fairs provided additional attractions, and revenue for the Quraysh. Although Muhammad had been orphaned in infancy, his uncle, Abu Talib, had raised the young lad in this environment and saw to his protection now; family connections were essential to tribal society. But effective protection wore increasingly thin when, after the Night of Power, Muhammad assumed the role of Prophet/Warner. At first he recited short piercing messages attacking the social injustices and pagan worship in which Meccan society had come to thrive. Then Abu Talib died in 619, as did Muhammad's beloved wife, Khadija. With two of his most important sources of human support gone, the next three years were extremely trying for the Prophet. Thus in 622 Muhammad and his followers made the fateful Hijra (emigration) to Yathrib (henceforth called the City of the Prophet, *madīnat al-nabī,* or simply Medina). This moment is reckoned as the beginning of year 1 (A.H. 1) in the calendar used in the Islamic world. It was a pivotal moment between failure and success for Islam, a poignant midway in sacred time.

Tradition tells us that at the time of the Hijra small groups of men, women, and children were quietly slipping out of the city of Mecca. Followers of the Prophet Muhammad, they were headed for the city of Yathrib and a new life of religious freedom without persecution. Earlier Muslim expeditions to nearby Ta^{c}if and far away Ethiopia had not produced an acceptable place for Islam to flourish. Two years before the Hijra, at age fifty, Muhammad had initialed an agreement with the town fathers of Yathrib pledging to help them overcome the tribal factionalism that sorely divided their city. This may seem odd since tribal sanctions and oppression were the very forces that drove Muhammad and his followers out of Mecca. Implicit in the warnings Muhammad had voiced to the Meccans, however, was a message of peace. In spite of the abuse this had earned him, Muhammad's honorific title, "al-Amin" (the trustworthy), was a recognized trait of his dealings, even with those who rejected him.

In Mecca, from the Night of Power until the Hijra, Muhammad had served in the role of Messenger/Warner to the few who would listen and respond. In Medina Muhammad was in a position to assume a role of leadership which enabled him to create an Islamic Umma or "commonwealth." The revelations continued to come to him, but now they had less to do with warnings about the Day of Judgment. The continued Guidance of Allah through His Messenger laid down the fundamentals of law for the Islamic Umma as well as other practical directives. Three problems confronted the Prophet during the remaining ten years of his life, which were spent in Medina. First, he needed to pull the Islamic community together and complete his role as a prophetic conduit of divine revelation as well as provide for the viability of an ongoing Umma through his own words and example. Second, he had to deal with opponents from other religions, primarily the Jews, but also continued resistance from Arab pagans. Third, his departure from Mecca did not end that city's general dislike of him or his goal of including it within the Islamic Umma. From the Hijra in 622 until his death in 632, the Prophet Muhammad succeeded in overcoming all three obstacles.

As leader in Medina, Muhammad served first as an arbiter to that city under a mandate to help end the quarreling among its chief clans. At first only the *Emigrants* from Mecca looked upon him as their Prophet. But slowly many Medinans also became Muslims; these were called *Helpers*.

Tribal factionalism also accounted in part for his trouble with the Jews, for some of the tribes in Medina were composed of Jews who had been living there for generations. At first the Prophet sought friendly terms with them, seeing much in common between Islam and their faith. During the earliest period in Medina, for example, Muslims joined the Jews in praying in the direction of Jerusalem. But the Jews mistrusted him and gave assistance to his enemies, the Meccans, against him. The matter became serious enough for Muhammad to have to deal harshly with the Jewish tribes in order not to have conspirators within his own ranks. In the end they were forcefully expelled from Medina.

The most serious skirmishes, however, were with the Meccans. Two major battles were waged between the Meccans and the Prophet's troops of Medina, one at Badr and the other at Uhud. The first limited successes of the Muslims evolved into definite victories, and by 630 the Meccans were forced to negotiate with the Prophet for terms of peace. The Muslims asked primarily for the right to make the pilgrimage to Mecca. At first the Meccans consented but arranged to be absent from the city when the Muslims arrived. But by 632, when Muhammad himself made the pilgrimage, the Meccans and many Arabs outside the two cities had been absorbed into Islam. Muhammad, the Messenger/Warner from God, had also become a statesman for the people of central Arabia.

Muhammad's death in 632 marked the closing of sacred time. He was a Messenger who ultimately had been received by his own people. The foundations of the Shari^{c}a were henceforth laid down for the historic community of Muslims. Earlier that year Muhammad had made the pilgrimage to Mecca, the first since the Hijra. It was a ritual that already had deep significance for the

Arabs. In a farewell sermon delivered from a small rocky promontory at one end of the Plain of Arafat, a sacred station of the pilgrimage just outside of Mecca, Muhammad is reported to have said the following: "I have left with you something which if you will hold fast to it you will never fall into error—a plain indication, the book of God and the practice of His prophet, so give good heed to what I say. Know that every Muslim is a Muslim's brother, and that the Muslims are brethren."[3]

Muhammad fell ill on his return to Medina, and he died at his home shortly thereafter. Sacred time had come to an end. Historic time resumed, but under a new dispensation. The historic community of Islam now held a world view which was to shape its response to the challenges that lay ahead. The sacred biographies that tell the story of Muhammad's life reverently express in historical terms the remembrance of what had taken place in sacred time. The most tangible results are the Koran, the Book of God, and the Sunna of the Prophet. We have seen that the Koran tells of how prophets of old had said to their people: Keep your duty to Allah and obey me! Now Islam as it faced the vicissitudes of historic time had a vision of its mission to do just that.

Sacred Time and Sacred Biography

At this point a word about interpretation should be entered. The foregoing biography of Muhammad's life is a composite drawn from several sources. Historians have long labored to sort out the underlying facts. But asking whether or not the founder or Prophet of a religion lived and did all that is ascribed to him is a question with limited value to our present concern. Even if it were answerable, we would not be much closer to understanding Islam. It is true that Muhammad is less ancient than such figures as Jesus, Moses, and the Buddha. Nonetheless, our information about his life comes from later generations of pious followers who proclaimed the story of Muhammad's prophetic role as a religious truth. Strictly historical assessments of this sacred expression of biography are difficult, if not impossible, to make.

The sacred time par excellence of Islamic history covers the twenty-two-year period (610–632) during which Muhammad served as the vehicle for Allah's revelation. Information about those years forms a sacred biography, for which the main source is the Koran. More information is contained in the transmitted traditions or Hadith about the Prophet's Sunna. Pious biographies about the Prophet appeared during the eighth and ninth centuries. These provided the next generations with fuller accounts of the life of one who continued to affect human affairs in times and places far removed from the revelation.

Muslims are very clear that the events of the Prophet's life form articles of faith that transcend history as it is usually judged. Most Muslims also assert the

---

[3] Alfred Guillaume, *The Life of Muhammad: A Translation of Ishāq's Sīrat Rasūl Allāh* (Lahore: Pakistan Branch, Oxford University Press, 1955), p. 651.

factual historicity of the biographical picture of Muhammad as presented in sacred literature. But another kind of question about Islamic conceptions of the Prophet is more pressing in the comparative study of religions. How have Islamic views of the Prophet served as paradigms for social and personal modes of behavior in cultures where Islam was and is a way of life? What important human concerns were being expressed in the ways the Prophet has been understood by those in different generations and cultural settings in Islam? When Muslims of the seventh and eighth centuries wrote the biographies we now possess, they communicated within a culture with which they shared a common world of symbols and meanings. These will seem strange to us if taken as bare facts without interpretation. The process of interpretation belongs to this entire study. It is appropriate, then, to view the biographical picture of the religious figure Muhammad with respect to the sacred time that his biography epitomizes.

In discussing the time of revelation in Islam, the term "sacred time" has been used. The meaning of sacred time as it applies to a wide variety of religions, past and present, has been described by the historian of religions, Mircea Eliade. Eliade holds that for many of humankind's religions the most sacred time is a "primordial mythical time made present."[4] In the religions of antiquity and among many nonliterate peoples, myths relate a course of events such as the creation of the cosmos out of chaos and the establishment of a world order. This mythical time is made present by the periodic retelling of the myth of Creation and by the performance of sacred rituals. At the beginning of each year the Sumerians and Babylonians recited myths of Creation in dramatic ritualized reenactment of sacred time. The original creation of an orderly cosmos out of chaos could be appropriated in ritual to revitalize historic time. The forces of dissipation and disorder in human life were thereby brought under control.

The matter is somewhat different in Judaism and Christianity, and especially in Islam. It has been noted that Creation and the divine sending of Messengers form an essential part of Islamic sacred history. But the most sacred time was an historic moment sanctified by the revelation to Muhammad, the Seal of the prophets. As such, the time of revelation to the Arabs through Muhammad was discontinuous with normal time. The second caliph, Umar, is reported to have said: "In the time of the Apostle of God, people were judged by revelation. Then revelation was cut off, and now we judge you by those works of yours that are apparent to us. . . . "[5] One historian of Islamic religion has noted:

> While Muhammad still lived and prophecy and revelation in Islam continued, an order of existence prevailed that was unattainable in subsequent times. Human affairs stood under the special "judgement" of the prophetic-revelatory event. . . . For most Muslims, the "cutting off" of revelation at the Prophet's death marks not only the end of one historical order and the beginning of another, but also the

---

[4] Mircea Eliade, *The Sacred and the Profane: The Nature of Religion,* trans. Willard R. Trask (New York: Harper and Row, Publishers, Inc., 1961), especially Chapter 2.

[5] Cited by Graham, *Divine Word,* p. 9.

> transition from one order of being to another. Once past, "the time of the Apostle of God" became—most vividly for those who had participated in it and the early Muslims after them, but in a real sense for all Muslims—a wholly different mode of time: a time made holy by divine activity, "a time out of time", what Mircea Eliade has called "sacred time".[6]

The religions of antiquity vivified the powerful paradigm of mythic time in their own lives through the retelling of myth and its ritual reenactment. Christians participate in the sacred time of Christ's incarnation in the ritual of the Eucharist or Last Supper. For Muslims the sacred time of revelation is most dramatically experienced in the proper recitation of the Arabic Koran. More will be said about this later. Let us now consider a few important "moments" in Islamic history.

SELECT PERSONS, PLACES, AND EVENTS

In the history of the world's great religions, the stories of key individuals are widely known. For Christians, the list may vary, but it probably includes the Apostle Paul, the conversion of the Emperor Constantine, the rule of Charlemagne, and the struggle between Martin Luther and the Roman Catholic Church. Stories about the lives of those who shaped the past are a popular form of historical knowledge. Stories about kings, saints, popular heroes, and fabulous places permit popular lessons to be drawn by the great majority who are not trained as academic historians. In the monotheistic traditions of Judaism, Christianity, and Islam, such stories function within a framework of sacred history that connects a sacred time in the past with the present moment in a learnable anthology of key persons, places, and events.

The annals of Islamic history record many such stories. Certain caliphs, saints, and other noteworthy figures appear as models to be emulated or avoided. To tell about them all here is neither possible nor necessary. Certain places—lands, cities, shrines—also became objects of stories, legends, and historical writing. A select few examples will suffice. We will focus on the "rightly guided" caliphs, on the city of Baghdad, and on Akbar, the Mughal emperor of India. The good and the bad that are attributed to them contain lessons that have served as meaningful illustrations within the Islamic tradition.

An attitude of critical skepticism toward all but the soundest evidence in reconstructing the past is not essential to our purpose here. Although the assumptions implicit in popular ideas about the past are often challenged in critical historical investigations, our present aim is to discover the popular assumptions operative within the Islamic tradition. What Muslims believe about the past is more appropriate to our present concern than the ascertainable facts of history.

---

[6] Graham, p. 9.

The Rashidun

Although for the more than thirteen centuries of its history Islam has been remarkably uniform in the expression of its main beliefs and practices, important divergences did occur after Muhammad's demise in 632. Muslims locate the source of these problems in the first major period following the death of the Prophet. This is known as the Age of the Rashidun, or "Rightly Guided Ones" (632–661). Much like the Emperors Constantine in Christianity and Asoka in Buddhism, these four Islamic rulers known as caliphs occupy an important place in the historical consciousness of Muslims. Theirs was the transitional age from a simple community established by the Prophet to a major religious tradition that constituted an empire. Such figures as Jesus, the Buddha, and Muhammad did not speak directly to the question of how and by whom their followers should be led in the years and centuries to come. There has been much debate within Islam about the legitimacy of the Rashidun caliphs and about their faithfulness to the mandate of the Shari^{c}a upon them as heads of the Islamic community. This discussion has had far-reaching consequences.

ABU BAKR. Islamic tradition relates that when Muhammad died in A.D. 632, survivors at his bedside were thrown into confusion. The Messenger of Allah's Word was mortal, as he himself had claimed. But the voicing of the Guidance of Allah's Word, the Koran, was now silenced—or discontinued—by his death. Who would lead the Umma which had formed around that Word and Guidance? How could those who had braved considerable abuse from their own clansmen continue without the Messenger of Allah?

Immediate steps were taken to choose a caliph to stand at the head of the Islamic Umma. Such a person would be a spiritual leader or Imam. He would also be a political figure. All agreed that Muhammad's function as Prophet and Messenger of God could not be served by anyone present. The sacred time of revelation had ended. Among the reactions reported of those present on this solemn occasion was that of Umar ibn al-Khattab, one of the Prophet's closest companions. Originally a fierce Meccan opponent of Islam, Umar converted four years before the Hijra to Medina, and he became one of Islam's most ardent adherents. Umar reportedly said: "By God, anyone who says the Prophet is dead shall have his limbs severed from his body."

More practical was the fatherly Abu Bakr, also a Meccan, and one of the first to have accepted Islam. He declared: "Let those who worship Muhammad know that he is dead and gone! Let those who worship God know that He is ever living, never dying!" Abu Bakr's realism was in keeping with the teachings of the Prophet about himself and about Allah.

We have already noted that Muhammad had not designated a successor, nor had he stated whether or how one should be chosen. The lack of guidelines was further complicated by vested interests within different parties. The Emigrants from Mecca claimed longer and closer ties as members of Muhammad's clan, the Quraysh. They too had been the targets of rejection by Muhammad's opponents in Mecca. Among the Emigrants from Mecca were some members of the Prophet's own family—notably his cousin Ali—who believed they stood closer to Muhammad than anyone else. Those who thought of Ali in this way came to be called the *Shi^{c}ites.* They believed Ali was the legitimate successor of the Prophet. The people of Medina, however, had made possible the Hijra by inviting Muhammad and his Meccan followers to their city. Known as the Helpers, the Medinan party preferred a caliph (who after all would rule in their city) from among their own ranks. Although each group had its special interests, the need for unity prevailed. The electors chose Abu Bakr to be Imam of the young Islamic Umma, Caliph of Islam. Some say it was Umar himself who urged the selection of Abu Bakr.

The choice of Abu Bakr was a good one. Other candidates such as Ali and Umar were more polarized. Abu Bakr was a middle-of-the-road candidate, an elder statesman, acceptable to the largest number, according to Sunni sources. In the two short years until his death in 634, Abu Bakr was able to consolidate Islamic rule in Arabia and to send forth his armies into Syria and Iraq, where they met with considerable success against the forces of the Byzantine and Sassanian Empires. Tradition pictures him as a modest man of high moral standards and humility regarding his role as leader. The main source of wealth for the growing community of Islam was the spoils gained in war, and most Muslims believe that Abu Bakr faithfully followed the Koranic teaching that all true believers had equal rights to booty thus gained.

UMAR IBN AL-KHATTAB. Much of tradition relates that the younger, more energetic Umar was Abu Bakr's designated choice of a successor. There is not total agreement about this, for according to Arab custom those men rose to power who possessed manly and fair-minded qualities that the rest were willing to recognize. Such a man became tribal leader when the rest swore allegiance to him. There is some indication that neither the Shi^{c}ite party, devoted to Ali, nor the Helpers of Medina were particularly happy with the choice of Umar, or with the principle of designating one's successor. Nonetheless, the majority of those who had been Muhammad's companions accepted Umar as the second Caliph of Islam. Once again the choice seems to have been fortunate, for during the ten years of Umar's reign (634–644) Islam became a world phenomenon. As military advisor to Abu Bakr, Umar already had demonstrated the expertise that enabled him to continue the conquests with brilliant success. His armies took control of Egypt in North Africa, and they had pushed Byzantine and Persian troops out of Syria and Iraq. By the time of Umar's death in 644, Persia was near total collapse. By 651 the last Persian king or *shah* of the Sassanian Empire had been assassinated. As one historian has put it: "The power which had been the colossal rival of Rome and Byzantium, both the dream and the nightmare of the desert nomads, was lying vanquished at the Arab's feet.''[7] Umar's role in setting this in motion is perhaps the reason he designated himself as ''Commander of the Faithful'' in addition to the title of Caliph.

Some historians have seen the military successes of Umar as almost inevitable given the changing balances of power in the Middle East at the time. Byzantium and Persia were exhausted after centuries of confrontation over the territory that lay between them, namely, Syria and Iraq. This was the Fertile Crescent of Biblical times. But other, more far-reaching institutional developments are assigned to the legacy of the second caliph of Islam. He is said to have adopted fair means of treating his non-Muslim subjects, particularly Jews and Christians. Islamic law referred to them as ''people of the covenant'' (Arabic, *dhimmī*). As conquered peoples who did not convert to Islam, they were guaranteed basic rights and freedom of worship in exchange for a poll tax paid into the central treasury in Medina. Umar's organization of the military included the founding of camp towns at strategic locations within the conquered territories. Many of these became important Islamic cities of a much different character than the urban centers that had been formed by the older, non-Muslim cultures. Umar provided for civil stability by appointing to each province a judge known as a *Qadi* to settle the inevitable disputes that arose especially in the more distant centers of Islamic population. Much of what already existed as Guidance in the Koran achieved under Umar the status of public ordinance. Pilgrimage to Mecca, the prayerful observance of the month of Ramadan, and punishments for drunkenness and adultery became matters regulated in the public domain by his command.

What sort of man could achieve all of this? We are not well enough informed to more than guess. As with so many patriarchal figures in the past, we are better informed of what tradition has made of Umar than we are about the real man. But the Islamic memory of this rightly guided caliph, as it was shaped and preserved by tradition, is nonetheless of value. The very fact that the Sunni majority and the Shi^{c}ite minority have perpetuated quite different pictures of each of the rightly guided caliphs is significant. Each strand of Islamic tradition could make use of Umar's reputation for astute political handling of generals who acquired too much power in the field, cutting them off when necessary. This could be seen either as being in the best interest of Islam or solely in Umar's self-interest.

Death came to Umar on November 3, 644, from the dagger of a Muslim governor's Christian slave. The motive was apparently bitter resentment of heavy taxes on those least able to afford them. Such resentment may have been widespread. Thus, as with so many shapers of history, the portrait of Umar contains many lines both light and dark, and the variety of interpretations of his

---

[7] Francesco Gabrieli, *Muhammad and the Conquests of Islam,* trans. Virginia Lulin and Rosamund Linell (New York: McGraw-Hill Book Company, 1968), p. 132.

achievements tells as much about the later painters of these portraits as about the man himself. But in an important sense that is exactly what we are looking for—Islamic interpretations of that period of sacred history when the Rashidun established Islam as a world religion.

UTHMAN IBN AFFAN. More controversial than Umar was his successor, Uthman ibn Affan, the third rightly guided caliph, who ruled from 644 to 656 in Medina. He was a member of the great Meccan family of Umayya, which would later rule Islam from Damascus, Syria, for nearly a century (661–750). It was the events surrounding his rule and eventual assassination that provided the Umayyad family with just the right motive for a parting of the ways with Ali, the fourth and final rightly guided caliph.

Uthman appears to have had much going for him. He was credited with having converted to Islam during the early Meccan period of Muhammad's prophethood. Uthman's family wealth was a product of the lucrative caravan trade that profited Meccan merchants. These families formed the aristocracy of Arabia. The aristocratic families had resented Muhammad's prophecy, much of which had been directed against them, and very few of them had become Muslim until they had been forced to capitulate to the forces of the Prophet near the end of his life. Even then, the extent of their piety has been frequently questioned. Thus the early conversion of Uthman, a Meccan aristocrat and man of the world, was all the more significant. It should also be noted in this context that even though Islam was ideally an egalitarian community that stressed the brotherhood of all believers, aristocratic families such as the Umayyads did not readily relinquish their political expectations.

During the period of Muhammad's prophethood and the reigns of the first two caliphs, Uthman had a reputation for being a loyal Muslim. Some have said his reputation was undistinguished by additional qualities that either favored or disfavored his selection as third caliph. He was chosen, in fact, by a council that Umar had appointed on his deathbed. There is speculation that Uthman was the council's compromise choice among other strong candidates. Uthman's policies as caliph were basically those established by Umar, and the difficulties Uthman eventually faced were bound to arise as Islam expanded rapidly from a local Arabian cult to a world religion and empire.

Tradition divides the reign of Uthman into six good years and six bad years. His detractors spread the story that halfway through his reign he committed the clumsy (but symbolic) act of dropping the prophetic emblem into a well. A more probable cause of the "bad years" was that far away in Iraq economic stability lagged far behind the rapid expansion of Islamic rule. By now the field generals of the conquests had become sufficiently powerful to pose a threat to the central caliphate in Medina. Lists of typical grievances made against Uthman have been preserved. One of the most serious charges was that of nepotism, that he favored his own family when he made appointments to lucrative posts. As with other events in the patriarchal period of the Rashidun, later tradition viewed these policies in different ways. Some regarded these appointments as grossly unfair. Others saw in them Uthman's clever move to diminish local thrusts toward independence. He simply invoked loyalties within his clan to preserve political cohesion, some have argued. In addition, Uthman is said to have required that some of the spoils of war be paid by the soldiers who took them to the governors of provinces and to other officials, many of them members of his own family.

Tradition also assigns to Uthman the decision to produce an official recension of the Koran. It is not known with certainty how much if any of scripture had been written down in the Prophet's own lifetime. During the early years of the Rashidun caliphs, certain individuals learned by heart the entire body of Muhammad's recitations. These individuals were known as *reciters,* and they enjoyed considerable prestige within the Islamic Umma. Soon written copies appeared in various locales, and tradition preserves some account of their textual variations. Uthman's effort to establish by central authority an official written version was marred by the suspicion in certain quarters of political maneuvering. Other versions of the text survived for a while. The Uthmanic recension may also have been resented by reciters, whose ritual function of oral recitation was thereby rivaled; they recited from memory, not from a text. The official Arabic text of the Koran that is used by Muslims today is traced to the Uthmanic recension. Again we have an example of a patriarchal achievement that was not without differences of appreciation within the Abode of Islam.

The third caliph also died at the hands of assassins. A contingent from Egypt bearing economic grievances angrily presented their case before the caliph at his home and headquarters in Medina. An altercation developed and the embittered Egyptian Muslims laid siege upon his house. Umayyad forces were dispatched by Mu^{c}awiya, Governor of Syria, but they did not arrive in time to save the caliph from an ignoble death. Nor does there appear to have been much of an effort on the part of important Muslims in Medina, including Ali and other members of the Prophet's family, to come to the aid of Uthman. This event began what Muslims call the *fitna,* the first civil war in Islam. It stands as a watershed in Islamic history, for after 656, religious and political loyalties flowed in different directions. The era of the rightly guided caliphs was not yet over, but the unity achieved by the Prophet was now a complex balance of differing loyalties.

ALI IBN ABI TALIB. When as a child Muhammad had been left an orphan, his uncle, Abu Talib (the father of Ali), brought him into his household. Thus began the lifelong association between the Prophet and his cousin Ali. Ali was among the first two or three Meccans to convert to Islam, and family ties were made stronger when Ali married Muhammad's daughter Fatima. In keeping with the tribal structure in Arabia, Ali was closely identified with the effect of Muhammad's actions upon others in Arabia. This was true of the difficulties faced by Muhammad. When Muhammad decided to leave Mecca for Medina under unpleasant pressure, it was Ali who provided a foil to divert attention from Muhammad's escape. After Muhammad's death, those devoted to Ali, if not Ali himself, believed Ali was the first and foremost successor to the Prophet. In fact, the partisans of Ali (Shi^{c}ites) have preferred the term "Imam" (religious leader) to "Caliph" as a designation for the position of leadership they believed Ali received directly from the Prophet. Among later Shi^{c}ites, Ali became something of a legend, characterized both as warrior and as saint. In one of the early battles he was typically credited with killing 523 enemies with his own bare hands in a single day. Along with heroic feats are legends of miracles which are held to be special signs of his divine favor.

Ali played only a modest role in attempting to soften the tempers of Uthman's enemies. When Uthman was murdered, Ali at first hesitated to assume the role of leadership that many thought should have been his in the first place. On Friday, June 5, in the year 656, many Muslims finally paid allegiance to Ali as caliph in the mosque of the Prophet in Medina. The fact that many others withheld or refused allegiance made Ali's caliphate the weakest politically of all the Rashidun. Shortly after his investiture Ali left Medina, never to return.

For the next five years Ali engaged in a series of attempts to force others to recognize his right to hold office. He first went to the Muslim camp town Basra, in Iraq, to put down the rebellion of certain Meccan Muslims who had been inciting feelings against him. This was called the Battle of the Camel. Next he went to another important camp town, Kufah, to establish allegiance there. Then he marched to the Plain of Siffin near the ancient Mesopotamian capital at Ctesiphon, where he engaged the forces of Mu^{c}awiya. Ali's troops fared rather well at first, but then Mu^{c}awiya ordered a rather curious stratagem. At the advice of a lieutenant, the Syrian troops under Mu^{c}awiya attached leaves of the Koran to their lances as they rode forth into battle. The troops of Iraq under Ali's command were intimidated by this sacred symbol of divine judgment. Ali was forced to accept Mu^{c}awiya's terms—to submit to arbitration the matter of Uthman's as yet unavenged murder.

The issue of whether or not Uthman's murder had been justified was a festering sore that infected Ali's caliphate. Uthman's aristocratic Meccan family, now the powerful Umayyads of Syria, followed Arab custom in demanding blood revenge for the third caliph's murder. But many other Meccans and Medinans, as well as a growing number of non-Arab Muslims outside of Arabia, especially those in Iraq, were in sympathy with the complaints against Uthman and saw his murder as just. The arbitration that took place between the negotiators for Ali and those for Mu^{c}awiya in 658 ended in Mu^{c}awiya's favor: Uthman's murder should have been avenged! Ali was held in contempt by Mu^{c}awiya for having failed to bring justice. Against the protests of many of those who had supported Ali, Mu^{c}awiya soon proclaimed himself the rightful Caliph of Islam.

The opposition to Mu^{c}awiya did not produce much support for Ali. Many seceded from his party, accusing him of weakness in his handling of the matter.

They had felt all along that Uthman had deserved his fate. Pursued by Mu^{c}a-wiya's troops to Kufah in southern Iraq, Ali was felled by an assassin's poisoned sword in an ambush in 661. Thus ended the brief Age of the Rashidun.

The *fitna* that ended the caliphates of Muhammad's close companions was to remain an important issue throughout Islamic history. However political these events may seem to the outsider, the presence of conflict in the formation of religious traditions was often a key element within each tradition. Whether more abstract as in the Persian dualism between the forces of Light and Darkness, or whether more concrete as in the ancient Israelite conquest of Canaan, the Near Eastern religions especially placed great emphasis on unity precisely because they faced enormous opposition.

For Islam, the religious dimension of the conflict raised questions that would have to be answered. What sins should exclude one from membership in the Islamic Umma? Who is a believer? The tension between defining right belief and achieving political cohesion was a chief legacy of the Age of the Rashidun to subsequent history.

Ali's legacy has been enormous. His followers have perpetuated a memory of him that is extremely pious. For some Shi^{c}ites the honors have reached divine proportions. For all of Islam, a favorable memory of the fourth caliph survived the ignominy of his five-year reign. Seen both as a warrior and as a saint, he is also remembered as an extremely self-giving person, attentive to the needs of others. His strength of character and pious devotion to Islam rank him among the authoritative sources of traditions about the Prophet's Sunna, especially among Shi^{c}ites.

The Golden Age of the Abbasids: Baghdad, City of Peace

History lends itself to explanation by comparisons. What was happening in Persia when Rome fell? What was the China of Confucius like as compared with the India of the Buddha (who were roughly contemporaries)?

A period of high cultural achievement in Islam took place during the first phase of the Abbasid Empire, which in its entirety lasted from A.D. 750 to 1258. Historians of Islam often choose the year 800 as a poignant moment for comparison. In that year on Christmas Day, Charlemagne was crowned Holy Roman Emperor in St. Peter's Basilica in Rome by the Christian Pope. Europe was emerging from the so-called Dark Ages to become a vast civilization for which the Christian religion would provide a unifying world view. The term "Christendom" designates Christian civilization in Europe during the Middle Ages.

In A.D. 800 Baghdad was the capital of Islamic power and culture, and al-Harun al-Rashid was its caliph. In almost every respect, the Abbasid Empire excelled the Holy Roman Empire. The Abode of Islam under Harun was first of all much greater in extent and population than European Christendom. Moreover, academies in the arts and sciences were established by Harun and his successor, the caliph al-Ma'mun, in which scientific, literary, and philosophical treatises from Greece, Persia, and India were translated into Arabic and seriously studied.

We owe a great debt of gratitude to the Abbasid scholars and to their enlightened royal patrons for preserving and furthering the great literary and scientific achievements of antiquity. For example, some of Aristotle's works would have been lost forever had not the Abbasid scholars made careful translations, often comparing several old Greek manuscripts and choosing the best reading, passage by passage. We have noted that Muslims held special respect for those they called "People of the Book," the people of scriptural religions, and often in these academies Muslims, Christians, and others worked together in a common scholarly search for truth about the past.

In addition to Aristotle and the Greek philosophers, Abbasid intellectual tastes ranged from mathematics, astronomy, geometry, and optics to medicine, pharmacology, music, poetry, and the literary arts. These studies were often implemented in special academies, "think tanks" we might call them, established by royal patrons. The House of Wisdom was built in Baghdad by the Caliph al-Ma'mun (reigning 813–833). It included a library and apartments for those appointed as "Fellows" to the academy, and a stipend was paid to the scholars who worked there.

The most famous appointee was the Christian Arab scholar, Hunayn ibn Ishaq (pronounced Iss-hak) whose knowledge of Greek and Syriac—the two languages in which much of Hellenistic philosophy was written at that time—proved to be invaluable to the task of translation. The genius of the Arabic translations of this period (there had been earlier literal translations into Arabic) was that the abstract conceptual ideas of Greek philosophy were rendered creatively and accurately into Arabic.

Many Muslim philosophers and theologians were to use these translations in the elaboration of Islamic thought. Perhaps the most famous figure to do so was Avicenna (a Medieval Hebrew corrupt version of the Arabic Ibn Sina), who lived two centuries after Ibn Ishaq. Avicenna wrote several commentaries on the Arabic translations of Aristotle's philosophy. These commentaries were not merely explications of the earlier texts, but were also probing philosophical exercises into the meaning these held for the intellectual understanding of Islamic belief. They produced a lively controversy among philosophers and theologians in Islam. Later Christian theologians such as St. Thomas Aquinas, and Jewish thinkers such as Moses Maimonides, were to take up the arguments that Avicenna and others had earlier advanced.

At the same time that the Abbasid scholars were championing what Muslims referred to as the sciences of antiquity, Muslim religious scholars were everywhere present in mosque schools, studying the roots of Islamic religion. These roots were discussed in Chapter 1: *Koran,* the *Sunna* of the Prophet, learned *consensus,* and reasoning by *analogy.* The scholars of the Abbasid Age continued to write valuable treatises on the meaning of the Koran. In the new intellectual environment of Baghdad these treatises developed sophisticated analyses of grammar and lexicography, and hence scholarly grammars and dictionaries of the Arabic language were written. In the time of the early Abbasid caliphs, important collections of Hadith, or sayings of the Prophet, were written down and codified. Islamic law had become an independent discipline and served as an important stabilizing force in Islamic society. Theologians endeavored to rationalize the roots of Islamic belief, and important theological controversies raged in the various schools that centered in Baghdad and elsewhere in the Abode of Islam.

It is important to remember that the Islamic Empire, like Christendom, was a total society comprising many ethnic groups and confessional religions. We use the term "Christendom" for the total cultural milieu of Medieval Europe and the term "Christianity" for the main unifying religion in that total system. The term "Islam," however, serves to designate both the total culture *and* the religion, and therein lies some confusion. One scholar has recommended the adoption of two separate terms, "Islamdom" and "Islam," to avoid this confusion.[8] Although this suggestion is not likely to be followed in discourse about Islam, the point is a good one. And nowhere is the distinction more appropriate than in the discussion of the Golden Age of the Abbasids.

Those Christians, Jews, and others who preferred to remain within their own religious traditions were allowed to do so by the Muslim authorities. The Arabic term for such persons is *dhimmī;* it means a person whose religious belief is included within the Islamic view of sacred history. Practically speaking, the Dhimmis had their own religious courts and intellectual institutions within Islamic society. Christians caught stealing were handed over to the Bishops' courts, Jews to the Rabbis'. Often under the Abbasids, Jewish, Christian, and even secular intellectuals would engage Muslims freely in argument over religious and philosophical matters. Caliphs such as al-Ma'mun enjoyed bringing the leading proponents of various doctrines into the royal chambers to debate such matters as the divinity of Jesus (opposed by Jews and Muslims) or the truth of Aristotle's philosophy (opposed by the orthodox scholars of all religions). In the cosmopolitan atmosphere of Baghdad many ideas from far and wide were aired. As noted already, when it came to establishing cross-cultural institutions such as academies, hospitals, and bureaucratic institutions, intellectuals were appointed on the basis of pertinent skills with little regard for religious persuasion. Such was the climate of Abbasid Baghdad.

BAGHDAD, CITY OF PEACE. It might be useful to ask what connection this unfolding of Islamic culture in the ninth century has with Islamic sacred history and the notions of sacred time described earlier. What Islamic symbols were appropriated and borne out in Baghdad, the City of Peace, which was deliberately constructed as an Islamic city? When the Islamic dynasty of the

[8] Marshall G. S. Hodgson, *The Venture of Islam,* 3 vols. (Chicago: University of Chicago Press, 1974), Vol. I, pp. 54–60.

Umayyads collapsed in 750, the seat of power in Damascus, Syria, was destroyed and the new capital was erected in Iraq. This change of location symbolized the decline of predominantly Arabic expressions of political and cultural modes, and the ascendency of other elements in Islamic society.

The city of Baghdad itself is interesting in this respect. The Abbasid caliph al-Mansur directed his architects to build a round city over a mile and a half in diameter encircled by a rampart wall. Towers were situated at the four points of the compass, and beneath these were the main gates into the city. The four entrances faced the main overland routes for which Baghdad served as a crossroads. While the Meccan Ka^{c}ba remained the most sacred focal point of the Islamic religion, Baghdad became the new cultural and political axis of the Islamic Empire, replacing Damascus of the Umayyads. The road between Baghdad and Mecca remained open and heavily traveled by Muslim pilgrims and religious scholars. But what bearing did the sacred space and time associated with Mecca and Medina have upon Baghdad?

The construction of the original city of Baghdad suggests that beyond its political and economic importance, it was intended to have special symbolic significance.[9] The city was regarded by some as the "navel of the universe," a designation that had been applied already to sacred cities such as Jerusalem. Yet Baghdad was basically a secular city. As one penetrated the walls through its gates, the first circle of buildings past the ramparts consisted of dwellings and shops. The homes were organized into neighborhoods formed of ethnic and tribal groups representing the wide diversity of peoples that comprised Islam under the Abbasids. The houses themselves appeared uninviting from the outside; these houses opened out only cautiously onto the street, where rougher elements were often about. The main functional access was to the courtyards where families and clans congregated in the traditional Middle-Eastern lifestyle.

In the center of the city were the caliphal palace and the royal mosque. Here architectural façades were richly artistic, and symbolic. It was to the center of the city that the great political, religious, and cultural figures of the day found their way. In the large reception hall of the imperial complex, statesmen, scholars, envoys, and travelers from around the world came to plead their cases and celebrate their causes. In the adjoining royal mosque one directional reminder indicated another center of high importance. The *mihrāb* or prayer niche, a common feature of all mosques, faced in the direction of Mecca. This directional orientation is called the Qibla. Five times each day in the royal mosque, as in all mosques and places where Muslims paused to perform the prayer, Islam pointed beyond its secular involvements to another, more sacred center: Mecca. All Muslim leaders of the Prayer would mention the name of the caliph in Baghdad, but when the caliph prayed, he joined all Muslims in facing the Meccan Ka^{c}ba.

It has been suggested that the circular city of Baghdad was a "conscious

[9] The point is made by Oleg Grabar, *The Formation of Islamic Art* (New Haven, Conn.: Yale University Press, 1973), p. 67.

attempt to relate meaningfully to the conquered world, by islamizing forms and ideas of old."[10] The history of Middle Eastern civilizations knows many examples of new sacred sites and cities built on top of old ones. In many cases older ideas and forms were given new expression and recognition. As we have seen, the older civilizations of the Jews and Christians were not obliterated by Islam.

The sacred history implicit in the Koran gave new meaning to the symbols of a basic world view shared by the peoples of the Middle East for four millennia. The sacred time of Koranic revelation was regarded by Muslims as the "Seal" of previous dispensations. With the building of Baghdad, Islam centered itself in Mesopotamia (modern Iraq), in which the Christian, Zoroastrian, Manichaean, and other religious cultures had flourished. Since the Babylonian Exile in the sixth century B.C., for example, great Jewish communities and academies of learning had lived on continuously in Mesopotamia, and before that, the great civilizations of Babylon, Akkad, and Sumer. Physically, much of the past had been buried by the winds of time. Culturally, each new civilization uncovered and gave new life to world views and cultural modes that had been long evolving.

The ideas of the day that were aired in ninth-century Baghdad reflected the diversity of peoples who streamed in and out of the Islamic capital. They reflected a long cultural history with sacred and secular dimensions. By inviting and absorbing these many influences, Islam (and "Islamdom") declared that human culture, since the dawn of time, had served a divine plan and Islam was now its culmination.

Beyond the Caliphate: Akbar of Mughal India

From the beginning of the sixteenth to the end of the eighteenth centuries the Abode of Islam comprised three politically independent regimes: the Ottoman Turkish, the Safavid Persian, and the Mughal Indian Empires. The caliphate which had been established by the Rashidun and which had risen to great heights of power under the Umayyads and the Abbasids had been destroyed by the Mongols in the thirteenth century. Mu^{c}awiya's victory over Ali had long before signaled the drifting apart of a new political center of Islam (Damascus) from the sacred geographic symbols of Islam's center (Mecca and Medina). With the later collapse of the caliphate, what changes in the religion and cultures of Islamic peoples actually occurred? Although Islam had run out of territory it could conquer and realistically manage within one political system, it nonetheless was able to *Islamize* those who invaded its borders. Thus the Mongols who ravaged central Asia and sacked Baghdad ended up becoming Muslims, even as Turkish and Persian warlords had done earlier. The Ottoman, Safavid, and Mughal Empires that arose in the sixteenth century, however, established new Islamic capitals: Istanbul, Isfahan, and Delhi. These cities were located at or beyond the outer circle of the Abode of Islam as it had existed at the end of the Age of the Rashidun.

---

[10] Grabar, *Formation*, p. 72.

The relocation of political capitals brought about a flowering of culture as Islam acquired new patrons and confronted new ideas. Probably the most dynamic area of religious ferment was that of India. Back in the Age of the Rashidun, Muslim troops had already penetrated the Sind in Northern India, thus bringing limited Arab influence to the Indian subcontinent. Later, extremist Shiᶜite missionaries also gained some footing. But it was Islamic mysticism that proved to be the most fertile expression of Islam on Indian soil. In turn, Muslim travelers such as the great al-Biruni brought back to the Islamic heartlands amazing accounts of Indian culture and ideas. Until the sixteenth century, however, Islamic political involvement in India was managed chiefly by Turkish warlords in Afghanistan. Then in 1524 a central Asian Turkish lord named Babur established the empire of the Mughals in India. The challenge of this enterprise for Babur as a Sunni Muslim was considerable. Consolidating the vast territory of India into an Islamic empire, and working out a cultural symbiosis with Hinduism, was a political task without precedent.

AKBAR. One of the most fascinating stories of Mughal rule concerns Akbar (reigning 1556–1605), grandson of Babur. Under Akbar, the Muslim royal court in Delhi became a center of radical religious eclecticism in which elements of Hinduism, Jainism, Zoroastrianism, and Christianity were combined with Islam to create what Akbar intended as a new religion known as the Divine Religion. By most measures of orthodoxy in both Sunni and Shiᶜite Islam, Akbar's unrestrained policy of religious eclecticism was an affair of appalling license and apostasy. His experiments in amalgamating elements of the various religions of his subjects, a venture in which he took a personal interest, did not long survive his death. The very failure of this attempt is significant to the history of Islam. It showed that even though the caliphate could no longer serve as the central symbol of Islamic unity (the Meccan Shrine and the Arabic Koran remained such symbols), and even though Muslim rulers were frequently tempted to act independently of the constraints placed upon them by the Shariᶜa, the Islamic Umma was able to resist and overcome harmful ruptures.

We should not dismiss Akbar as a malevolent fool. Nor should we overlook the possible motivations he might have had in creating the Divine Religion, precisely because it did draw from the various traditions of the people who came under his rule. Under the Rashidun, the majority of non-Muslim subjects had been Christians, Jews, and Zoroastrians. As we have seen, Islamic sacred history regarded the Christians and Jews as People of the Book and they enjoyed a special status as Dhimmis. Most of the Dhimmis of the Middle East adopted the Arabic language, even for writing their own religious literature. Islamic sacred history was more hostile to the Zoroastrian religion of the Persians. The Arabic term *zindīq* became a broad term for heresy, especially the various forms of dualism and skepticism that took root in Persia.

The Mughals of India were not directed by a central Islamic caliphate in Medina, Damascus, or Baghdad. India had for centuries been a pluralistic society of Zoroastrians, Hindus, Jains, Christians, and Muslims. Like other religions in India, when Islam became the religion of the rulers, it formally became the state religion. But it could not form the same kind of natural symbiosis with Hinduism and Zoroastrianism it had with Judaism and Christianity in Mesopotamia during the days of the caliphate. Nor could Muslims realistically declare a state of siege against religions not recognized in the Koran, as they had earlier with the Zindiqs of Persia. In view of these changes in the situation in which Muslims found themselves in India, Akbar's experiment appears less damning. Even his Muslim subjects were drawn into religious error from the point of view of strict orthodoxy, because of their everyday contact with the other religions of India.

Perhaps more significant than the cultural patterns of Mughal India was Akbar's own spiritual odyssey. Like the Abbasid caliphs of ninth-century Baghdad, Akbar invited representatives of the various religions of his subjects to debate their beliefs with one another in his presence. Until 1578 he remained a Sunni Muslim. But from that date he entered into a personal crisis that sent his courtiers scurrying for alternative religious views that might appease his spiritual restlessness. Certain influential mentors suggested that he might become the "Renewer of Religion" that Muslims expected to appear at the beginning of each century, and significantly, Islam was approaching the anniversary of its first millennium. Thus Akbar came to believe he was a prophet, and some say he conferred divine status upon himself. The call to prayer and exchange of greeting with the phrase *Allāhu Akbar*—"Allah *is* Akbar"—came to bear this meaning among his disciples.[11]

So into his new Divine Religion Akbar accepted many teachings which were by no means necessarily compatible. At one point he became persuaded of the truth of Persian dualism. At another, a Hindu teacher convinced him that since the longest *sūra* of the Koran was named the *Sūra* of the Cow, the Koran itself was proof of Hindu sanctity for that animal. He also came to share the Jain dislike for killing, and the Catholic Christian ideal of celibacy. Vegetarianism, foreign to Islam, was adopted. And he maintained within the confines of his palace a sacred eternal flame, the chief symbol of Zoroastrian Fire Temples.[12]

It is interesting to note that modern historians disagree about Akbar's relation to Islam. Sunni Muslims, of course, have located him outside the pale of Islam. Their reasons are easy to understand and require no comment. European historians regard him as an apostate, a denier of his own religion, while Indian historians see him as a liberal Muslim. Commenting on these two latter views, Aziz Ahmad has surmised that "the Western assessment is based on the polemical position that Islam is incapable of liberalism, and since Akbar was a liberal he must have necessarily ceased to be a Muslim. The Hindu historians

[11] Aziz Ahmad, *Studies in Islamic Culture in the Indian Environment* (Oxford: Clarendon Press, 1964), p. 171.

[12] Ahmad, *Islamic Culture*, pp. 170–171.

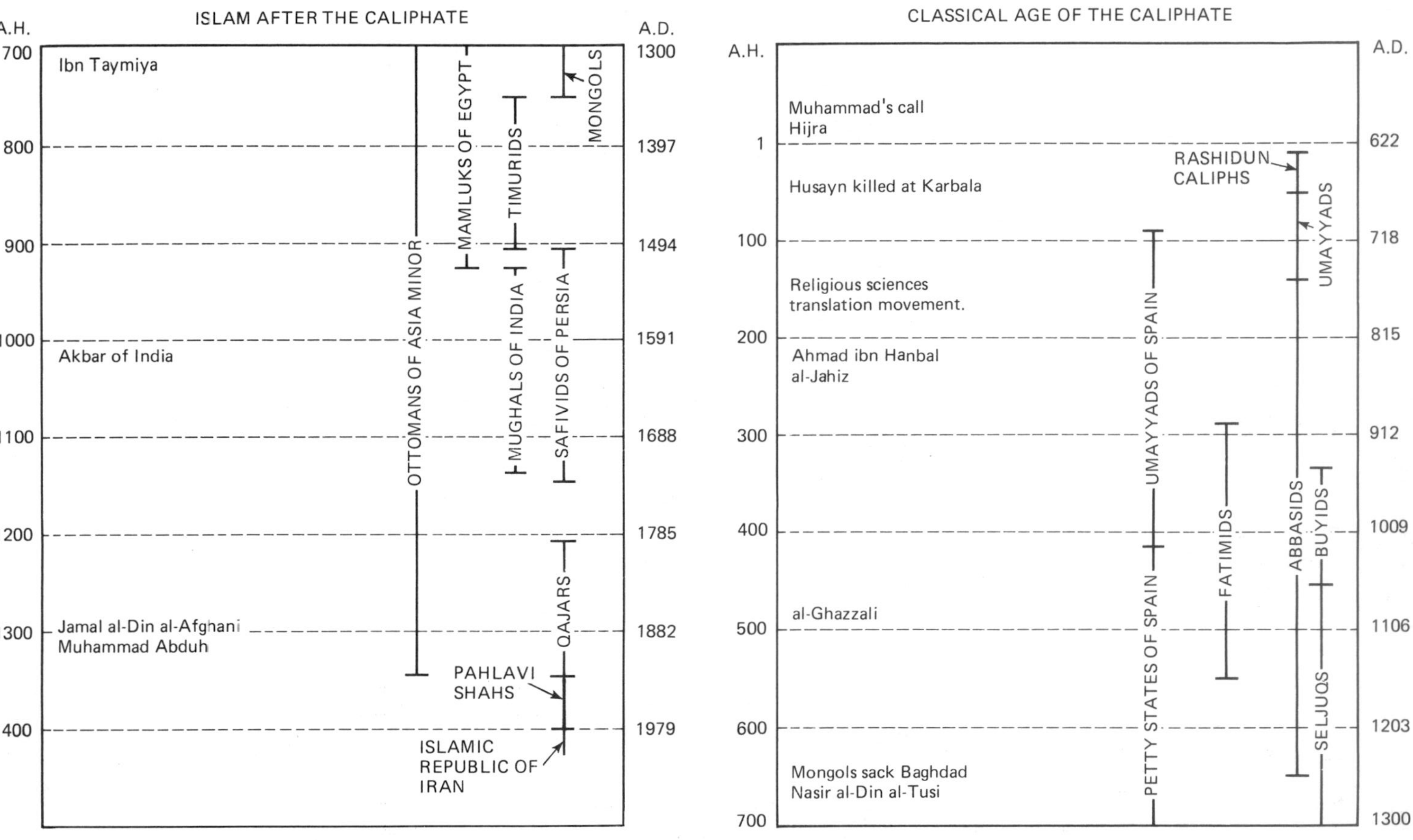

FIGURE 2.4. Chronology of Islam.

who wished to evolve a *modus vivendi* with Islam in India regard Islam as a liberal religion and Akbar as a good Muslim with some heretical views.''[13] Ahmad's view is itself polemical, but his judgment is not without merit, for the tenets of Sunni Islam, especially among the Arabs, are usually taken by Western scholars to be the norm, and all other expressions of Islam, including Shi^{c}ite Islam, are then dismissed as deviations from that norm.

Akbar died in 1605 and was succeeded by his son, Salim, who became known as Jahanjir. Akbar's several close disciples in the Divine Religion did not long perpetuate his eclectic religion. For one thing, Islam, Hinduism, Jainism, Zoroastrianism, and Christianity were much too traditional and firmly rooted in Indian soil to be drastically altered in popular piety for very long. The pluralism that has always been characteristic of Indian culture did not require the different traditions to dissolve into one another. Yet non-Muslim religious beliefs and practices, forbidden by strict Sunni and Shi^{c}ite law, were at the popular level of religion in India to be found among common folk, especially those drawn to Islamic mysticism. Those affected did not regard themselves as non-Muslims or heretics. Perhaps Akbar simply believed that the ambiguous boundaries between the different traditions could be freely crossed to the enhancement of all. Or perhaps his failure to achieve a lasting new religion is the lesson to be learned here. In any event, his story is an indication of the kinds of problems and opportunities created by the expansion of Islam into lands and cultures that were much different from the central Islamic lands of the Middle East.

[13] Ahmad, p. 175.

3

boundaries of community, faith, and practice

Measures of orthodoxy in religion and politics are matters of perspective. One is regarded a heretic, dissident, or subversive if he or she does not adhere to religious and political norms that prevail within a given group. Prevailing norms of right belief indicate how a community chooses to define itself. Along with some sociologists of religion, we may say that communities establish religious and political *boundaries,* beyond which those persons and movements that threaten the collective sense of identity are exiled. This exile can take the form of actual physical expulsion, but more often it is expressed in subtler forms of alienation such as labels applied to those who don't conform. In our own culture, terms such as "God-fearing" and "private property" signal the existence of boundary concepts. Verbal attacks against these concepts are viewed with alarm by many people. When labels such as "godless communist," "bleeding-heart liberal," or "racist" are used, they indicate that both the accuser and the accused have different definitions of right belief and action in a given social, political, or religious community.

The term *zindīq* (heretic, dualist) signifies a conceptual boundary drawn around the Islamic tradition as a whole. "Sunni" and "Shi^cite" are labels indicating divisions within Islam. Other terms exist, including ones for social and cultural distinctions. The process involved in the use of these terms is a very important one in the study of the religions of humankind. It is possible to argue that orthodox articles of faith are often the result, not the cause, of internal religious conflicts. If we take the view that countermovements against the mainstream of a tradition may express real human needs and aspirations, then we must be prepared to look beneath the surface when pejorative labels are used.

Islamic history has been a dynamic drama of different social, political, and religious movements, each searching to define its own legitimacy in terms of the central symbols of the Shari^{c}a. Where there was stress between groups, boundary concepts and labels came into use. A few persons and movements in particular are characteristic of countercultural movements in Islam. In our discussion of these paradigm cases, lines between religious heresy and political dissidence cannot be sharply drawn. The language employed to deal with all perceived threats to the collective identity within Islam has usually been religious.

However much in contempt they may be held by a community, dissidence and counterforces often play a significant role in the formation and consolidation of the beliefs and practices within the public consensus. Heresy calls for greater clarity on such matters as "Who is a Muslim?" and "Who is a member of the Islamic Umma?" Dissidence can serve to raise public consciousness of instability and inequity within the social fabric. As in other religious traditions, Islamic religious language about heresy and unorthodox ideas assumed a particular world view. Basic to that world view was the Shari^{c}a with its central symbols of the Koran and the Sunna of the Prophet. The sacred history of which these symbols formed the central core provided a means by which to identify threats to the collective identity and to explain the import of their dangers to the common people.

EARLY SECTARIAN BOUNDARIES

Sectarian Divisions During the Age of the Rashidun

The religious significance of the assassination of Uthman and the unsatisfactory arbitration between Ali and Mu^{c}awiya lay in the subsequent emergence of three sects: Kharijites, Murji'ites, and Shi^{c}ites. Each developed a different notion of its collective identity, and thus each saw differently the boundaries of right belief. The *Kharijites* believed that faith was demonstrated in righteous acts; without faith made explicit in public behavior, one could not claim to be a Muslim. Conversely, sinful acts committed by any Muslim, including the caliph, breached one's confession of faith and claim to be a Muslim. Uthman, the Kharijites argued, had acted contrary to the mandate of the Shari^{c}a. Therefore he—and all who committed grave sins—should be expelled from the Islamic Umma. When Ali lost the round of arbitration with Mu^{c}awiya on this matter, the Kharijites were those who withdrew from Ali's forces to form a separate sect. Mostly Arab, Kharijites had nonetheless resented the aristocratic families of Mecca such as the Umayyads.

The *Murji'ites* held that outward acts of faith and sin could not be judged by man except insofar as the common good was affected. They believed that the decision regarding Uthman's or any Muslim's status as a believer or sinner must be left to Allah, that is, postponed until the Day of Judgment. The Murji'ites believed that sin did not imply that one should be excluded from the community. Those who held this more moderate attitude fell more or less in line with Mu^{c}awiya and the Umayyad caliphs, though not without criticism of their alleged lack of piety.

The *Shi^{c}ites* or partisans of Ali were not happy with either development after the arbitration at the Plain of Siffin. In their view, the office of the caliph had already been greatly abused. But they also mistrusted the Kharijites, who wished to let the Umma as a whole be responsible for judging whether or not human acts were contrary to God's will (in keeping with Arab tribal custom). Shi^{c}ites further believed that Ali possessed special charisma and the proper understanding of how to apply the Shari^{c}a to everyday life, and that this gift had been passed on to him, but not to the other Rashidun caliphs, by the Prophet himself. Thus the proper source for interpreting the Shari^{c}a was the Imamate—the true line of successors to the Prophet through Ali—not the caliphate or the Ulema. Although the Shi^{c}ites soon found themselves in opposition to both the central caliphate of the Umayyads in Damascus and the sternly resisting Kharijites, many of the non-Arab peoples in Iraq who became Muslims were drawn to their cause. Both religious and social explanations have been offered for this, but it is fair to say that the various groups of Shi^{c}ites became the main bastions of resistance to Arab hegemony in Middle Eastern politics after the rise of Islam. Whether viewed religiously or politically, many of the early Shi^{c}ite groups seem to have been underground movements that gave vent to the hopes and aspirations of both Arabs and non-Arabs who felt oppressed by the policies of the Umayyad caliphate.

The Imamate

Whereas the Sunni *caliphate* can be discussed in the political terms of dynasties, the Shi^{c}ite *imamate* focuses on Ali and the descendants of his family (known as Alids). For the next several generations after the Rashidun, the Shi^{c}ites swore allegiance to Alid Imams, often in opposition to the caliphate and to the political and religious sensibilities of the Sunni majority. The complex history of the Imamate cannot be told in detail here. The many inconsistencies between Sunni and Shi^{c}ite accounts of that history make the task extremely complicated. The general picture that emerges in the sources shows that Ali's two sons, Hasan and Husayn, became the second and third Imams after Ali. They and their followers suffered persecution, resulting in the martyrdom of Husayn at Karbala in Iraq in 680 (see Chapter 1). Far from suppressing the movement, Husayn's murder by the Umayyad caliph Yazid gave impetus to the Shi^{c}ite cause.

After 680, nine more Imams of the Alid line became the spiritual leaders of the main body of Shi^{c}ites. The twelfth and final Imam, Muhammad al-Muntazar, disappeared as an infant in the year 878. For the Twelver Shi^{c}ites—the main body of Shi^{c}ism in the Islamic world today—this disappearance or *occulta-*

tion of the twelfth Imam constituted a separate notion of sacred history. The Imam, though absent from human affairs since that time, is expected to return as the *Mahdi,* the divinely "Guided One," the restorer of religion and faith to the Islamic Umma. In fact, the doctrine of a future restorer is found in some Sunni works, although the term Mahdi is not always used. The idea has been popular among Shi^{c}ites and among the masses of Muslims, particularly in times of stress and turmoil within the Abode of Islam. Actual leadership within the Twelver Shi^{c}ite community since the occultation of the twelfth Imam has been conducted by living representatives of the Hidden Imam and a structure of religious notables not unlike that of the Sunni Ulema. From the middle of the tenth to the middle of the eleventh centuries, Twelver Shi^{c}ism gained important political footings from time to time, especially during the reign of the Buyids. The Safavid Persian Empire that arose in the sixteenth century was Shi^{c}ite, and the present state of Iran is predominantly Twelver Shi^{c}ite.

Tension within the early Shi^{c}ite community resulted in divided loyalties and differences of opinion about the succession of the twelve Imams. In the eighth century some claimed that a Zayd, a grandson of Husayn who was not in the succession accepted by the majority, was the real Imam. The Zaydis, as his followers were called, established strong communities south of the Caspian and in the Yemen for a number of centuries. Although some Zaydis believed that in theory the Imam must back his claim to office by force if necessary, they were considered the moderate branch of the Shi^{c}ites while they flourished in the Middle Ages. Many of their political figures were accomplished religious leaders and theologians.

The more revolutionary Sevener or Isma^{c}ili Shi^{c}ites trace their spiritual heritage to Isma^{c}il, a son of the sixth Imam. The Isma^{c}ilis contest the legitimacy of the other son, the seventh Imam in the Twelver line, Musa al-Kazim. The Isma^{c}ili Shi^{c}ites believed that Isma^{c}il did not die but went into occultation. More aggressive than the other Shi^{c}ites, the Isma^{c}ilis believed that their Imam was the spiritual leader of all of Islam. As a result, after Isma^{c}il's death late in the eighth century, his living representatives sent missionaries throughout the Islamic world, challenging the religious leadership of the Sunni Ulema. Basic to the teachings of the Isma^{c}ili missionaries was the assertion that the genuine truths of religion were derived from the esoteric wisdom of God. The main symbols of the Shari^{c}a, the Koran and Sunna, are merely exterior forms of knowledge for the masses. The true interior meaning of religion was in the possession of the Isma^{c}ili Imams and their representatives and missionaries. For a while the Isma^{c}ilis presented a revolutionary force within Islam, attacking Sunni strongholds, sometimes with deadly consequences. For example, a sect of Isma^{c}ilis known as the Assassins conducted suicidal raids on the leadership of Islam, killing many important political and religious figures. Eastern Arabia was for a time under the political control of the Isma^{c}ilis. Also a branch of the Isma^{c}ilis known as the Fatimids established its own caliphate in Egypt and North Africa in the

CHART 3-1. SHI^{c}ITE IMAMS

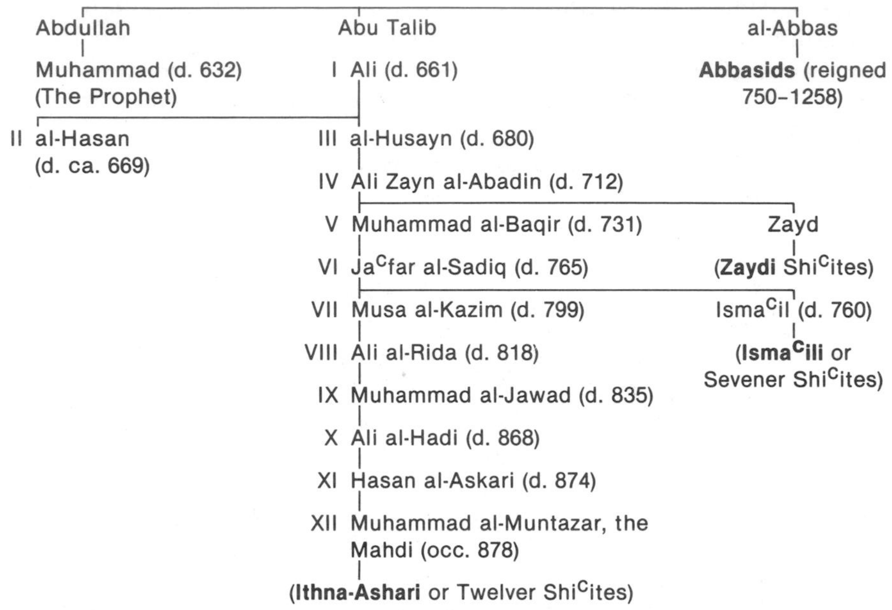

Abdullah — Abu Talib — al-Abbas

Abdullah
Muhammad (d. 632) (The Prophet)

Abu Talib
I Ali (d. 661)

al-Abbas
Abbasids (reigned 750–1258)

II al-Hasan (d. ca. 669)

III al-Husayn (d. 680)
IV Ali Zayn al-Abadin (d. 712)
V Muhammad al-Baqir (d. 731) — Zayd
  Zayd → (**Zaydi** Shi^{c}ites)
VI Ja^{c}far al-Sadiq (d. 765) — Isma^{c}il (d. 760)
  Isma^{c}il → (**Isma^{c}ili** or Sevener Shi^{c}ites)
VII Musa al-Kazim (d. 799)
VIII Ali al-Rida (d. 818)
IX Muhammad al-Jawad (d. 835)
X Ali al-Hadi (d. 868)
XI Hasan al-Askari (d. 874)
XII Muhammad al-Muntazar, the Mahdi (occ. 878)
(**Ithna-Ashari** or Twelver Shi^{c}ites)

tenth to twelfth centuries. Today in India, East Africa, and the Yemen there are still Isma^{c}ili Shi^{c}ite communities. Many are businessmen whose religious activities are nonviolent, including such programs as providing relief to the needy.

CULTURAL BOUNDARIES

Although the Rashidun had established an empire inspired by the Prophet's message of the unity of God and the equality of all believers, the texture of Islamic civilization was richly variegated with many ethnic and religious groups. As conquerors, the Arabs at first dominated other peoples. Arabic was the sacred language in the worship of the conquerors, centered in the liturgical recitation of the Koran. But Arabic did not significantly replace the languages of the conquered peoples for several decades after the Rashidun. Certain literate classes of functionaries, such as the professional record keepers in the Rabbinical academies, the Christian churches, and the Sassanian Persian chanceries became indispensable civil servants in the bureaucracy of the Islamic Empire. The Jews and Christians could preserve their confessional status by paying a special poll tax. As noted earlier, they were known as Dhimmis. Although these People of the Book enjoyed a special status in Islamic sacred history, social tensions occasionally arose among Muslims, Dhimmis, and other religious subgroups within the Islamic Empire.

Another important class of people was comprised of non-Arabs who chose to convert to Islam. Because the clan structure of social organization among the Arabs was still functional after the rise of Islam, those who converted to Islam were regarded as *mawālī (singular, mawla)* or ''clients'' of a particular tribe that absorbed them after their conversion. Many of the Mawali were soon heard to complain of being second-class citizens, possessing less than equal rights with Arab Muslims. By virtue of their traditionally important roles in Middle Eastern public life, the limits of their integration into the Arab social structures presented a serious impediment to the achievement of social and political equilibrium.

The Shu^{c}ubi or People's Movement

Among the Dhimmis, and among the Mawalis in particular, there were signs of cultural resistance to the Arab Muslims' having a privileged place within the Islamic society. One movement became a form of counterculture, waging war with the Arab intelligentsia in the field of *belles-lettres*. It was known as the Shu^{c}ubi or People's Movement. Originally Shu^{c}ubi was a term indicating that no tribe or race among Islamic peoples was superior to any other; all were to enjoy equal status under the Shari^{c}a. By the eighth and ninth centuries, Shu^{c}ubi came to designate the anti-Arab slurs of non-Arab peoples living in the Abode of Islam, including Mawali converts. Within the vast caliphal bureaucracy were many Persian Mawalis, a class of scribal functionaries which had for centuries been masters of courtly literature and etiquette. In view of the enormous pride the Arabs had in their language, the claim of Persians and other Mawalis to be able to become more lettered in Arabic than even the Arabs was defiantly provocative.

By the end of the Umayyad and the beginning of the Abbasid caliphates (eighth and ninth centuries), the Islamic Empire had produced two classes of literati. The Ulema consisted largely of Muslims, including many Arabs, who were devoted to the elaboration of religious sciences. These included the study of Koran and Sunna, Islamic law, and Arabic grammar and lexicography. The other class of lettered professionals, the court secretaries employed by Islamic officialdom, were drawn largely from the social class of Persian Mawalis. Around the beginning of the eighth century, Arabic was made the official language of the Empire. Persians and other Mawali scribes learned it as a second, official language. There was no comparable class of professionals among the native-speaking Arabs, although some Arabs did serve within the secretariat of the government. Though mostly Muslim, some of the Mawali secretaries held thinly disguised contempt for the Arabian prophet and his religion.

The ensuing conflict was waged on paper, itself introduced from China at about this time. Paper mills were soon built in Baghdad, providing inexpensive material means for the circulation of books. The Shu^{c}ubi movement among the Persian secretaries now produced works in Arabic that had little to do with Islamic religion. New genres of literature focused on manners and culture, not religious truths. Some Arabs responded by producing secular prose and poetry, an expression of their own cultural heritage. The urbane and romantic themes of Bedouin Arab poets were embellished to provide a literature of entertainment.

At the base of all this there seems to have been a fundamental conflict between Arabic and Persian cultural traditions. Although the Islamic religion and the Arabic language by the middle of the Umayyad Age were the predominate cultural vehicles of the Abode of Islam, tensions between the Arab aristocracy and the Mawali intelligentsia were abundantly evident. In a battle of words, the Arabs praised generosity and the simpler virtues of their tribal origins. Finding these qualities to be primitive, the Shu^{c}ubi literati esteemed high culture and courtly etiquette. Arabs viewed Persians as niggardly and haughty; Persians regarded Arabs as crude and uncultured. It would not be difficult to think of examples of this sort of cultural conflict in other times and societies, including twentieth-century America.

The mood of the Shu^{c}ubi Muslims is typified in the following verse by the Persian poet and satirist Abu Sa^{c}id al-Rustami:

The Arabs boast of being master of the
world and commanders of peoples.
Why do they not rather boast of being
skilful sheep and camel herders?[1]

Another poet, Mu^{c}bad, could be even more outspoken about his longing for the return of bygone days of Persian empire:

I am a noble of the Tribe of Jam—he called
in the name of the nation—and I demand
the inheritance of the Persian kings.
Tell all the sons of Hāshim [the Arabs]:
submit yourselves before the hour of
regret arrives.
Retreat to the Ḥijāz [in Arabia] and resume
eating lizards and herd your cattle
While I seat myself on the throne of the kings
supported by the sharpness of my blade
[heroism] and the point of my pen
[science].[2]

---

[1] Ignaz Goldziher, *Muslim Studies,* ed. S. M. Stern, trans. C. R. Barbar and S. M. Stern, Vol. I (Chicago: Aldine Publishing Co., 1967), p. 150.

[2] Goldziher, *Muslim Studies,* vol. I, pp. 151–52.

Commenting on the import of this literary manifestation of dissent, one scholar has said:

> The dangers of the shuubi movement . . . lay not so much in its crude anti-Arab propaganda (in spite of its appeal to the still lively hostility to the Arabs amongst the lower classes in Iraq and Persia) as in the more refined scepticism which it fostered among the literate classes. The old Perso-Aramaean culture of Iraq, the centre of Manichaeism, still carried the germs of that kind of free thinking which was called *zandaqa* [i.e., Zindiq], and which showed itself not only by the survival of dualist ideas in religion, but still more by that frivolity and cynicism in regard to all moral systems which is designated by the term *mujun.*[3]

The Arabs were hardly unequal to the challenge. In addition to pious contempt and religious condemnation, expressed by the Ulema and tradition-minded Muslims, many Arabs gave vent to cultural pride in ways that were more artistic and literary. A ninth-century writer whose devastating humor was expressed at the expense of Mawali, Dhimmis, and others who made light of Arab Muslims was a theologian and man of letters named al-Jāḥiẓ (777–869). In his several books that have survived, Jahiz ranges beyond the discussion of mere dogma to show himself to be a shrewd moralizer and keen observer of the manners and customs of virtually every ethnic and political subgroup within the Abode of Islam. In one passage he noted with irony:

> . . . this is what the non-Arabs have come to, what with the Shu^cūbiyya and their doctrines and the *mawālī* with their claims to superiority over the Arabs. . . . What could be more vexing than to find your slave claiming that he is nobler than you, while in the same breath admitting that he acquired this nobility when you emancipated him![4]

The cultural symbiosis Islam was able to achieve within its borders is all the more remarkable because such movements as the Shu^cubi were bound to arise, and did from time to time. But Islam is ideally a brotherhood of believers, not a melting pot of ethnic groups. Thus the cultural boundaries that existed and still exist in Islam have presented the Umma with the ongoing task of ameliorating cultural conflict with the ideal of religious unity. No society can boast of existing without these conflicts, but few can boast of meeting them with more success over the centuries than Muslims have.

[3] Hamilton A. R. Gibb, *Studies on the Civilization of Islam,* ed. Stanford J. Shaw and William R. Polk (Boston: Beacon Press, 1962), p. 69.

[4] Charles Pellat, *The Life and Works of Jāhiz* (Berkeley: University of California Press, 1969), pp. 85–86.

BOUNDARIES OF BELIEF

Ibn al-Rāwandī

The most infamous atheist in Islam was Abu l-Husayn ibn al-Rawandi. So hated is his memory among orthodox Muslim thinkers that an accurate historical biography is now impossible. Even the determination of when he flourished is difficult. Some sources say he died or was killed around 900, but an earlier date around 850 is just as plausible according to others. Information about him comes mainly from those who labored to refute his arguments. Their concern was with the greatness of his impiety, and thus their accounts of him well reflect the boundaries that the orthodox community felt to be most threatened by the likes of him.

Basic to the Islamic notion of human creatureliness is that man ought to be *shākir,* that is, in a posture of gratitude for Creation and for the divine blessings contained therein. The opposite, *kāfir* (ingratitude toward the Creator), is often translated "unbeliever." But it is especially in the sense of "defiant ingratitude" that Ibn al-Rawandi was held by subsequent generations to be one of the most dangerous Kafirs in Islamic history.

One feature of the Sunni version of Ibn al-Rawandi's life that clearly emerges is his alleged association with Jews, Christians, and Zoroastrians. Christian and Jewish polemics against Muslims (and vice versa) were particularly intense in the ninth century. Muslim thinkers usually attributed expressions of religious error to non-Islamic influences. Some said Ibn al-Rawandi's family was Jewish. Others said the Jews hid him from the police in their homes. His sharpest critics accused him of hiring out to Jews and Christians to write damning critiques of Islam for them. The image of an intellectual Judas appears throughout Sunni biographical remarks about him.

Ibn al-Rawandi apparently spent his early life in the eastern Islamic province of Khurasan, where religious ideas had always been more adventuresome than in capitals such as Baghdad and Damascus. Gnostic dualism, Manichaeism, Buddhism, and Hinduism were among the many religions that had settled in Khurasan in earlier times, leaving their traces in the Islamic era. Also in ninth-century Khurasan a Jewish arch-heretic named Hiwi became notorious for his devastating critiques of pious Jewish belief in the Torah and the prophethood of Moses. Perhaps there was something of a model or paradigm of ultra-atheism being played out in the traditional accounts of figures such as Hiwi and Ibn al-Rawandi.

Ibn al-Rawandi studied Islamic theology in the school of rationalism known as the Mu^{c}tazila, about which we will have more to say in Chapter 5. He learned well their defensive arguments against Islam's critics. At some point he appeared in the Islamic capital, Baghdad, and for reasons that are not entirely clear the Mu^{c}tazilites there snubbed him. In retaliation, he joined their Shi^{c}ite adversaries. In the name of Shi^{c}ism, he wrote several treatises in which he argued that belief in the Koran and the prophethood of Muhammad was the height of mental weakness. This was an extreme view which the majority of Shi^{c}ites, of course, did not avow.

One of his most interesting ploys was apparently a literary fiction in which he attributed some of his most damning criticisms to the Brahmins, the priestly caste of intellectuals in Hinduism. The basis of the so-called Brahmin critique was a logical dilemma between reason and revelation: If the truths of revelation can be known by reason, then revelation is unnecessary; if they cannot, then revelation is irrational and thus unworthy of human credence. The first horn of the dilemma was directed against the rationalist Mu^{c}tazilite theologians. The other was aimed at blind Sunni piety. Taken together, the dilemma attacked the cornerstone of all three monotheistic religions—Judaism, Christianity, and Islam—making belief in God, prophets, and scriptures a source of ridicule for rational human beings.

Along with others accused of impiety, Ibn al-Rawandi attempted to silence orthodox theologians with a technique called "the equivalency of proofs." Taking their arguments for God's existence, for the authority of scripture, and for the Prophet's mission, he showed the contrary of each to be equally logical. In effect, he was trying to demonstrate that if both the pro and con arguments for any article of faith are equally valid, they are ineffectual demonstrations of truth. He also delighted in pointing out contradictions in scriptures, especially the Koran, though the Bible was shown to be just as vulnerable. The chief Islamic test of Muhammad's prophethood was the Koran itself, a miracle in the eyes of Muslims for its inimitable Arabic linguistic qualities. Islamic dogma asserts that like the miracles of Moses and Jesus, such as dividing the Red Sea and raising the dead, the inimitable Koran is a supernatural sign of Muhammad's prophethood. Ibn al-Rawandi countered that if this were the case then Euclid's *Geometry* and Ptolemy's *Almagest* (on astronomy), which were admired as incomparable books of learning in those fields, must be miracles; hence, their authors must be prophets from God. This tactic of forcing an opponent to absurd conclusions with his own arguments was widely practiced, even among Muslim theologians.

Later literature has attested that Ibn al-Rawandi ended his life a hunted and despised man, some say killed by government agents. The Mu^{c}tazilites claimed that he recanted late in life and that he wrote works refuting his earlier atheism. It is even possible to see him as much abused and misunderstood in his own lifetime, and to say that what he was trying to do was to show that the so-called rationalism of the theologians was a weak disservice to Islamic faith because it attempted to prove the unprovable. Be that as it may, his life and writings had the effect of focusing Islamic attention on some of the most critical problems of belief. Whether in fact or in fiction, he was truly a paradigmatic figure in Islamic intellectual history. Through the refutation of his pungent criticisms, Muslim theologians were better able to achieve a more articulate understanding of the intellectual boundaries that guarded the religious life against dangerous forces of disunity.

BOUNDARIES OF PIETY

In the early days of the Islamic conquests, many Muslims developed an inherent distaste for the corrupting influence of the personal wealth these wars had brought. From this more simple expression of faith arose an ascetic form of piety, that is, a life of devotion to the teachings of Koran and Sunna unmarred by quest for worldly gain. The life of the Prophet lent itself to this interpretation: his frequent retreats into the hills to meditate; his total trust in God through many years of hardship and oppression; and the utter simplicty of his house and possessions. Among those who preferred more ascetic forms of piety were some known as ''People of the Bench'' because they used to spend their time in prayer and devotion on benches near the Prophet's house in Medina. They believed that the riches of God were accessible only through a life of poverty and abstention. Many ascetics adopted the habit other Middle Eastern holy men had of wearing unostentatious white garments made of wool (Arabic, *ṣūf*). This may be the origin of the term ''Sufi'' that is widely applied to the mystics of Islam.

The Sufis sought to discover the interior meanings of the Koran and Sunna. Their interpretation of scripture and their performances of prayer and other religious duties were noticeably at variance with the popular consensus on these matters. The mystics' rejection of the worldly life and the outward forms of piety practiced within the orthodox community brought mistrust and alienation. The struggle against the mainstream of Islam earned for many Sufis oppression and even martyrdom. Such negative reactions, however, usually came from the orthodox Ulema. Often the Sufis were quite popular among the masses, and many of the Sufi masters were respected scholars in the religious sciences.

Sufism is not properly a sect of Islam; most Sufis regard themselves as Sunni or Shi^{c}ite Muslims. But through their mystical orientations they express a mode of piety that distinguishes them from the larger community. This mode of piety is still to be found among Muslims, and it has had some appeal outside the Islamic world as well. Non-Muslim Sufi groups have formed in Europe and the United States. Such groups are eclectic, drawing much more on mystical lore from other religions than from the Koran and Sunna of Islam.

The Prophet Muhammad and other early figures became important models of piety in the saintly biographies the Sufis used for their spiritual edification. A Sufi of the ninth century could say of the Rashidun:

> When Abū Bakr succeeded to the leadership, and the world in its entirety came to him in abasement, he did not lift up his head on that account, or make any pretensions; he wore a single garment, which he used to pin together, so that he was

known as the "man of the two pins." ᶜUmar b. al-Khattab, who also ruled the world in its entirety, lived on bread and olive-oil; his clothes were patched in a dozen places, some of the patches being of leather; and yet there were opened unto him the treasure of Chosroes and Caesar. As for ᶜUthman, he was like one of his slaves in dress and appearance; of him it is related that he was seen coming out of his gardens with a faggot of firewood on his shoulders, and when questioned on the matter he said, "I wanted to see whether my soul would refuse." When ᶜAli succeeded to the rule, he bought a waistband for four dirhams and a shirt for five dirhams; finding the sleeve of his garment too long, he went to a cobbler and taking his knife cut off the sleeve level at the tips of his fingers; yet this same man divided the world right and left.[5]

These statements about the Rashidun may seem surprising in view of what was said in the last chapter about their involvement in the *fitna.* The Sufis in particular, however, developed an important genre of literature known as the "Lives of Saints." In these anthologies about their spiritual founders, pious and sometimes even miraculous legends served important instructional purposes. In this way, earthy and much maligned figures were transformed into saintly personalities.

Sufi leadership and social organization differed somewhat from the orthodox communities of Sunnis and Shiᶜites. A spiritual master known as the "Shaykh" was the focal point of the Sufi orders that developed widely in the Middle Ages. Muslim aspirants would present themselves to a Shaykh and ask to receive his spiritual guidance. Often the Shaykh presided over a compound of buildings, known as Zawiyas, within whose walls several disciples were led in spiritual exercises by the Shaykh. The several spiritual devotions or "stations" to which each disciple was assigned included private experiences, such as the constant repetition of the divine name, Allah, over long periods of time. Some Sufi orders also had public liturgical orations in which poetry and dancing served to create ecstatic feelings of nearness to God. Those who practiced piety in this manner were known as the "intoxicated" Sufis, that is, they were drunk on the spirit of God. For all Sufis, the desired goal was to achieve nearness or union (Tawhid) with God. Most Sufis have held that *God is the only reality.* Thus their exaggerated forms of poverty, their prayerful remembrances or *dhikrs* of the divine name, and their ecstatic and sometimes erotic love poetry all sprang from the single purpose of striving for union with God.

Abu Yazid of Bistam

Bistam in northeastern Persia is the site of a shrine to which pilgrims have streamed for more than a thousand years. The hamlet of Bistam was the home of Tayfur ibn Isa, known as Abu Yazid, the son of a Zoroastrian convert to Islam. Except for occasional ambiguous statements about a pilgrimmage to Mecca and

[5] Cited in A. J. Arberry, *Sufism, an Account of the Mystics of Islam* (London: George Allen & Unwin Ltd., 1956), p. 32.

Medina, it seems that Abu Yazid led a life of seclusion in his home town. He died there in 874. Yet the fame of this spiritual recluse has spread far and wide. The shrine in Bistam that commemorates this celebrated Sufi saint is not unique in the Abode of Islam; hundreds were built in those lands to which Islam spread in the centuries following the death of the Prophet. They were the tombs of Muslim saints, many of whom were barely known outside their immediate locales. Sufis called them Friends of God. The people who have visited these shrines over the centuries have done so hoping to receive *baraka,* a divine blessing richly associated with the saint both in life and in death. Abu Yazid differs from the majority of the other saints only in the extent of his fame. That branch of Sufism known as the Intoxicated Sufis traces its heritage to the recluse of Bistam. His story illustrates important boundaries of piety within Islam.

Abu Yazid was intensely devoted to God, so much so that he labored to extinguish any expression of a ''self'' separate from God. Yet the path to God was through self-realization, shorn of all external distractions. Consider the following anecdote:

> A man came to the door of Abu Yazid and called out.
> "Whom are you seeking?" asked Abu Yazid.
> "Abu Yazid," replied the man.
> "Poor wretch!" said Abu Yazid. "I have been seeking Abu Yazid for thirty years, and cannot find any trace or token of him."[6]

The search for self *is* the search for God. Yet, ironically, to find God is to lose one's *self.* Abu Yazid's paradox of self *annihilation* (Arabic, *fanā'*) was later elaborated in theory and technique along different lines in the various schools of Sufim. Abu Yazid's intense preoccupation with the central content of Islamic faith—God—was accompanied by occasional and notorious disregard for the standard forms of expressing that faith, including the obligatory prayers, pilgrimage, and fasting. This earned him a reputation for madness in the orthodox community. Some have said he was a flagrant heretic. But like those of other Sufi saints, his biography contains solid credentials in the study of the Sunni roots of the Shari^{c}a. This aspect of his story is as essential to his place in Islam as is his irreverence, for as Jesus quarreled with the Pharisees (a term Abu Yazid used on occasion), the saint from Bistam said outward forms of piety are not enough. They may even act as a shield against the interior experience of the God they are prescribed to serve.

Sacred biographies of Sufi saints report that once when Abu Yazid was returning to Bistam from a pilgrimage to the holy city of Medina he was greeted by throngs of townsmen eager to see the now famous Sufi Shaykh from their town. It was during Ramadan, the month of the obligatory fast. As they approached, Abu Yazid pulled out a loaf of bread and defiantly devoured it before

---

[6] Farīd al-Dīn ^{C}Aṭṭār, *Muslim Saints and Mystics: Episodes from the Tadhkirat al-awliya'* ("Memorial of the Saints"), trans. A. J. Arberry (Chicago: University of Chicago Press, 1966), p. 121.

their astonished eyes. The crowd shrank away in horror and disgust. On another occasion:

> "A man encountered me on the road," Abu Yazid recalled.
> "Where are you going?" he demanded.
> "On the pilgrimage," I replied.
> "How much have you got?"
> "Two hundred dirhams."
> "Come, give them to me," the man demanded. "I am a man with a family. Circle round me seven times. That is your pilgrimage."
> "I did so, and returned home."[7]

The many stories about the Shaykh's notorious lack of piety serve as insights into a man deeply concerned not to let the outward forms of piety build up his own ego to the eclipse of God. The reputation for madness this earned him is itself significant. We need only recall that the Arabs of Quraysh in Mecca had accused the Prophet of madness and of poetic enthusiasm. He was also said to be poor and illiterate. But madness, poetic enthusiasm (ecstasy), poverty, and illiteracy did not become extolled as Islamic virtues in the Sunna of the Prophet. The contrast between Muhammad as pagan Arabia saw him and Muhammad as model for his community (Umma) indicates the ironies of his sacred biography. The illiterate Muhammad had been chosen to recite the incomparable linguistic masterpiece, the Koran. The poor orphan of Mecca had become Prophet of God and the inspiration for a new political order. The mad, poetic-like utterances of this oft-rejected Prophet had become the rationale for a new world religion.

So then with Abu Yazid we find no effort to expunge from his life story the signs of madness and alienation from the community in which he lived. His stance over and against the norms of the Islamic Umma was a message to later Sufis. It was also an explicit declaration of boundaries of piety that existed within Islam. Sunni Islam could not accept Abu Yazid's flagrant abuse of normal religious practice, and Abu Yazid could not find in the external forms of worship a final introduction into the mystery of God's being. Both the orthodox Ulema *and* the Sufis relied upon the Koran and the Sunna as sources of religious piety. There came into focus a distinction between external, observable forms and internal, secret meanings. For the orthodox Umma, these were one and the same. For the Sufis, the outer forms were ciphers. One must start there but must go on to penetrate inner meanings. For many, such as Abu Yazid, this called for the rejection of external forms of worship, at least as a provocation to jolt the masses out of the slumber of their pious formalities.

Ultimate truth for Abu Yazid was God. God is the All, and union (Tawhid) with God is total. Willing as they were to dismiss most of his antics as madness, later generations of the Sunni Ulema could not forgive Abu Yazid's infa-

[7] Aṭṭār, *Muslim Saints, p. 114.*

mous declaration: "Glory be to *me!*" The *gloria* in Arabic is restricted solely to God. Applied to one's self, it amounted to self-deification, and a heinous denial of God. For Abu Yazid, only the annihilated self could so praise God. For the many who saw only blasphemy in this phrase, only one who ceased to be Muslim could declare such sacrilege. Between the polarities that were thereby highlighted, the Sufi Shaykhs, the orthodox Ulema, and the masses of spiritually motivated Muslims have struggled to define the boundaries of piety appropriate to the mandate of the Shari^{c}a.

4

islamic expressions of form and beauty

Muslims often ask their Western acquaintances who have read the Koran (usually in translation) whether or not they liked it or were persuaded by it. The question is perfectly natural, but those who read a scripture as outsiders to the language and culture in which it was originally expressed have little reason to appreciate it, and they may find it unappealing without intending disrespect. If the initial assignment is not to read the Koran in translation, but to listen to the melodic Arabic chant of a trained reciter, or to look at the beautiful pages of the Koran in stylized calligraphy, the reaction can be quite different. Calligraphy and chant greet the senses, leaving an artistic rather than a pedantic impression. Art rises above the limitations of specific languages and captures the eye or ear of any beholder or listener. Full appreciation of another religion and culture cannot come from paintings, concerts, recordings—in short, not from art through the senses alone. But, as one writer on art and religion has said, artistic expression "opens up the possibility of communication between people who are separated by distances of space or time."[1] Without requiring us first to learn another language, art offers us insight into how others have seen the world—what kind of world created the artist and what kind of world he or she was creating through a specific medium of expression.

In previous chapters we reflected upon many of the diverse elements which come together to form the mosaic of the Islamic world. The diversity of artistic traditions found within the Abode of Islam is no less varied than other customs

[1] James W. Karman, "Art," in *Introduction to the Study of Religion,* ed. T. William Hall (New York: Harper & Row, Publishers, Inc., 1978), p. 110.

and traditions, and yet there exist some distinctive Islamic art styles which articulate the vast cultural unity formed by Islamic peoples.

THE UNIFYING FACTORS OF ART

Several unifying forces contribute to form an Islamic art style. The most important of these is the Islamic religion itself. Islam as religion serves as a common foundation upon which other aspects of culture are built. The bond of a common faith creates a certain attitude and a certain world view which are to be found throughout the centuries and the regions of the Islamic world. Common expressions of belief, ritual, and social pattern are in turn reflected in the arts, giving rise to "Islamic" forms of architecture, visual art, and music. Arabic, the language of Koran and Sunna, becomes a major vehicle for expression in poetry and prose, and its script becomes the medium of the arts of the calligraphers throughout the Islamic world.

Another unifying factor was the high mobility of the population. Trade between peoples of diverse cultures brought them into contact with one another. We have seen in Chapter 2 how population mobility played an important role in the rise of Islam. This theme will be expanded in Chapter 5. A ritual process that had enormous social and economic implications for the circulation of goods and ideas was the annual pilgrimage to Mecca from all parts of the Islamic world. The pilgrimage will be studied in full in Chapter 6.

Through social contact and a common religious faith, an Islamic art style arose which served to embody these attitudes and beliefs in concrete form. The sense Muslims shared in the ultimate meaning of their world found expression in the arts, and the specific beliefs unique to Islam actually gave rise to a distinctive art style. Such traits as the extensive use of calligraphy and the use of intricate interwoven linear designs can be seen to have been influenced by the importance Islam has placed upon the written word and by the reluctance of Islamic artists to render realistic human and animal forms. In this chapter we will discuss the various arts in the Islamic world, paying special attention to the roles of religious belief and cultural traditions in shaping each particular art form.

THE VISUAL ARTS

Arabesque

One who views Islamic art becomes immediately aware of the importance given to patterns of abstract design. By avoiding representational motifs, a purely abstract design succeeds in breaking ties with the concrete world. There are no figures or other recognizable forms which relate to one's everyday environment. There is no sense of three dimensions, only an intricate pattern on a flat plane.

By seeking to avoid realistic representations of the world around us, abstract art becomes especially suited to symbolize spiritual or sacred views of reality rather than the material and concrete views. By this means, in the case of Islam, abstract art approaches the true reality—the sacred dimension of the spirit—more closely than could any representational artwork. This notion is related to the fact that the rise of Islam also necessitated the rejection of the previously existing nature cults and their pagan mythologies. The art of the nature cults relied heavily upon works depicting natural phenomena, and therefore with the Islamic rejection of pagan cults, artistic representations of nature also fell from favor. Those attitudes, in combination with a precedent of abstract design in earlier Byzantine art, partially account for the preference in Islamic art for abstract design.

Abstract designs find their expression in two different yet compatible modes—the straight line and the *arabesque.* The straight line is used in creating geometric patterns. Closed, static forms composed of straight lines represent what is fixed and stable. The geometric forms in their mathematical regularity exhibit clarity and a sense of order. The arabesque, on the other hand, represents growth and change. The curving, interwoven lines of the arabesque call to mind the rampant and vivacious growth of an ivy plant; spreading, twisting, and branching off in numerous directions. Geometric and arabesque patterns of line are often used together, the designs overlapping and interlacing into a complex of intricate configurations which dazzle the imagination as well as the eye. The two modes complement each other, giving a sense of growth and life within a

FIGURE 4.1. Arabesque panels. (Courtesy of Creswell.)

framework of order. The student of religions finds an analogy in arabesque with the order that Islamic teachings provide in directing what would otherwise be a random existence. In art as in religion, human beings create a *cosmos* that yields meaning to their lives.

A precedent for the arabesque can be found in the marginal page illuminations of pre-Islamic Coptic (Egyptian) and Sassanian (Persian) art. In these earlier cultures vegetal design patterns were used, and the interweaving of stems and leaves for a decorative effect eventually gave way to more abstract forms extended over entire surfaces. Found on mosque and shrine walls and façades, arabesque is frequently used in combination with another basically linear art form that gained supreme importance in the Islamic world, calligraphy.

Calligraphy

Calligraphy is considered the ultimate achievement in the Islamic arts, for it has the power to render the spoken word in a concrete form. The religions of the Middle East have placed high importance upon the power of the *word.* The Koran echoes the Biblical and ancient Mesopotamian and Egyptian mythical notions of divine creation by words of command. The sending of prophets, so essential to the sacred histories of the monotheistic traditions, was the divine mode of communicating the word to humankind. In Chapters 1 and 2 we saw

FIGURE 4.2. Koranic calligraphy, Kufic. (Courtesy of Staatliche, Museen, Berlin.)

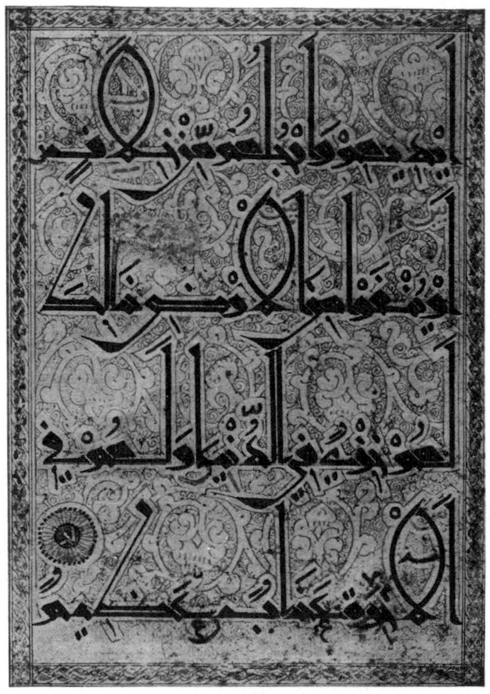

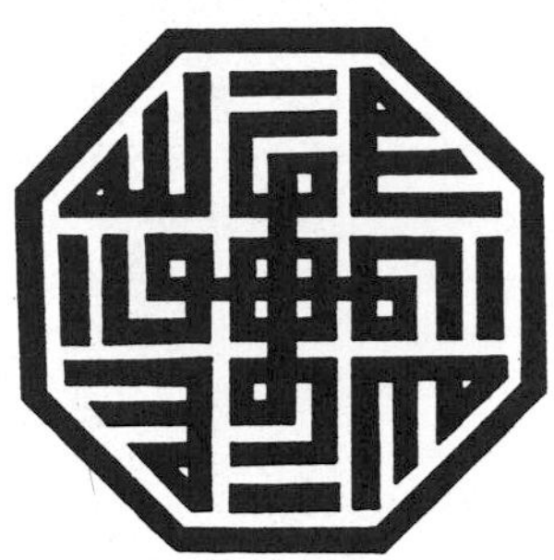

FIGURE 4.3. *Left:* "Allah" in abstract calligraphy. *Right:* "Allah" in normal calligraphy. Can you detect the abstract form of "Allah" in the octagonal rendering?

how important the revelation of the Koran through Muhammad is to Muslims; its revelation forms a sacred time in history, a "time out of time," to repeat Eliade's phrase. Through the spoken word of Allah, communicated through Muhammad, revelation was rendered visible and preserved in the Arabic script. Since Muhammad claimed only to be a messenger of God, an ordinary human being, the miracle of the Koran takes a position of primary importance that touches religious belief, literature, and art as well as calligraphy itself. For in the artistic modes of Koranic recitation and calligraphy, the supernatural role in the historical appearance of Islam is borne witness.

The skillful copying of the sacred words of the Koran became a highly cherished talent; the exercise of writing the words themselves became a sacred occupation that required years of patient apprenticeship with a noted shaykh or master. Often words from the Koran are elaborated in calligraphy to the point where, like the arabesque, they become abstract patterns interwoven and interlapped into ciphers whose meaning requires careful study to discover. Also like the arabesque, calligraphy is nonfigural, and thus it is better suited to express the spiritual, nonmaterial side of humankind declared in the message of Islam.

An interesting characteristic of Arabic calligraphy is that it is often difficult to read. We have already mentioned the elaboration of script into abstract design. Consider also that calligraphy may be painted or carved high up on a wall or dome of a mosque where even with sharp eyesight the viewer on the ground has difficulty visually resolving the lines into a script of words. Thus calligraphy, both in design and distance, is neither blatant nor obvious, but subtle, requiring thoughtful reflection. As with the message of God and the Messenger who brought it, it is believed that some will hear it and pay no heed, see it and fail to understand its sense. Rather than detracting from the meaning of the Word by making it appear to be illegible, calligraphy enhances the symbolic quality of the Word. The Word becomes elusive and mysterious. These qualities reinforce the Islamic belief that the true and total meaning of the Koran is known only to God.

Calligraphy was also used for more straightforward purposes, such as copying non-Koranic manuscripts; decorating buildings and mosques with inscriptions. In the case of the manuscripts of literary and scientific works, legibility was of course important. In such works the calligraphy was stylized and artistic, but rendered more obvious to the reader. Inscriptions on buildings were often written in the more angular and difficult Kufic script. Reminding worshippers who enter, Koranic inscriptions grace the border façades around the large gates and doors leading into mosques.

Architecture

Although secular forms of architecture abound in the Islamic world, as elsewhere, the mosque stands as the example par excellence of an architectural form created to serve religious functions. There is really no standard form of the Islamic mosque, because different regions have developed different forms. Forms common to each region reflect in large part pre-Islamic and local customs. Artistic expression, like language itself, varies from region to region. Different people have different ways of "saying" the same things.

The general mode for the mosque in most Arabic countries is based upon the form of the Prophet's house in Medina. Tradition teaches that Muhammad's house was a square building with wide arches and a courtyard, much like the typical houses of Baghdad, described in Chapter 2. One functional consideration produced a change over time. The wall which faced in the direction of Mecca, known as the Qibla, was itself faced by worshippers standing tightly shoulder to shoulder during the prayer. The broader shape of a rectangle better served the function of worship, and in time many mosques, especially in the Arab world, assumed a rectangular shape.

The great mosque of Córdoba, Spain, exemplifies many features of mosques throughout the Arab world. Inside the mosque, in the wall facing Mecca (the Qibla wall) is a small niche known as the *mihrāb,* which forms the focal point of the mosque. The Mihrab is cut into the center of the wall. As in all mosques, it is highly decorated in the styles customary in the geographic region in which it was built. Near the Mihrab there is an area set aside for royalty or aristocracy, covered by a canopy. Inside the mosque the limits of the inner space are obscured by rows of columns, by elaborate decoration that uses calligraphy and arabesque designs, and by carvings and stucco decorations. The effect is that one cannot clearly define the space within the mosque. Therefore the space appears possibly limitless, and this adds to the feeling of mystery.

In front of the main building of the mosque is a courtyard, where there is a large fountain for the worshipper to perform ablutions (Arabic, *wuḍū'*), the ritual cleansing before the prayer. The courtyard is large in order to serve as a central gathering place for the community. Famous teachers have met their students in this area. The mosque as a whole is a focal point of communication.

Outside most mosques there are one or more minaret towers. Like the church bells tolling from a steeple, the call of the muezzin from the minaret beckons Muslims to the prayer five times each day. Minarets vary greatly in style throughout the Islamic world. Squares, spirals, and tapering cylinders grace skylines in different regions. Some rise up from the mosque building itself, others are freestanding. In the absence of a minaret, a platform located on the roof of the mosque can serve the same purpose.

The main mosque in each city is known as the cathedral or "Friday" mosque. Often it is the largest mosque in town, more elaborately decorated than the others. Each Friday the leading religious figure climbs the stairs of the *minbar,* an elevated pulpit structure that stands in front of the Qibla wall facing the worshippers, to deliver a sermon.

In Iran, mosques have acquired features somewhat different from those of the Arab type just described. In the courtyard of Iranian mosques are features derived from the style of courtyards in the traditional Persian home. Each wall of the mosque's courtyard has at its center a high *eyvan,* which is a deep hallway, the opening of which is a large niche-shaped chamber that may be decorated with elaborate honeycombed vaults. One eyvan leads into the courtyard itself, one leads to the prayer hall, and the two side eyvans lead to other halls. The Iranian courtyards became more elaborate as the style developed, culminating in mosques such as the Masjid-i-Jum^{c}a (Friday mosque) in Isfahan. Also characteristic of the Iranian mosque is the brilliant blue color of the ceramic tile. The

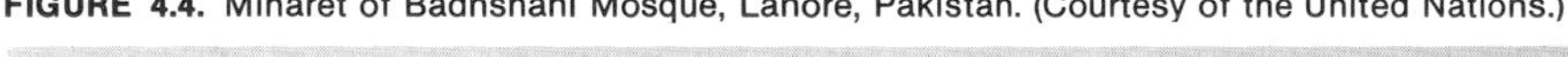

FIGURE 4.4. Minaret of Badhshahi Mosque, Lahore, Pakistan. (Courtesy of the United Nations.)

FIGURE 4.5. Minbar (pulpit) of mosque in Egypt. (Photo by Elizabeth Gottschalk.)

blue of the mosque contrasts sharply with the stark surrounding desert environment, and it gives the mosque a sense of cool restfulness.

The Turkish mosques may have had a domestic precedent in the domed tent which seems to have served as a model for the Anatolian domed prayer hall. The style was further developed when the Ottomans captured Constantinople and were impressed by the architecture of the Byzantine church, Hagia Sophia. In the sixteenth century an architect by the name of Sinan further developed the Turkish style, creating a mosque dominated by a great dome and flanked by half-domes. The half-domes functioned as supports for the main dome, thus making the usual maze of columns beneath unnecessary. The interior space of the Turkish mosque therefore had a different visual effect; the mihrab was visible to all, pointing more boldly toward Mecca. The mosque known as Iskele Jami^{c} at Uskudar exemplifies this style.

Painting and Sculpture

It has already been established that Islamic art proliferated in vegetal and geometric designs, shunning the representation of especially human figures. Not only was nonrepresentational art considered more suitable for portraying the spirit, but the portrayal of figures was at times even suppressed. When Muhammad returned to Mecca in 632 and took over the Ka^{c}ba, he removed the idols and destroyed them in condemnation of idolatry. The idols were statues, and the Koran specifically mentions statues of idols among the works of Satan. But what about other kinds of statues and figures in paintings? The Koran did not specifically mention these. In popular religious feeling, statues of any kind were abominated, but early Islamic art contained images of animals and even nonfigural Hellenistic landscapes were used as wall decorations in mosques. Sassanian Persian styles in art also influenced the Mosque, and eventually there arose a school of painting in Islam. Sculpture, however, is almost totally lacking from Islamic art.

We might reflect for a moment on why Islamic art was generally nonrepresentational and yet in certain periods and regions human and animal figures came to dominate the exquisite miniature paintings, especially in Persia.

Robert Ellwood, a historian of religions, has defined religion from two essentially different perspectives, the *temple-oriented* and the *prophet-oriented* perspectives.

> The first approach is basically cultural, starting with an awareness of society's art, architecture, music, poetry, rites, and philosophy. . . .
>
> The second—the "marketplace" or "prophet"—approach is more related to that side of human nature which makes words, which argues, which sees the separateness of man from man and of man from God. It is highly aware of the conflict between what one is and what one thinks one ought to be. It is less interested in the religion of esthetic expression, or of feelings of bliss, than in faith for moments of crisis and decision, in the inner agonies of guilt and anxiety and moral choice.[2]

Ellwood's description of the prophet-oriented religion of the marketplace aptly characterizes the original Arabian impetus of Islam. The social context was a market economy. The moral demand conveyed by the Prophet Muhammad was a verbal delivery, in keeping with the highly prized oratorical and poetic skills of the Arabs. And, as we have seen already, the primary visual art form of early Islam was calligraphy. Again, the "word" was the best expression of the divine. However, both the Byzantine and Sassanian cultures, whose lands and peoples fell largely into Muslim hands, were largely temple-oriented. Art for art's sake commingled with religion in the churches of Eastern Christianity and of Zoroastrianism. Thus, in time, Islam brought religion into the Persian marketplace (the bazaar), but the temple-oriented aspect of Persian culture brought into Islam expression in the visual arts. The most noteworthy effect was in painting.

From ca. 800 onward strict injunctions against representational art appeared in Islamic religious literature. Behind such injunctions lay not a deprecation of works of art themselves so much as fear that the artist would create images of living things. In Islam, the creative act is one reserved for God alone;

---

[2] Robert S. Ellwood, Jr., *Many Peoples, Many Faiths: An Introduction to the Religious Life of Mankind* (Englewood Cliffs, N.J.: Prentice-Hall, Inc., 1976), pp. 8–9.

God's power can not be usurped by man; this is a doctrinal matter we will discuss more fully in the next chapter. The Sunna of the Prophet, written down in the Hadith collections, reinforced this concept. In one such Hadith it is said that on the Day of Judgment an artist who had dared to create images of living creatures would be enjoined to breathe life into them. If he failed, as he surely would, he would be condemned by God.

The ban against representational art was effective against works intended for public display, but in the more private sectors of society representational art was created and appreciated. Gradually there appeared to be a willingness to permit artistically represented living things so long as they were not shown to cast a shadow (thus not really there), or were applied to objects of daily use, such as carpets, pottery, and other household implements. Human and animal figures also came to be represented in abstract arrangements as a part of decorative patterns so that they carried no more importance than vegetal or geometric ornament. By portraying men and animals in this fashion, the artist proved that he had no intention of creating a replica of a living form.

Very little is known about Islamic painting from the eighth to the thirteenth centuries. Not much has survived from that period, and the only evidence we have comes from literary sources, not the works of art themselves. The minor arts, however, flourished. The nomadic social element of the Abode of Islam preferred ornaments that were portable, such as carpets, pottery, decorated boxes, and the like. The illustration of texts in the margins was another form of minor art of this period. As we saw in Chapter 2, the Muslim world translated and studied Greek and other foreign works on science. Arabic manuscripts with

FIGURE 4.6. Pottery, sixteenth century Ottoman. (Courtesy of the Museum of Fine Arts, Boston, and Victoria and Albert Museum, London.)

ample margins provided "canvases" for Muslim artists while often the content of the books only suggested but did not determine the real subject matter of the illustrations. The information on the page might be Greek in origin, but the illustrating artist might create his own or an Islamic story in the picture he painted.

Illustrations of literary manuscripts were particularly prevalent in Persia from 1300 onward. East of the Arab heartland the ban against representational art was not felt quite so strongly. Particularly in Persia the figural paintings of China had a strong impact. Eventually even the painting of religious subjects became acceptable.

It is interesting to note that in connection with the production of illuminated manuscripts the social position of the calligrapher, as a transmitter of words, was very high; the social position of the illustrator painting on the very same text and subject matter was by contrast very low. The artist's craft was considered less honorable and less skilled than that of the calligrapher. The power of the *word* retained its conceptual importance even in Persia, where painting came to be a form of artistic expression. The calligrapher was thought to transmit not only the form of the word but its inner meaning as well. The artist, through the use of line and color, merely embellished the scene conveyed. An artisan of words, the calligrapher held the status of a learned man, while the painter was merely a workman. Some theologians argued that the painter was worse than the sculptor of images, to be ranked with money lenders and tattoo artists. It was only during the Mongol rule, beginning in the thirteenth century, that artists gained a measure of social esteem.

The Persian miniatures (taking chiefly the form of manuscript illuminations) of the Timurid dynasty carried on the traditions already established for Islamic art. The Timurids succeeded the Mongols as rulers of Persia. The figures painted in that period rendered no sense of substantiality; the artistic goal was still to decorate. All objects appearing in the picture are equidistant, with no attention paid to perspective or natural shading. Often the viewpoint changes as one looks from one element in the painting to another. For example, carpets may appear spread out as if one were looking down on them from above even though the view is otherwise from the side. The closer side of an object may be shown smaller than the farther side. An object or person, such as the hero of the scene, may appear much larger than the other figures in order to give emphasis to that particular figure. Symbolic gestures may be used to indicate mood. In fact, symbolization and abstraction are important characterizations of such paintings.

These remarks should not be taken to suggest that the Muslim artists of this period lacked skill or technique. The artists wanted and were able to create visually pleasing designs while at the same time giving symbolic content to the objects in the painting. An illustration from Rumi's poem "Mathnawi" may serve as an example. A group of travelers, after eating an infant elephant (which symbolized righteousness), is trampled to death by the mother elephant (Judg-

FIGURE 4.7. Fifteenth century Timurid miniature painting. Note that perspective is represented by means other than size of figures. (Courtesy of the Iranian Institute.)

ment). It is evident in this painting that the artist did not intend to portray a gory, realistic picture of an elephant trampling human beings. Instead, the artist is concerned with the visual pattern of the illustration and with emphasis upon the significance of the mother elephant through her size and white color.

Despite attempts to suppress representational art, it nonetheless continued to exist, after a fashion. One should note, however, that even figural art conformed to the influence of Islamic belief, and the figures themselves are not so much representational as they are decorative and symbolic. Such paintings still belonged somewhat to the abstract modes of arabesque. Like arabesque, Islamic painting tended to convey a meaning beyond the surface appearance of form, and it relied on ornate patterning to present a pleasing visual effect.

OTHER ART FORMS

Music

The music of the Islamic world is a unique blending of styles from four different sources: Arab Near Eastern, Iranian, North African (Maghrebi), and Turkish. Because of the widespread use of the Arabic language as a medium of expression in speech, writing, and poetry, vocal music has tended to be preferred over purely instrumental music. Often the rhythmic or melodic structure of a piece is determined by the vocal inflections in the lyrics and is arranged according to the rules of prosody. The two main types of music in Islam are *folk music* and what we will call *art music.*

"Folk music" arises in a popular environment and is closely associated with the lives of common people and their everyday concerns. The same melody may occur over and over with new words to fit new occasions, which may range from weddings to birthdays to the adventures of a villager on the pilgrimage to Mecca. Folk music is often sung without instruments. With the exception of Central Asia, there is virtually no tradition of a purely instrumental peasant folk music. Even for the dance the music is often purely vocal. Again, this is due to the importance placed upon the word, especially poetry, and to its significance in the social life of the people.

"Art music," on the other hand, is usually performed for the aristocracy, and thus it is more common in urban centers. Unlike folk music, art music requires a trained professional musician for its performance and it adheres to certain melodic and rhythmic rules. The musicians are trained individually by a master until they reach a high level of virtuosity. As with folk music, the singer is foremost in importance. A concert usually consists of a singer accompanied by one—never more than just a few—instrument.

Islamic music differs greatly from Western music in the manner in which it is performed. In the West, composers write their music down on paper exactly as it is to be played. A great deal of a Western musician's training is aimed toward learning to play music exactly as it is written. In the Islamic world, on the other hand, the key to music virtuosity is the ability of a performer to improvise on a particular melody or rhythm in an innovative way. Several musicians playing the same melodic line will each add their own variations in the tempo or in the ornamentation of the melody. Therefore, the performer is allowed a great deal of freedom as to how a piece will be played. The judging of a performer's artistic ability is based upon the amount of creativity and imagination displayed in the improvisation. A musician is not expected to compose new melodies, but to improve and embellish traditional ones. Even in music, the very concept of *sunna* and tradition reminds us of just how Islam was woven into the fabric of culture. Enormous creativity is there, for like the religious scholar who must interpret and apply the Shari^{c}a to ever new situations, the musician working in traditional modes also gives creative self-expression. Art and religion require interpretation in order to bring contemporary meaning.

Islam has not entirely favored music as a legitimate form of expression, especially in the context of worship. Because of its association with the aristocracy, especially in the early days of Islam, music was viewed by some as a frivolous luxury. Women also took part in the performance of music, or in dancing accompanied by music, thereby adding an element of sensuality. Another forbidden activity, the drinking of wine, was associated with music and dancing. The Koran and Sunna, especially under Sunni interpretation, saw each of these elements in association with the other, a threat to one's character. In fact, the Koran does not forbid music as such; rather, it is in the Prophet's Hadith that the music, especially of the aristocracy, is condemned.

In orthodox Sunni and Shi^{c}ite Islam, music does have some important functions. The call to prayer, for example, can be classified as chant or music. On certain festivals and holy days hymns are sung. Even the recitation of the Koran is very highly stylized so as to qualify as a type of music. This quality enhances both meaning and memorizing.

Outside of orthodox Islam, music and dance play more important roles, especially among the Sufis. Mystical orations called in Arabic *samā*^{c}, meaning "listening," are spiritual exercises done in the mode of music. The oration may include singing, dancing, and instrumental music as aids to the Sufis' attempts to reach higher and higher levels of ecstatic experience of union with God. The music serves both as an aid to heightening the emotions and as a symbol or ritual gesture of transcending the material world. Sufis believe that music can lead to spiritual knowledge by echoing the beauty and the harmony of the universe, urging the worshipper to go beyond the pedestrian feelings and concerns of this life.

Poetry

The supreme example of literature in Islam could be said to be the Koran, but the Koran actually ranks in a class by itself, as scriptures often do. As revelation, Muslims do not judge the Koran along with works by humans. Even to attempt to imitate the literary quality of the Koran was a matter of sacrilege. Other prophets had brought miracles such as Moses' dividing the Red Sea and Jesus' raising of the dead. The evidence of Muhammad's prophetic mission was the inimitable Koran. In keeping with the pre-Islamic Bedouin Arab's high appreciation of poetry and skill in spoken eloquence, the miracle of the Koran was seen at first in terms of its poetic, oratorical eloquence. The art of proper recitation was from the first days of Islam an important religious calling. Eventually, as the Arabic language passed into the medium of literature, the Koran also served as the model or paradigm for establishing rules of literary criticism.

Pre-Islamic poetry falls into two categories. The first is a type of poem composed in preparation for battle and is called the *rajaz*. It contained eloquent insults hurled at the enemy tribe. A more elaborate style is called the *qasida*. The Qasida is written according to strict rules of composition and has three parts. The first part is a lament for the tribe of a loved one that has gone away. Part two describes a journey into the desert. Part three offers a eulogy to a person or a tribe that is friendly, or the denunciation of an enemy.

With the rise of Islam, the basic form of the Qasida acquired some variations. Instead of the old tribal wars of the desert, the Islamic conquests provided new subject matter. Instead of lamenting a lost loved one, Arab soldiers carried far from their homeland in battle remembered poetically the desert that had once been home. Pride in Islamic victory formed another new theme. Political poetry emerged as an expression of conflicts within and between religious communities. Skill in poetic polemics, as earlier in tribal wars of revenge, roused emotions and renewed commitments. Even some philosophers and theologians composed their more academic subject matters in poetic rhymes in order to aid the memory.

Like music, some poetry developed in a frivolous and decadent style. Many poets valued the power of words not only to inform and teach, but also to entertain. Such a precedent was also to be found in a pre-Islamic form. Similar to the first part of the Qasida, which lamented the loss of a loved one, some poetry was more arrogant and explicit about sexual exploits. The pleasures of food, wine, and women, hardly topics to be encouraged by Islamic religious idealism, nonetheless found some expression in poetry. The aristocracy in Islamic cities resurrected interest in this more sensational poetic genre.

Non-Arab parts of the Abode of Islam developed still other forms of Islamic poetry. In Muslim Spain a type of poem called the *muwashshah* was developed. The Muwashshah ignored the metrical structures of classic Arabic poetry. Actually, part of the poem is in classical Arabic, part in vernacular Spanish. The Persians also developed independent forms of poetry in an attempt to break with Arab traditions.

Literature

By the term literature, we normally think not of poetry but prose, and Islam also came to regard prose composition highly even though it lent itself to oratory less dramatically than did poetry. In the last chapter we spoke of al-Jahiz, the great Arab littérateur of the ninth century. The term meaning worldly knowledge and the witty use of it in composition and conversation was *adab*. A man of letters was an *adīb*. This was something different from the training of the Ulema, which was steeped in the religious sciences. Adab is considered the earliest form of secular Arabic prose writing and it contains fables and treatises of a didactic nature. Al-Jahiz' best remembered work, still read in the Islamic world, is a book entitled (and largely about) *Animals*, but the lines and pages contain lively diversions about the manners of foreigners, love, religion, and a whole host of topics, all very entertaining and informative about the customs of the times.

After the tenth century another form of prose writing, the *maqāma* genre of literature, appeared. It was developed by Badi al-Zaman al-Hamadhani (968–1008). His name means "Wonder of the time from Hamadhan." A Maqama tells of imaginary events that involve two principal characters, a hero and a narrator. Through rhyming prose the narrator relates the adventures of the hero. Al-Hamadhani's hero was a certain Abu l-Fath of Alexandria, whom the narrator represents as a witty "Renaissance Man" of his age; his exploits as told by Hamadhani delighted the reader, whether peasant or professor. Perhaps the best known author of Maqama literature was al-Hariri of Basra (1054–1122). His works, known as *al-Maqāmāt* [the maqamas], had as its hero Abu Zayd of

Saruj. The following account, in Hariri's own words, tells of what led him to write about Abu Zayd.

> Abū Zayd of Sarūj was an importunate old beggar, full of eloquence, who came to us in Basra and one day stood up in the mosque of the Banū Ḥarām (the quarter in which Ḥarīrī lived) and after pronouncing a greeting begged alms of the people. Some of the magistrates were present, the mosque being crammed with eminent men, and they were charmed with his eloquence and wit and the beautiful phrasing of his speech. On this occasion he related the capture of his daughter by the Greeks, as I have related it in the Maqāma called 'Of the Ḥarām'. That same evening a number of the eminent and learned men of Baṣra were gathered at my house and I told them what I had seen and heard of this beggar and of the elegant style and witty allusiveness which he had employed to effect his purpose. Thereupon every one else there told of how he too had seen this beggar, each in his own mosque, what I had seen, and how he had heard him deliver on other subjects a discourse even better than the one I had heard, for he used to change his dress and appearance in every mosque and show his skill in all kinds of artifices. They were astonished at the pains he took to gain his object and at the cunning in changing his appearance and at his ingenuity. So I wrote the "Maqāma of the Harām" and thereafter constructed upon it the remainder of the Maqāmāt.[3]

The primary purpose of Hariri's tales about Abu Zayd was to amuse. Storytelling had long been a high art in Middle Eastern cultures. Hariri transformed this form of entertainment into the best remembered works in literature to come out of the Middle Ages. Many editions of his Maqamat were illuminated by Persian miniature paintings, thus preserving in one volume the art of storytelling, a rich literature of entertainment, and treasured paintings from the hands of gifted artists.

Both poetry and prose played a significant role in the traditions of Sufism. The Sufi poets found poetry to be an eloquent mode for expressing the intoxicating joys of experiencing nearness to God. The Sufis orally transmitted narratives and the sayings and events from the sacred biographies of saints and holy men. From the ninth century onward, these narratives were written down and became a type of religious prose. These sacred biographies also included passages from the Koran and the Hadith of the Prophet, interwoven into the legendary accounts of the saints' lives. Sufi prose literature also contained treatises of a more theological nature that sought to explain mystical doctrine. Another type of literature belonging to this class was the confessional type with eloquently described individual mystical experiences. Perhaps one of the best examples of mystical prose is the *Manṭiq al-Ṭayr* [Conference of the Birds] by Farid al-Din Attar (d. 1230). The *Conference of the Birds* describes the allegorical journey of thirty birds in search of the Simurgh. This allegory of the mystical search for

---

[3] Cited and translated from Yaqut's *Irshād* by H. A. R. Gibb, *Arabic Literature: An Introduction*, second (revised) ed., (London: Oxford University Press, 1963), p. 124.

God is revealed in the symbolic meaning of Simurgh, which means "thirty." That is to say, their journey was in search of themselves. As we have seen in the last chapter, Sufis such as Abu Yazid al-Bistami had taught that the journey to God is an interior one. Sufi literary artists such as Attar explored this abstract notion in memorable literature.

Two important conclusions may be drawn concerning the function of the arts in Islamic culture. First, they served to crystalize the abstract concepts of Islam into concrete form. Second, they integrated these concepts into the daily life of the people. We have suggested that many of the arts attempt to convey the difficult-to-grasp concept of God's transcendence beyond the material world. In the visual arts this concept is emphasized by an avoidance of representational forms. In music the nonmaterial quality of sound itself points to the spiritual experience of man, and that experience is extolled also in the mystical poetry and prose of the Sufis, albeit in a quite different way. Didactic prose, on the other hand, sought to establish morals for everyday life. Calligraphy rendered visible the spoken Word of God.

We have also seen that Islamic principles have done much to formulate the styles of Islamic art. From the unity of the Islamic faith comes a unified purpose to art. Cultural differences from region to region have accounted for differences in taste and style. Thus an important unifier, classical Arabic, finds its way into poetry in vernacular Spanish, on the façades of Persian mosques, and within the biographies of Sufi saints. The unifying force of Islam is felt in many cultural aspects of a Muslim's life, and the arts give evidence to this unity.[4]

[4] The following works offer a good introduction to the arts of the Islamic world: Oleg Grabar, *The Formation of Islamic Art* (New Haven, Conn.: Yale University Press, 1973); *Islam and the Arab World*, ed. Bernard Lewis (New York: Alfred A. Knopf, Inc., 1976), especially the chapters on Islamic art and architecture by Richard Ettinghausen, literature by Charles Pellat, and music by A. Shiloah; David Talbot Rice, *Islamic Art* (New York: Praeger Publishers, Inc., 1965).

part 2

FAITH, WORSHIP, AND COMMUNITY

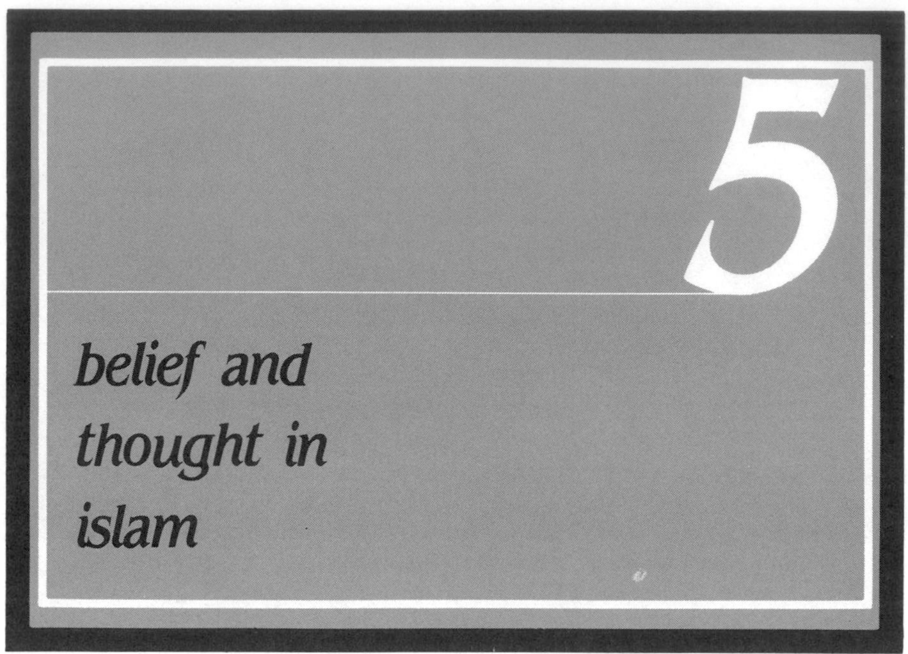

When people talk about religion, the phrase "I believe . . ." is a frequent utterance. Believe what? What are the objects of belief? Holding beliefs is not unique to the devoutly religious person. All of humankind understands the world in which it lives on the strength of a variety of beliefs. Some people believe that the country is a better place in which to live than the city. Others firmly believe the contrary is true. Proponents have argued the matter both ways. Although beliefs may be personal, they may also prove to be views widely shared within a particular group. Among the cohesive elements of ethnic, social, and religious groups are the beliefs shared by the group as a whole. Such beliefs are rationalized and discussed in persuasive language. World views formed of myths and symbols, credal statements of belief, and cogent discourse and reflection about these matters are products not of nature but of culture.

The planet Earth, with a finite range of possible climatic, geographic, and other physical conditions, has been the habitat of numerous cultures for thousands of years. World views (culture) vary just as much if not more than physical environments (nature). Each culture develops its own world views and official sets of beliefs, and each witnesses the rise of schools of thought that defend one set of beliefs against others to the contrary. The very ability to live within the world beyond the level of instinct and mere physical needs requires world views, beliefs, and systems of thought; this requires human beings to create, adapt, and change these mental concepts when it is appropriate to do so.

When we approach Islam as a field of study, we want to know why and how the Islamic religious tradition has been and continues to be a persuasive, meaningful way of life for Muslims. The next three chapters will focus on Islamic thought, worship, and social organization. Essential to these studies are beliefs involving myths and symbols. In addition to patterns of thought and conceptualization, religion and religious behavior can be discerned in the social patterns of kinship, occupations, and communities. Between these two areas of our studies—the ideals of thought and the realities of social organization—lies the study of worship and ritual. The tension between normative beliefs and actual social experiences is meditated through the rituals of life crises and of worship. All of these areas must be taken into consideration in order to address properly the question: why and how is the Islamic religious tradition a persuasive, meaningful way of life to Muslims?

EMPHASIS UPON DIVINE UNITY

I witness that there is no God but Allah. We have seen in Chapter 1 that these words form the basis of the fundamental Muslim creed and that they are invariably followed by a second affirmation: *I witness that Muhammad is His Apostle.* Muslims utter this simple declaration of faith often. Some express its words many times each day. What does it mean and why is it so important?

The answer lies in part in historical considerations. In seventh-century Arabia there were other gods besides Allah to be worshipped. In addition, the Middle Eastern milieu had produced many prophets and holy men. These two background elements, the pagan culture and language of Arabia and the monotheistic traditions of the Middle East, stimulated each other in Islam, giving profound meaning to the First Pillar of faith: "There is no God but Allah; Muhammad is His Apostle." The achievement of Islam can be appreciated all the more when we consider that the religious cosmologies or world views inherent in Arabian culture on the one hand, and in the monotheism of Judaism and Christianity on the other, were quite different, if not incompatible until Islam arose.

From Many Gods to One

Arabia in Muhammad's time was polytheistic in its conception of the cosmos and tribal in its social structure. Both the Koran and other sources suggest that until Muhammad's time Allah was thought to be a supreme god, but much more attention was paid to local deities and spirits.[1] At special locales throughout central Arabia, gods were enshrined in sacral surroundings. During the sacred months each year nomadic tribesmen made pilgrimages to these shrines to pay homage to their gods. Within the sacred territories of the gods there could be no killing of anything—plants, animals, or human beings. These sacred times and

[1] See the articles "Allāh" and "Nabī" in *Shorter Encyclopaedia of Islam,* ed. H. A. R. Gibb and J. H. Kramers (Ithaca, N.Y.: Cornell University Press, 1953).

spaces were coordinated with commercial and other cultural activities. At or near the shrines, huge fairs provided occasions for celebration, for the sale and exchange of goods, and for social intercourse. Poetry and skillful oratory, the pride of Bedouin culture, often took the form of tribal contests between distinguished bards. In pre-Islamic times the Plain of Arafat outside of Mecca had been the site of important annual fairs. Within Mecca were enshrined the idols of some of the most important gods in Arabian culture. The Ka^{c}ba which housed these idols was distinguished by a black stone, itself thought to be extremely sacred by pagan worshippers.

ETHICAL MONOTHEISM. About a thousand years before Muhammad appeared in Arabia, other prophets were challenging the religions of antiquity in China, India, and the Middle East. In China it was Confucius and Lao-tze, in India the Buddha and Mahavira. In the Middle East the ancient Persian religion was challenged and reformed by the prophet Zoroaster. In Israel the Hebrew prophets preached messages about the one God, Yahweh, and the religion of Judaism evolved from their moral demand that the people honor an ancient covenant of faith with Him. All of these prophets and reformers inspired the rise of religious traditions that have survived now for 2,500 years. The philosopher Karl Jaspers has referred to the original period of this prophetic activity as the *axial age.* Between 800 and 200 B.C. along the great river valleys of China, India, and the Middle East (the Nile and Tigris-Euphrates), civilizations arose based upon an agrarian economy.

In the Middle East, Zoroaster and the Hebrew prophets had warned their people that God was just and righteous and that He demanded morality and obedience. These prophetic warnings were regarded as messages from God, and the prophets' words were cherished as scriptures. The scriptures also contained laws (for example, the Torah of the Old Testament), and these laws, regarded as divinely sent, became the fundamental bases of new religious civilizations. The Ten Commandments encapsulate the Law of ethical monotheism that was promulgated in the Middle East during the axial age. Between the axial age and the rise of Islam, the religions of Judaism, Christianity, and several other offshoots of ethical monotheism had become well established in the lands the Muslims would later conquer.[2]

SOCIOPOLITICAL IMPLICATIONS OF COSMOLOGY. In order to understand the import of Muhammad's prophetic role as Apostle of God in Arabia during the seventh century, it might be useful to refer to a theory recently advanced in another context by a scholar of religions, Robin Horton. An anthropologist, Horton has sought to explain why African peoples have converted in large numbers from tribal polytheism to the monotheistic religions of Christian-

---

[2] The importance of the axial age to the rise of Islam within the Middle Eastern environment is discussed by Marshall G. S. Hodgson in *The Venture of Islam,* 3 vols. (Chicago: University of Chicago Press, 1974), vol. I, pp. 103–45.

ity and Islam during the past century. Most of Africa has held traditional polytheistic world views, very similar to those of Canaanites prior to the rise of Judaism, and to those of the Arabians prior to the rise of Islam. *Local gods* and spirits command the attention of the Africans in their sacred rituals, even in their less ceremonial, everyday concerns. More remote, usually, is a *high god* who is always there but who seldom functions in the rituals and concerns of everyday life. Horton has noticed that as these local African tribes come more into contact with other societies and peoples (through warfare, trading, migrations to natural resources, and incursions from the outside world), the high god comes more into focus. At the same time the local gods and spirits function less explicitly, and they may even be abandoned for all practical purposes. In other words, as tribal societies become absorbed and drawn into communication with other civilizations, a more universal god who rules and orders the cosmos becomes more functional and meaningful in concept and worship. Conversely, if the situation reverses itself and a group should become culturally isolated from the rest of the tradition, we should expect local gods and spirits to regain parochial importance.[3]

Arabia in the seventh century A.D. is pertinent to Horton's discussion of traditional African cosmologies. The Arabs were Semitic people who worshipped many gods. Like the Africans, the Bedouin peoples of Arabia had lived for centuries in tribal social groupings, fairly well isolated from the rest of Middle Eastern civilization. When the Byzantine and Sassanian Empires sought to exert military and economic influence over Arabia, success was only partial. In the desert, foreign armies were at the mercy of Bedouin raiders. Caravan routes bringing the spices and exotica of India to markets in the Mediterranean, and Byzantine products back to the East, were in the effective control of the Arabs.

The eventual impact of the outside world upon Arabia was nonetheless inevitable. Men, goods, and ideas from faraway urban civilizations began to circulate in Arabian market towns. Monotheism, and perhaps more significantly, a cosmology that presented a unified world view, began to appeal more to those Arabs affected by these social, economic, and political changes. The message of Allah delivered by Muhammad developed into a system of thought that proved to be appropriate to the growing international awareness felt by the Arabs.

Of course, many Arabs in Muhammad's time were not eager to abandon their local gods and religious customs. As among the Africans, many of the tribal leaders of Mecca, who were devoted to established pagan polytheistic beliefs, resisted such changes. We saw in Chapter 2 that Muhammad's role as Prophet/Warner among the Quraysh was deeply troubled by old tribal resistance. The Koran classified tribal polytheism and the culture this entailed as *Jahiliyya,* a "Time of Ignorance (of God)," that is, a time in which the original pure monotheism of Abraham had been forgotten. The tribesmen living in distant regions

---

[3] Robin Horton, "On the Rationality of Conversion," *Africa,* 45/3 (1975), 219–35, and 45/4 (1975), 373–99.

of the central Arabian desert were the most remote from the changing world views of Meccan traders and caravan merchants. It was precisely these tribes that most fiercely resisted accepting Islam. During the early years of the rightly guided caliphs, "Wars of Apostasy" were waged by Muslim troops against these recalcitrant tribesmen. Eventually, however, the tribesmen were settled by the expansion of Islam into lands outside of Arabia. Soon they too were persuaded by the Islamic doctrine of one, all-powerful God, the creator of an all-encompassing cosmos.

These remarks about the changing social, economic, and political situation in Arabia in the seventh century place in perspective the cardinal concept of Islamic belief mentioned in Chapter 1, the doctrine of God's unity, "Tawhid." Among the monotheistic Western religious traditions, Islam has most insistently asserted the unity and oneness of God. As Islam spread into other Middle Eastern lands, the doctrine of Tawhid, at first articulated against tribal world views among the Arabs, became a rigorous monotheistic world view that challenged the dualism of Zoroastrianism and the tri-theism of Christianity. The theological writings of Muslims have usually begun with carefully reasoned chapters on Tawhid, God's unity.

One God, Many Worlds and Beings

We have already gained some sense of the Islamic experience of the cosmos. Its structure is compelling in its simplicity, created and governed by the one God, Allah. The cosmos is geographically centered around the sacred Ka^{c}ba, the directional focus or Qibla of the canonic prayers that are performed each day at prescribed times. The pilgrimage to the Meccan Ka^{c}ba annually brings Muslims from every direction around the world to this focal point of Islamic religious consciousness. The sacred center of Islam has persisted in spite of the fact that the political capitals of the Islamic world have located at such far-flung places as Baghdad, Istanbul, Delhi, and Córdoba. As the political fortunes of Islamic civilization have fragmented and shifted, the sacred center in Mecca has persisted as a powerful symbol of the unity of Islam.

Islam affirms the Judaeo-Christian doctrine of the divine creation of the world out of nothing *(creatio ex nihilo)*. The earth is filled with the fullness and goodness of Allah's creative act. Adam, the first man, was a special creature, but humans were not the only beings created to inhabit the cosmos in obedience to Allah. The first *sūra* of the Koran, entitled "The Opener," begins with the phrase, "Praise be to God, Lord of the Worlds." The plural, worlds, does not refer to other planets and stars as we think of them but rather to other sacred realms of angels and unseen spiritual beings. The most important of the angels is *Jibrīl* (Gabriel), whose function it was to convey the message of Allah to Muhammad, who in turn recited it to the Arabs. Jibril is sometimes called the "Faithful

Spirit'' and he occupies an important place within the Islamic conception of cosmos.

Among the angels was also the figure of *Iblīs,* who, as in other Near Eastern traditions about the Devil, had fallen through disobedience into disrepute among the heavenly host. According to the Koran, the cause of Iblis' fall was his refusal to pay homage to Adam, the first man:

And when We [Allah] said unto the angels:
Prostrate yourselves before Adam,
They all fell prostrate except Iblis.
He demurred through his pride,
and so he became an unbeliever. (Koran 2:34)

Iblis and his legion of seducers were granted a reprieve from punishment until the Day of Judgment, at which time they will be cast into the fiery pit of hell. In the meantime it is within the power divinely granted to Iblis to lead astray those who believe not in Allah. The paradigm example of this seductive power is the Koranic story of Iblis tempting Adam and Eve to eat of the forbidden tree of immortality and power (Koran 20:116–122).

Other angels appear in Islamic cosmology. Michael, Israfil, and Azrael were mentioned in Chapter 1. Others appear with special functions. Hārūt and Mārūt were thought to have possessed the secret knowledge of ancient Babylonian magic. In the myths of earlier Near Eastern peoples, including the Hebrew, human knowledge about the secrets of nature and the use of civilized tools was communicated to humankind through divinely sent sages and kings (cf. Genesis 4:17–22). Harut and Marut also possessed the means of creating disharmony between men and women (Koran 2:102). Here again the student of religion notices a correspondence between cosmological views and social realities. Thus the pursuit of a life of faithful obedience to Allah is seen as a cosmic drama that engages the many realms, visible and invisible, that are felt to impinge upon the phenomenal world of reality and social experience.

Early Muslims inhabited a world felt to be filled with other unseen creatures of God. Angels played an important role in the mythic times of origins and in the revelation of Allah's word to humankind. The Arabic term for angel, *malak,* means ''messenger.'' Other unseen creatures included the *jinn* (known in the West as ''genies''). Along with humankind and the angels, the Jinn appear in the Islamic tradition as intelligent beings who, like humankind, are subject to being led astray or saved. They are usually defined as imperceptible creatures, although they have the power to assume visible, creative form from time to time. Muhammad's role as Messenger/Warner was to the Jinn as well as to humankind, for the salvation of the Last Day comprehends the many realms of Allah's lordship. Thus some of the early Islamic juristic works entertained a number of questions regarding legal status in matters of property and marriage between humankind and Jinn. Islamic folklore has associated the Jinn with fabled performances of magic. Many of the stories in the popular romances of the *Thousand and One Nights* portray Jinn as agents of marvelous feats of magic. Related to the Jinn are the *shayāṭīn* (singular *shayṭān,* i.e., Satan). They appear in the Koran as proud and rebellious demons who, through their disobedience, will suffer punishment in hell-fire. The Koran (*sūra* 26) had suggested that the poets and the other Arab contemporaries of Muhammad who persisted in the cultural and religious attitudes of the ''Time of Ignorance'' were inspired to go astray by the satans.

Another aspect to the Islamic conception of the cosmos is the notion that the Word of God is inscribed on a heavenly tablet, sometimes referred to as the ''Mother of the Book.'' The Koran, and the earlier scriptures of the Christians and Jews, are spoken of as having been ''sent down'' to humankind through angels to prophets. The prophets mentioned in the Koran are mostly figures that appear in the Old and New Testaments of the Bible. Thus the original Torah, Gospel, and the Koran are all believed to be revealed scriptures in the Islamic world view. On the historic occasions with which the prophecies of Moses, Jesus, and Muhammad are associated, the Islamic view is that Allah's heavenly inscribed word was sent down to select human civilizations. These recipients of Allah's Word through His messengers are the People of the Book. The obvious cultural and religious affinities among Judaism, Christianity, and Islam have their religious bases for Muslims in such cosmological doctrines as that of the Heavenly Tablet.

The domains or ''worlds'' inhabited by all creatures—angels, humankind, and demons—are basically three: the heavenly Paradise, the Earth, and fiery Hell. In addition, there are the ''seen'' and ''unseen'' realms. Later Islamic cosmologies, especially among the Shi[c]ites and Sufis, greatly expanded the number of distinct realms within heaven and hell. The Earth is the center stage. It is created for humankind and it is good, filled with sufficient signs that it is God's creation. The Koranic motif of the tension between those who recognize the signs of Allah and accept his messengers, and those who do not and are led astray, involve all domains. Adam's fall from Paradise, the threat of punishment in Hell, and the promise of reward in Paradise determine the human predicament and opportunity within the cosmos. Some of the angels, humankind, and the Jinn refused to obey the will of Allah and were led astray. Such a person or creature is, as we have seen, regarded a *kāfir,* an unbeliever who is defiantly ''ungrateful.'' The Earth, the natural realm in which the drama of salvation history is played out, is balanced by the realms of Paradise and Hell. Living within this view of the world, Muslims perceive their lives with special meaning. The cosmos had a beginning, and it will have an end, and thereby a purpose. The revelation of God's Word in the Koran and other scriptures of the People of the Book, and the guidance of the prophetic Sunna, chart the way of the believer to that end.

Prophetic Religion and the Koranic View of Humankind

Humankind's purpose in the world, according to Islamic religious thought, is to receive Allah's messengers and to obey His commands and prohibitions. Human beings are created with the faculty of reason, which is sufficiently developed at the age of puberty for one to be held "accountable" (the Arabic theological term is *mukallaf*) for his or her obedience to Allah and His messengers. Thus, in traditional Islamic society, formal education beyond rote memorization of the Koran began at about the age of eleven or twelve (in modern times elementary education begins for children at a much earlier age). A child was first instructed in the Koran and taught how to recite it properly. Later the student learned the Prophet's Hadith, the roots of Islamic law, and other religious sciences. In all of this, the human faculty of reason is held in high esteem by most Muslim thinkers. It complements knowledge gained through revelation. *Reason* teaches humankind in general to be thankful to God, and it teaches the general moral precepts and practical matters that are essential to a good life. *Revelation* teaches the specific ways of expressing grateful obedience to Allah, such as the five prayers daily, the fast during Ramadan, pilgrimage to Mecca and so on. Thus the basis of the Islamic view of humanity is that men and women are under obligation to live lives of faithful obedience. The Islamic emphasis on revelation *and* reason implies the importance of education and learning in both spiritual and worldly affairs.

Although Islam teaches that Muhammad and all prophets were fully human, in no way divine, the figure of the Prophet plays an important role in

FIGURE 5.1 The Mosque is a place of worship and learning. (Courtesy of the United Nations.)

Islamic humanism. The Koran says, "Truly you have a good example in the Messenger of Allah for those who regard Allah and the Day of Judgment, and remember Allah often" (Koran 33:21). Believed to be the most noble of humankind, the Prophet Muhammad possessed all the human qualities that should be emulated by his community (Umma). Those who had the closest contact with the Prophet, known as Companions, became revered sources of his Sunna or path. Along with the next two generations of Followers, these Muslims of the first century of Islam were largely responsible for shaping the subsequent Islamic idea of humanity, based as it was on the formation of a living tradition about the Prophet's Sunna.

From the Hadith literature and other aspects of the Shari^{c}a there emerges a total way of life for Muslims. It touches upon religious duties as well as secular responsibilities. Indeed the Shari^{c}a does not recognize a distinction between these two realms. In modern times many Muslim countries have instituted civil law courts, but the religious Shari^{c}a courts have remained a force, especially in the lives of pious Muslims. One's duty to Allah and His Messengers extends to government, neighbors, and family. A well-known Hadith of the Prophet has it that a man's responsibility to take care of his family is just as much a religious duty as, say, the prayer. Thus even in the sphere of social and political ideals the experience of God's unity (Tawhid) is strongly felt: ideally, Islam presses for unity at every level.

The question of sex, marriage, family, and the role of women is of contemporary interest to students of human cultures. It should be remembered that Islamic society arose out of kinship patterns characterized by extended families. This was typical of the tribal structure of Arabia and elsewhere in the Middle East in the seventh century. The effect of the Prophet's teaching was to emphasize the importance of the family while at the same time replacing tribal loyalties with loyalty to the cohesive notion of an Islamic Umma. This task required an ordered sense of humanity and society. The Prophet's example, contained in his Sunna and Hadith, is the basis of Islamic conceptions of humanity and society.

HISTORICAL DEVELOPMENT OF ISLAMIC THOUGHT

Scripture serves the needs of basic beliefs. It tells the story of how a community came into being and for what divine purpose. It establishes the liturgical rituals of worship and the legal modes of social behavior. The Koran thus served its proper function in the early Islamic community. With the expansion of Islam into lands already dominated by Jews, Christians, Zoroastrians, and other religious groups, simple declaration of belief proved to be insufficient for the discussion of Islam, both among Muslims and by Muslims with non-Muslims. With the help of Greek philosophy and established schools of thought, the other religious traditions had developed systematic articulations of their beliefs as well as arguments against the beliefs of rival traditions. For example, by the time of Islam, Jews and Christians had already engaged in sophisticated *polemics* with each other in the attempt to prove the truth of one tradition against the claims of the other. Into this theological activity, established in the towns and cities conquered by the Arab armies, Muslim intellectuals found themselves drawn to respond in kind.

Islamic thought had another, more indigenous impulse, in the view of many scholars. The two sources of Koran and Sunna required considerable interpretation for each generation of Muslims after the Prophet, and differences of opinion inevitably arose. The expanded Islamic community in the newly conquered lands of the Middle East experienced numerous threats of internal disruption. The sectarian groups of Shi^c^ites, Kharijites, and Murji'ites, described in Chapter 3, each sought to define and clarify the meaning of crucial concepts such as faith, sin, and the nature of human freedom. From these early disputes came schools of thought that in time produced important theologians and theological works. Islamic thought, then, centers around religious ideas that sprang from the historical circumstances of early Islam. The chief language of discourse during the early centuries—Arabic—was soon adapted to the theological and philosophical discussions of contemporary Christian, Jewish, and other religious thinkers. The result has been a rich literary history of religious thought which we shall briefly survey.

Early Theological Problems

The monotheistic religious traditions—Islam, Judaism, and Christianity—have each wrestled with a common set of theological problems. For example, the problem of evil has occupied the minds of religious thinkers in all three traditions. God is described as good and all-powerful in the creeds of all three faiths. The question then arises: given the nature of God, is there a source of evil in the cosmos other than God? If not, why is there suffering? Another problem that divided early Muslim thinkers was the seeming contradiction between free will and predestination. In this case, not only the nature of God but the nature of man was at issue.[4] The problem which drew the most attention was free will versus predestination, to which we shall turn brief attention.

GOD'S DETERMINATION OF EVENTS. During the Umayyad Age (661–750) many religious thinkers attempted to define God's "power" to determine events. The real problem arose when it came to defining acts done by human beings. To what extent is God involved in the doings of humankind? Who is the efficient cause, say, of an act of murder, or of saving a life? One group of thinkers took the position that God is all-powerful and thus the ultimate

---

[4] An excellent history of the early period of Islamic thought is W. Montgomery Watt, *The Formative Period of Islamic Thought* (Edinburgh: Edinburgh University Press, 1973).

source of the power behind all events in the cosmos; humans act under the compulsion of God's power. This group was known as the "Predestination" party. Another group argued that human morality would be thereby undercut; thus humans must be held responsible for their own acts. This latter group became known as the "Free Will" party.

These early theological debates did not take place in a historical vacuum. They were related to claims, especially of the later Umayyad rulers, that their control and conduct of the caliphate was divinely willed, that is, a matter of God's power, not man's. Many Muslim thinkers, regardless of their personal offense and distaste for the impiety and secular interests of several of the Umayyad caliphs, defended the current state of political affairs and thus accepted the Umayyad caliphate on theological grounds. The others, the Free Will party, held the Umayyads accountable on the ground that human beings (including the caliph) are responsible for their own acts. The Free Will party of the Umayyad Age, then, was political as well as theological in its opposition to the mainstream of thought. Many of them paid for their stubborn resistance by imprisonment and even execution.

Both the Free Will party and the Predestination party claimed that the Koran and the sayings (Hadith) of the prophet supported their views. Islamic theology, like Christian and Jewish theology, accepts scripture and tradition as authoritative sources on which to build decisive arguments. The problem is that scripture and tradition can be read both ways on most theological problems that divide the religious community. The Koran, like the Bible, is not a systematic theological or philosophical treatise.

Many passages of the Koran suggest that if God decides that a person shall be a polytheist or unbeliever, there is nothing that person can do; he or she must die an unbeliever. Other passages appear to say that humankind is to be held accountable for its sins on the Last Day, with the obvious implication that human beings are masters of their own acts. The matter could not be decided on scripture and tradition alone. The process of theological argumentation, already highly developed by Christian thinkers who used Greek philosophy to support their claims, was soon adopted by Muslim thinkers. On the other hand, internal political problems led to sectarianism in early Islam and thus provided an urgent need for theological reflection.

The Classic Schools of Islamic Thought

By the middle of the eighth century, when the Abbasid caliphs came to power in Baghdad, Islam was entering its golden age. Baghdad became an intellectual marketplace for many new ideas, religious and secular. The Free Will party was no longer politically suppressed. Shi[c]ite theologians more openly argued their claims that Ali, not the first three rightly guided caliphs, was the true successor to the Prophet. Christians, Jews, Manichaeans, and even atheists with schooling in Greek philosophy, gained established reputations in the Abbasid court. During the eighth through the early eleventh centuries the various theological trends in Islam produced noteworthy figures who gathered many pupils around them in Baghdad and elsewhere.

THE MU^c^TAZILITES. One of the most powerful theological movements in the early Islamic Middle Ages was known as the Mu^c^tazilite school. In reality the Mu^c^tazilites were not a unified school at all, but rather various groups of intellectuals with common but not identical sets of views. In a sense, the Mu^c^tazilites were the continuation of the Free Will party, and like that party, they soon ran afoul of both the religious and the political establishment. Yet in the teachings of the early Mu^c^tazilites, much of which has been cited in later works we now possess, we find these theologians to be extremely sophisticated in their articulation of Islamic thought. They were among the first Muslims to challenge heretics and non-Muslim thinkers. Their attempt to systematize Islamic thought in a way that was intellectually defensible had the effect of identifying the most essential doctrines of the Islamic religion.

The Mu^c^tazilites organized their discussions around five fundamental principles. First was the doctrine of Tawhid, God's unity. Most Mu^c^tazilites denied any resemblance between God and His creatures. Against more popular conceptions, the Mu^c^tazilites argued that God could not be conceived in human terms; that is, they "deanthropomorphized" the notion of God in order to be more clear about His unity and uniqueness. This view had implications for Koranic interpretation as well. In one famous passage of the Koran God is described as sitting on the throne of Heaven. In this and all such passages, the Mu^c^tazilites argued, it is best to give the verse an allegorical interpretation for it could not be an accurate literal description of God. The early Mu^c^tazilites developed their understanding of Tawhid particularly in arguments against the Zoroastrians and Manichaeans, who held dualist notions of the godhead. But their arguments were also a challenge to those Muslims who read the Koran literally and thus understood God in anthropomorphic terms. Thus we see how early mythical world views of monotheism versus pagan polytheism were translated and developed into a sophisticated theological doctrine.

Second was the doctrine of *^c^adl,* divine justice. In Western theological terms, Adl has to do with the problem of *theodicy*. Given the existence of evil in the world, how can the notion of an all-powerful, good God be justified? Here the Mu^c^tazilites carried the arguments of the Free Will party to its logical implications about the moral nature of God's being. The basic Mu^c^tazilite premise under the doctrine of Adl is that God is just, and therefore He must do what is best for His creation. It also means that God, though all-powerful, cannot (or does not) do evil or require human beings to do what is evil. Human beings, then, are responsible for their own acts, which they commit under their own power.

The third fundamental doctrine of the Mu^c^tazilites was *al-wa^c^d wal-wa^c^īd,* the Promise and the Threat. Under this heading, theologians discussed religious beliefs concerning the Last Day or Day of Judgment. Western thought uses the term *eschatology.*

The fourth fundamental Mu^{c}tazilite principle was *al-manzila bayn al-manzilatayn,* meaning roughly "the position between the two positions." Under this category came the discussion of what we might call *political theology.* The Arabic phrase refers to the early period of conflict when many Mu^{c}tazilites adopted a middle position between the extremes of the Kharijites on the one hand and the Murji'ites on the other. All questions concerning the caliphate and imamate were discussed here, as well as the nature of the Islamic state or community, that is, the Umma.

The fifth and final Mu^{c}tazilite principle was *al-amr bil-ma^{c}rūf wal nahy ^{c}an al-munkar,* which roughly means "commanding the known (good) and prohibiting evil." Here the missionary enterprise of spreading the faith came under discussion. Islam first grew under the impulse not just to conquer, but to spread the faith. The Mu^{c}tazilites had been especially active helping the Abbasid family overthrow the Umayyads in the middle of the eighth century. This they did through their interpretation of Islam which denied the predestinarian views supported by the Umayyads. Mu^{c}tazilite political and missionary doctrines were especially popular in the Abbasid court until the middle of the ninth century.

These five fundamental principles—the doctrines of God, theodicy, eschatology, political theology, and missions—formed the five subdivisions of most early works on theology. Even the opponents of the Mu^{c}tazilites adopted these categories, if only to refute their main arguments. Before long, however, opposing trends of thought became powerful enough to challenge the Mu^{c}tazilite schools in Baghdad, Basra, eastern Persia, and elsewhere.[5]

THE ASH^{c}ARITES. Toward the end of the ninth century Abu l-Hasan al-Ash^{c}ari was born in Basra. He began his early career as a brilliant student of one of the leading Mu^{c}tazilite theologians of the day. Later biographers report that one night al-Ash^{c}ari had a dream in which he was divinely advised of the errors of Mu^{c}tazilite thinking and interpretation. Henceforth he left the Mu^{c}tazilite camp and founded the so-called Ash^{c}arite school, which came to be regarded as an orthodox school of theology in Sunni Islam.

Until al-Ash^{c}ari's time, the main opponents of the Mu^{c}tazilites had been a pious group of thinkers among the Ulema known as the "Traditionists." The traditionists had great contempt for independent reasoning and reliance upon Greek thought which was characteristic of the theologians. The Traditionists argued for sole reliance upon literal interpretation of the Koran (including its anthropomorphic passages) and upon the authority of the Prophet's Sunna; these, they argued, must be the sole sources of religious knowledge *bilā kayf,* "without (asking) how." The opposition between the Traditionists and the Mu^{c}tazilites raised the very important question of the relation between reason and tradition

---

[5] On the Mu^{c}tazilites, see Watt, *Formative Period,* pp. 209–50.

as sources of religious knowledge. In the West we usually comprehend this problem as reason versus revelation. In both Islam and Christianity during the Middle Ages the problem was very much the same.

Al-Ash^{c}ari and his successors in the Ash^{c}arite school accepted reason as a legitimate tool or instrument in understanding the sources of Islamic faith. But the Ash^{c}arites were more careful to defend and explain popular Islamic beliefs, that is, tradition, rather than subject these matters to the criticism of reason. Whereas the Mu^{c}tazilites had fallen into political disfavor with the Abbasid court, the Ash^{c}arites became for the next few centuries the leading thinkers of Sunni Islam.[6]

THE SHI^{c}ITES. During the eighth and ninth centuries, as the Traditionists, Mu^{c}tazilites, and Ash^{c}arites were striving to clarify Sunni Islamic religious doctrines, the Shi^{c}ites were also engaged in the theological enterprise. Even more than the Mu^{c}tazilites, the Shi^{c}ites were motivated by political considerations. At first the Abbasid court had seemed much more friendly toward Shi^{c}ite groups than had the Umayyad court. Against the prevailing view of the Abbasids and of Sunni Islam, however, Shi^{c}ite theologians argued that Ali, not the first three rightly guided caliphs, had been the rightful successor to the Prophet, designated by Muhammad himself. The Shi^{c}ites preferred the term "Imam" to "Caliph," and their religious thought sprang from the twelve (five or seven) Imams whose teachings were regarded as sources of inspiration along with Koran and Sunna. Most of the early Mu^{c}tazilite and Ash^{c}arite writings contained refutations of the political and religious views of the "imamite" Shi^{c}ites. For their part, the Shi^{c}ites were not silent. Many of them wrote important theological and philosophical treatises about the various Shi^{c}ite world views and doctrines.

The terms each group used for the others were seldom polite, often extremely deprecating. The Isma^{c}ili branch of the Shi^{c}ites spread esoteric doctrines throughout the Abode of Islam using highly trained missionaries (see Chapter 3). Thus during the classical period of Islam, the theologians of all branches formed a class of intellectual elites whose function it was to articulate interpretations of Islam commensurate with distinct religious and political groups within the Abode of Islam. Looking backward into those turbulent moments of intellectual history, we see that the categories of heresy and atheism, bandied about with emotion and conviction, were related to the articulated political convictions that each group of Muslims established for itself.[7]

One of the most important Shi^{c}ite thinkers of the late classical period was Nasir al-Din al-Tusi (1201–1274). Born in Tus, Persia, Tusi managed to gain a solid education in the religious, philosophical, and physical sciences before the destructive armies of the Mongols marched across the Islamic East. In his early

---

6 Watt describes the Ash^{c}arites and other orthodox schools in *Formative Period*, pp. 279–318.

7 On the Shi^{c}ite theologians in early Islam see Watt, *Formative Period*, pp. 252–78.

professional career he served as an astrologer to an Isma^{c}ili Shi^{c}ite prince, but when the Mongol invasions posed a threat to libraries and academies he gained the confidence of the famed Mongol lord, Hūlāgu. Tusi was thereby able to save many libraries containing intellectual treasures of the past. Much of the Mongol "loot" of this type was brought to Azerbaijan, where, with the support of Hūlāgu, Tusi founded an important institution that housed an observatory, library, and academy of scholars. Tusi's keen analytical mind ranged over a variety of subjects about which he wrote over one hundred books. He is best known in the West for his work in astronomy and mathematics. In the Islamic world, particularly among the Shi^{c}ites, Tusi's works (written in Arabic and Persian) in theology, philosophy, ethics, and logic mark an important stage in intellectual history. Not only did Tusi save books and libraries from extinction, but he revived the achievements of philosophers such as Avicenna from the intellectual decline of the thirteenth century.

The Late Middle Ages

Despite the efforts of Tusi and others to preserve the rich heritage of the classical period and to build upon it, the Mongol invasion and the destruction of the caliphate proved to be a moment of decisive intellectual as well as political change in Islam. Major theological schools and philosophical movements either declined and vanished or simply perpetuated the more creative achievements of the past. An important exception to this trend was Sufism. Among the most important "speculative" sufis were Shihab al-Din Suhrawardi (d. 1191), Jalal al-Din al-Rumi (d. 1273), and Ibn al-Arabi (d. 1240). The lives and works of these figures belonged to a new trend in Muslim thought known as "Illuminationism," from the Arabic term *ishrāqī,* meaning "eastern." Illuminationist philosophy had already been expounded by such important figures as Avicenna. Illuminationism was infused with the symbolism of light, which had traditionally played an important role in Persian reflections on the nature of the divine. Another strong influence on this trend of thought was Neoplatonic philosophy, which conceived of the cosmos in gradations of being from the most perfect and abstract (God) to the material, corruptible realm of earthly existence.

The most important orthodox Sunni thinker of the late medieval period was Taqi al-Din ibn Taymiya (1263–1328). Ibn Taymiya's intellectural heritage came not from the prevailing Sunni school of theology, the Ash^{c}arites, but rather from the more conservative Traditionists inspired by the Hanbalites (see the next main section, "Two Formative Thinkers in Islam"). Against the Traditionists, however, he argued that individual Muslims must follow the teachings of Koran and Sunna with reason, not in blind acceptance of the authority of the Ulema. He also accepted the Mu^{c}tazilite teaching that moral responsibility for human acts must be accepted by each person and not relegated to God alone. Unlike the majority of the Sunni Ulema, Ibn Taymiya did not condemn outright the popular teachings of the Sufis of his day, although he did criticize them on many points. While recognizing the importance of the Sufi focus upon the spiritual reality *(al-ḥaqq)* of God, he also faulted the Sufis for what he saw as their moral laxity when they claimed that the ideal of union with God placed them beyond the ritual requirements of the Shari^{c}a.

Despite such figures as Ibn al-Arabi and Ibn Taymiya, some non-Muslim and Sunni Muslim scholars have characterized the period from the thirteenth through the eighteenth centuries as the "dark age" of Islam. This is perhaps a misconception that is due to the predisposition of both groups to appreciate more readily the intellectual achievements of the classical period of the caliphate. The specter of stagnation during the late Middle Ages is raised by the ongoing conflict between the Sunni Ulema and Sufism. The sultans, lords, and princes who ruled the various regional empires during this period often gave less support and authority to the Ulema. Sufi orders and brotherhoods, on the other hand, gained popular support throughout the Abode of Islam. The Ulema often bickered with Sufis when the latter defied orthodox interpretations of the requirements and restrictions of the Shari^{c}a. Illuminationism and Sufism were "inward" religious trends of thought and practice which during this phase of Islamic history found ready acceptance by great numbers of Muslims.

The Modern Period

Islamic thought experienced a "revival" of classical interests in the nineteenth century. Two main reasons are usually given for this revival. First, as we have seen, the dominance of Sufism during the late Middle Ages had led to what many orthodox Muslims regarded as a drifting away from the teachings of the Shari^{c}a. Second, the West, once overshadowed by the unity and power of the Muslim world, was now attempting to control it. The answer to both trends for many Muslim intellectuals was to recapture the vital force of the Islamic past. Like the Humanists of the late Middle Ages in Europe, nineteenth-century Muslim reformers sought to rediscover their true heritage as they believed it had been during the classical ages of the Rashidun and Abbasids.

Many of the reformers, such as Jamal al-Din al-Afghani (1838–1897), Sir Muhammad Iqbal of India (1876–1938), and Muhammad Abduh of Egypt (1845–1905), had received traditional Muslim educations as well as training in Western thought. Al-Afghani traveled widely throughout the Muslim world giving speeches and writing pamphlets that urged Muslims to reform their educational curricula and to take their Islamic heritage with intellectual seriousness. Iqbal and Abduh argued in their influential writings for modernist reforms through the cultivation of science and reason. Both men argued that Islam, not the West, had been the champion of philosophy and science when other civilizations had been in decline. Both men argued, in different ways, that the Koran and the Muslim world view encourage the use of reason. To put it differently, reason and faith are complementary requisites to the life prescribed by the

Shari^c^a. Also, both men were deeply suspicious of the influence of Western, materialistic values upon the Islamic world.

Islamic thought in the twentieth century has been dominated by social and political concerns. Political and economic control of the regional empires of the late Middle Ages was in the hands of Western powers in the modern period, and as each "colonial possession" has sought and gained its independence, the struggle to retain or regain "Islamic" identity has intensified. Many of the reforms sought by Afghani, Iqbal, Abduh, and others like them are now being implemented, with differing stress from one country to the next being given to the Islamic heritage, modernization, and educational reforms. Despite the growing communication between Muslim and non-Muslim cultures, the West is still relatively uninformed about the vital intellectual currents of Muslim thought that are shaping the future of Islam.

TWO FORMATIVE THINKERS IN ISLAM

The Islamic religious tradition is characterized by a vast literature, much of which survives in modern times. Each century has produced outstanding thinkers whose teachings have been carefully recorded and expounded by generations of disciples. The lives of these individuals are extremely colorful and interesting as we meet them in the facts and legends that have been preserved about them. Just as every Christian knows something about such figures as Saint Augustine and Saint Thomas Aquinas, so every Muslim reveres the seminal thinkers of the Islamic religious tradition.

Ahmad ibn Hanbal (780–855)

One of the most influential early figures in Islam was the noted Traditionist and religious leader of Baghdad, Ahmad ibn Hanbal.[8] There is hardly any aspect of the religion of Islam upon which the stamp of Ibn Hanbal's name and influence does not appear, either positively or negatively. His collection of the Sayings (Hadith) of the Prophet became one of the six canonical works that comprise the literary record of the Sunna of the Prophet. But Ibn Hanbal was more than a Traditionist. As a jurist he offered penetrating insights that drew a large following, and the Hanbalite school of Islamic law became one of the four orthodox branches of religious jurisprudence in Sunni Islam. Ibn Hanbal also became a legend in his own time by refusing to subscribe to the Abbasid court's official pronouncements on Islamic doctrine. As a Traditionist, Ibn Hanbal held views that were much closer to those of the pious masses of Sunni Muslims, and soon his heroic resistance and refusal to recant his views, even in prison and under

---

[8] See "Ahmad ibn Hanbal," *Encyclopaedia of Islam,* 2nd ed., ed. H. A. R. Gibb et al (Leiden: E. J. Brill, 1960–).

physical punishment, forced the government to release him and eventually to condemn his theological opponents. Throughout the Middle Ages the term "Hanbalite" was almost synonymous with "Traditionist." A revival of Hanbalism in the fourteenth century was headed by Ibn Taymiya, as we have seen. The conservative reform movement in Saudi Arabia in modern times traces its spiritual heritage to Ahmad ibn Hanbal.

Ibn Hanbal's family had descended from a prominent Arab clan. His grandfather and father had participated in the conquest and pacification of Iraq and Persia. By the time of Ibn Hanbal's birth in 780, the family had settled in the recently built city of the Abbasids, Baghdad. The social and intellectual climate of the Abbasid capital must have been quite stimulating for the bright young son of a retired military figure. Most of the great religious teachers of the day found their way to Baghdad, and Ibn Hanbal was to become the pupil or teacher of many of them.

The main focus of his education was the sayings (Hadith) of the Prophet, Muhammad. Until Ibn Hanbal's time these had been preserved mainly by oral tradition. The early Abbasid period, however, produced an environment in which Islamic religious knowledge turned increasingly to literary forms. Such scholars as Ibn Hanbal were still known for their extensive memories and wide travels to gain comprehensive command of the thousands of sayings attributed to the Prophet. With the expansion of Islamic civilization came the growing need for an established literature about the Prophet's Sunna. Judges, lawyers, teachers, and other religious writers were to profit greatly from the work of Ibn Hanbal and others in classifying and writing down the prophetic sayings that played such an important role in the life of the Islamic Umma.

THE UNCREATED KORAN. The divinely given message of the Islamic way of life, contained in Koran and Sunna and known as the Shari^{c}a, was viewed in a very particular way by the Traditionists. Soon they came to be known as the "People of the Sunna." Against the Mu^{c}tazilite theologians and others, the People of the Sunna argued that innovations through reasoning and individual judgments had no part in religious matters. The Shari^{c}a was a total way of life. To thinkers like Ibn Hanbal, it was not necessary to go beyond Koran and Sunna to establish the Islamic way of life. This is why Ibn Hanbal was so extremely popular among the common people, and less so among Muslim and non-Muslim intellectuals who were not ready to accept the Koran and Sunna as the sole authoritative sources of belief. Thus, as we have seen, tradition and reason emerged as two different, sometimes incompatible, sources of religious knowledge.

The conflict surfaced during Ibn Hanbal's lifetime, creating a whirlwind of controversy that swept the entire sociopolitical structure of the intelligentsia of Baghdad into the eye of its storm. The caliphs, their large staffs of civil servants, famous Mu^{c}tazilite teachers, eminent philosophers, and many others became involved. Fortunes and reputations were gained and lost almost overnight. At the center of the storm stood two men of immense public stature: the Caliph al-Ma'mun, and the Traditionist Ibn Hanbal. Both men claimed deep commitment to the Islamic religion. The confrontation between them was a poignant reminder that religious ideas do not just inhabit the minds of pious recluses; the controversy over right belief (orthodoxy) can affect the whole social and political order.

The theological issue that brought Ibn Hanbal and al-Ma'mum into public conflict had political and social dimensions, but it was the Koran that stood at the center of the controversy. Al-Ma'mun, in addition to the matters of state for which he was directly responsible, took a personal interest in Islamic theology. He gathered around him many of the eminent Mu^{c}tazilite theologians of the day. He even wrote several treatises on theology that were decidedly influenced by Mu^{c}tazilite arguments. He thus came to favor the Mu^{c}tazilite view that the Koran was God's revelation to man, created and recited to the Arabs in their own language at a particular and finite moment in history. The Mu^{c}tazilites had further argued that the notion of God's unity (Tawhid) would be compromised if it were regarded, as it was in the popular view, as an eternal, preexistent document inscribed in Heaven. The question that exercised so many minds, then, was this: Is the Koran eternal or created? The Mu^{c}tazilites, whom the Caliph al-Ma'mun supported, said that it was created and that it could not be otherwise. The Traditionists and People of the Sunna, whom Ibn Hanbal supported, said that the Koran was the eternal, uncreated Word of God. The arguments that raged back and forth were sometimes subtle and elusive, but the social and political effects were not.

Al-Ma'mun took decisive steps to implement the Mu^{c}tazilite views as state policy. He required his chief civil servants to state publicly that the Koran was created. Many were willing to submit to this imperial meddling in matters of belief in order to save their jobs, despite their own convictions to the contrary. Along with a few others, Ibn Hanbal chose imprisonment over subversion of religious conviction. The rounding up and conviction of dissenters was known as the inquisition, *(miḥna).*[9] Outside the prison in which ibn Hanbal was incarcerated the streets filled with common folk who supported his resistance to the caliph. Most of them were devoted to the popular belief in the uncreated, eternal Koran. Soon the caliph, al'Ma'mun, died, and under his successor Ibn Hanbal was held in prison for two more years. During that time the additional measures of scourgings could not persuade him to accept the doctrine of the created Koran. And so he was released on his own recognizance to live in retirement in his own home. There he remained in seclusion until the accession of Caliph al-Mutawakkil in 847, when Ibn Hanbal was able to resume his lectures on Traditions. Five years later Ibn Hanbal was invited to the new royal palace in Samarra, a town not far up the river from Baghdad. In the royal compound he tutored the caliph's son and, in sharp contrast to much of his public career in

[9] On the Mihna and Ibn Hanbal's role in it, see "Mihna," *Shorter Encyclopaedia of Islam.*

Baghdad, Ibn Hanbal enjoyed the last years of his life as something of a celebrity in the highest echelons of government, where he was guaranteed independence of thought. He died at the age of seventy-five in A.D. 855, and his body was interred in a cemetery near one of the main four gates of the city of Baghdad. Thousands of Muslims mourned at his graveside, and for generations his grave was a shrine for the large segment of Sunni Islam that in law and orthodox interpretations of the Shari^ca goes by the name Hanbalite.

Ahmad ibn Hanbal's legacy in the Abode of Islam has been considerable. As a personality he has been remembered in history and legend as a heroic resister of doctrinal innovations and of rationalism, where these appeared to threaten popular, Traditionist notions about the Koran and Sunna. In theology, the widely accepted view that the Koran is the eternal, literal word of God found its most popular champion in Ibn Hanbal. Throughout the Middle Ages many of the Ash^carite theologians defended such Hanbalite doctrines, although not all Ash^carites followed or studied the Hanbalite branch of Sunni law; and to many Hanbalites, the Ash^carites erred on the side of the rationalism as opposed to Tradition. Historically, the Hanbalites have reappeared from time to time as the inspiration behind religio-political attempts to reform Islam. The terms "fundamentalist" and "puritan" are often applied to the Hanbalites and to Ahmad ibn Hanbal himself. Accurate as these terms may be, it would be unfortunate if such terms were taken to mean that a great religious and theological figure such as Ahmad ibn Hanbal (and his followers) should be overlooked in the intellectual history of Islam.

Abu Hamid al-Ghazzali (1058–1111)

Ibn Hanbal, along with many contemporary ninth century Muslim thinkers, both Sunni and Shi^cite, laid the foundations for Islamic intellectual history. Henceforth in the fields of Islamic law, theology, Koranic studies, and traditions, Islamic thought developed along lines and trends established by the Ulema and by other thinkers of Ibn Hanbal's time. Also by the mid-ninth century the translation of foreign works in philosophy, science, and the arts added new dimensions to Islamic thought. For the next two centuries Muslim theologians and philosophers struggled to define the proper relationship between the religious sciences, such as Koranic studies and traditions, and the more rational and empirical sciences, such as philosophy, mathematics, logic, geography, and medicine. The Hanbalites, and the "People of Tradition" generally, devoted themselves to the religious sciences. Their chief pedagogic institution was the mosque, which, in addition to being a place of prayer, was a place where pupils gathered around noted teachers. Learning in the sciences and the arts, as in the translation movement, was done by individuals in their own homes or in special academies established by the caliphs and other wealthy patrons. The relationship between the mosque and the academy was often troubled.

Ninth-century questions regarding free will and predestination, the problem of good and evil, and the proper form of Islamic government were, by the eleventh century, answered according to definite systems of thought by Sunni and Shi^c^ite theologians. This produced what historians of thought refer to as *scholasticism.* Schools of thought became doctrinaire in posture, abstract in modes of expression. The religious and the nonreligious sciences became much too sophisticated for the average Muslim to grasp. By the eleventh century most Traditionists and some theologians believed that it was harmful to the faith of the average person to study theology. Others believed that religious knowledge and secular knowledge were incompatible. The average Muslim regarded the abstract study of most of these sciences, secular *and* religious, as irrelevant to his or her personal spiritual life. By the eleventh century the time had arrived for a religious and intellectual synthesis of these repellent trends. Abu Hamid al-Ghazzali (1058–1111) looms large in Islamic intellectual history for providing such a synthesis.[10]

Al-Ghazzali was born in Tus near the modern city of Meshed in north-eastern Iran. Like most Muslim boys, he obtained his early education with a Shaykh at a mosque, where he learned to recite the Koran by rote memory. Later he was sent to the college at the provincial capital of Nisapur. There he advanced through the usual religious curriculum of Koran, Traditions and Law. His greatest teacher was an Ash^c^arite theologian at Nisapur, Imam al-Haramayn al-Juwayni. By this time the Ash^c^arite school was the leading school of theology in Sunni Islam, and the Mu^c^tazilites were no longer influential.

Al-Ghazzali wrote numerous books, many of which have survived and have been translated into Western languages. One of the most interesting was his autobiography, *Deliverance from Error.* As we read through it we gain glimpses of a searching, often deeply troubled quest for peace of mind on religious matters. Al-Ghazzali's lifelong scholarly pursuit of an intellectual grasp of the truths of religion reminds us of the great Christian theologian Saint Augustine.

Like that of Augustine, al-Ghazzali's religious faith as a young man was severely tested by the conflicting intellectual currents of his day. In the eleventh century orthodox Sunni and Shi^c^ite religious thought were by no means the only religious world views circulating in the abode of Islam. Many Muslims were being drawn into the "errors" of rival and heretical religious groups. The more devout Sunni Muslims remained persuaded of the Traditionist path of accepting the authority of Koran and Sunna "without asking how," that is, on faith alone. Others were persuaded by the arguments of non-Muslim and radical Muslim heresies.

As with Augustine's intellectual odyssey, al-Ghazzali was for a while drawn into the semi-philosophic movement known as Skepticism. Both in Augustine's and in al-Ghazzali's times, the Skeptics advanced arguments that seemed to shatter religious and scientific assumptions. In the West, Skepticism had originated in Plato's Academy. In the East, a similar philosophical trend of

[10] An excellent historical and intellectual biography of al-Ghazzali is W. Montgomery Watt, *Muslim Intellectual: A Study of Al-Ghazali* (Edinburgh: Edinburgh University Press, 1963).

thought had flourished in the Sassanian court of the Persians. By al-Ghazzali's time the radical Isma^cili Shi^cites had assumed many of the doctrines of the Skeptics, especially their political tactics. These radical Shi^cites were known as *Bāṭinites,* which means "esoterists." As a philosophical movement, Skepticism raised serious questions about the reliability of reason and sense perception for determining knowledge and truth. As a religious movement, Skepticism substituted absolute faith in the teachings of a charismatic leader for the more usual reliance of the faithful upon the face value of tradition and the teachings of the Ulema. As a political movement, Skepticism created cadres of propagandists and missionaries devoted to the subversion of the established government and their supporters, the leading figures of the Sunni Ulema.

One of al-Ghazzali's early works was a treatise against the Batinites. The Batinites claimed that their teachings came from the Koran and Sunna of the Prophet. But *bāṭin* means "secret," "gnostic." The literal meaning of Koran and Sunna urged by the Traditionists, and the more abstract meanings argued by the Mu^ctazilites and other theologians, were replaced by the Batinites with secret meanings that bore no literal or obvious rational relation to the actual words of the texts. The Imam or semi-divine head of the Batinites assumed absolute authority to interpret the sacred texts of Islam in ways that the average Muslim, the trained members of the Ulema, and the rational arguments of the theologians could not refute. Appealing to the emotional devotion of the masses to Koran and Sunna, the Batinites fomented social and political anarchy with secret teachings. Whether seen as an attack from without or within the Islamic Umma, the effect upon the political and intellectual stability within the Abode of Islam was profound.

For this reason, in 1094 the caliph in Baghdad commissioned al-Ghazzali to write a refutation of the Batinites. In this and several books written much later, including *Deliverance from Error,* we see the complexity of issues—religious, theological, and political—that the Isma^cili Shi^cites and Batinites stirred up within the Abode of Islam. Al-Ghazzali recognized that at the level of the simplest minds he would have to show that the Koran urges humankind to follow logical principles in clarifying religious truths, not the illogic of secret teachings. In another line of attack (or polemic) against the Batinites, al-Ghazzali argued against the general Shi^cite notion of a charismatic leader in the Imam, by pointing out that Islam has such a leader in Muhammad. The Sunna of the Prophet is, along with the Koran and the consensus of the Ulema, a sufficient source of charismatic leadership, al-Ghazzali argued. It seems that al-Ghazzali was trying to restore the intellectual appeal of Sunni Islam by showing that in the traditional sources and in the Prophet himself Islam has a spiritual source and figure par excellence.

THE CASE AGAINST THE PHILOSOPHERS. In 1091 al-Ghazzali received an appointment to a theological college in Baghdad known as the Nizamiya. It was named after the famed Sunni Muslim statesman Nizam al-Mulk. The college had opened in 1067, and its faculty was dominated by theologians of the Ash^carite school and legal theorists of the Shafi^cite branch of canon law. The more conservative Traditionists and Hanbalite legal theorists resented its opening. But the real target of Nizamiya faculty teachings, especially after al-Ghazzali arrived, were the philosophers and the Batinites.

Resuming our comparison of al-Ghazzali with Saint Augustine, we may note that both men were attracted to the intellectual discipline of philosophy. The Neoplatonism that was so prevalent in the Mediterranean world in Augustine's lifetime (A.D. 354–430) was still influential in the eleventh and twelfth centuries, when al-Ghazzali lived. Unlike Aristotle's philosophy, which had first inspired the philosophical movement in Islam, Neoplatonism was more conducive to religious systems. For this reason, many of the Muslim philosophers, such as al-Kindi (ca. 800–873) and Avicenna (Ibn Sina, 980–1037), combined the more logical characteristics of Aristotle's philosophy with the religious doctrines of Neoplatonism. Thus, for example, Aristotle had held that matter, the basic substance of the world, was eternal and indestructible. This view was difficult to reconcile with the monotheistic doctrine of creation out of nothing. The Neoplatonists, on the other hand, held that the cosmos was made up of a succession of grades or realms of being from matter to pure Spirit. The world of human experience was the result of emanations downward from the One (pure Spirit) into the corruptible many in the realm of matter. But the process reverses itself as the many seek to escape the corruption of the realm of matter and return to the One. Thus Neoplatonism offered a philosophical (and very abstract) way of rationalizing the monotheistic doctrines of creation and salvation.

Although Traditionists and Hanbalites would accept only the literal concepts of creation and salvation as found in the Koran and Sunna, philosophers argued that scriptures such as the Koran were allegorical explanations of divine, philosophic truths, aimed at simpler minds. Only philosophers understand the full rational truth of God's revelation to humankind (scripture). Prophets, in the view of Muslim philosophers like Avicenna, are the most perfect philosophers, for they comprehend both the rational truths of the divine mind and the simpler expression of those same truths in the stories and allegories of scripture. The Muslim philosophers in the Middle Ages believed, with Plato's *Republic,* which had been translated into Arabic, that the best founders and rulers of society were philosopher-kings (prophets). Prophets, then, in the view of many Muslim philosophers, were conceived of as Plato had conceived of kings in the *Republic.*

Al-Ghazzali carefully read and considered the works of Muslim philosophers such as Avicenna, as well as the works of Greek philosophers translated into Arabic. He was not unmindful of the lack of intellectual sophistication that a religion may have when truths and beliefs are claimed without justification. Philosophers attempt to be systematic and logical in their treatment of thought. One thing troubled him about philosophy, however. Even those philosophers who claimed to be Muslims, such as al-Kindi and Avicenna, were accused of not explaining, but of explaining away Islamic beliefs. While he was teaching at the Nizamiya in Baghdad, al-Ghazzali wrote *The Incoherence of the Philosophers,* a point-by-point refutation of several inconsistencies he found in the writings of Avicenna. His basic argument was that reason, so highly exalted by the philosophers, works very well in disciplines such as logic and mathematics, but when philosophers attempt to rationalize divine truths and metaphysics, their arguments are filled with confusions and inconsistencies. In a word, they become unphilosophical. Thus al-Ghazzali did not deprecate rational thought, as the Traditionists and some theologians were accused of doing, but he carefully restricted the limits of reason in apprehending divine truth.

THE INFLUENCE OF SUFISM. Toward the end of his teaching career in Baghdad, al-Ghazzali underwent a severe period of mental and emotional unrest, brought about in part by his inability to find intellectual peace of mind in any of the intellectual disciplines and movements to which other intellectuals were devoted. Even the theology of the Ash^{c}arite theologians he found spiritually bankrupt and intellectually stagnant. Moreover, his worldly success as a famed teacher, to whom even the caliphs turned for professorial guidance, was distasteful to him. In a work that was given the English title of *Faith and Practice,* al-Ghazzali reflects on the final moments of despair before he turned to the mystical understanding of Islam which was professed and practiced by the Sufis. Al-Ghazzali's own words speak best at this point.

> Lastly I turned to the way of the mystics. I knew that in their path there has to be both knowledge and activity, and that the object of the latter is to purify the self from vices and faults of character. Knowledge was easier for me than activity. I began by reading their books . . . and obtained a thorough intellectual understanding of their principles. Then I realized that what is most distinctive of them can be attained only by personal experience ("taste"—*dhawq*), ecstasy and a change of character. . . . I saw clearly that the mystics were men of personal experience not of words, and that I had gone as far as possible by way of study and intellectual application, so that only personal experience and walking in the mystic way were left.[11]

The moment in his life to which al-Ghazzali was referring occurred about 1095. He reports that some days he was so disturbed that he couldn't even utter words during his lectures, and soon his health declined so far as to require physicians. But there could be no physical antidote for a malady that was psychological and spiritual. Finally, in a drastic move inspired by Sufism, he resigned his teaching post, made arrangements for the maintenance of his family, and left Baghdad for Syria. He spent two years in Damascus exploring mystical doctrine and ways of life. He received much criticism from the Ulema, for here was one of the most famous intellectuals of the day shirking his duties and responsibilities as a professor, husband, and father, in order to retire to the

[11] Cited in Watt, *Muslim Intellectual,* p. 135.

suspect life of the mystic. What did al-Ghazzali hope to find in "the Path" of Sufism?

Sufism, to which we have referred in earlier chapters and to which we shall return in Chapter 7, promised a certainty of faith, but not through reason, theology, or philosophy. It drew Muslims from all walks of life into practices and states of mind that produced the felt experience of nearness or union with God. The Koran, the Sunna of the Prophet, and the obligatory duties of worship, as understood in Sufism, had special mystical meanings. Tawhid, the cornerstone on which Islamic theology is laid, meant for Sufis the *experience* of union with God. The Sufis who sought this experience found it either as solitary wanderers or as disciples, gathered in special communities that were directed by a renowned "Friend of God" or saint. In both cases—on the road or gathered in communities—the Sufis withdrew from normal society. Society, even at best when structured according to the demands of the Shari^{c}a, causes one to forget God, they felt. Al-Ghazzali finally realized that even the most honored discipline of society—teaching in a respected theological academy—was pulling him in the wrong direction. And so he took up the Path.

After some years with Sufism, al-Ghazzali finally resumed a state-appointed teaching post, this time in Nisapur, where he had first studied with al-Juwayni. Shortly before he died in 1111, he retired to his home town of Tus, where he continued to write until the end.

AL-GHAZZALI'S ACHIEVEMENT. Scholars, both Muslim and non-Muslim, have argued the overall achievement of al-Ghazzali in Islamic intellectual history. Some have found him rather overbearing in his frequent statements of self-esteem. Others have doubted the sincerity of his conversion to Sufism or the extent to which he actually adopted its path and discipline. But almost all historians agree that he had a profound effect upon the history of thought in Islam, and many would say that the spiritual dimension of Islam as a living faith was revived by al-Ghazzali. In what is perhaps his greatest work, *Revivication of the Sciences of Religion,* al-Ghazzali carefully worked out both the rational and spiritual bases of the Islamic religion. The work is a magnificent achievement in the history of religious thought. It has been cited by Muslim intellectuals and common folk alike down to this day, so well known and read has been this work and others by one of Islam's most brilliant thinkers.

6

worship and ritual in islam

It is Friday noon on campus. Students are hurrying to have lunch, to attend class, or to celebrate the end of the school week with friends. This bustling activity, so familiar to American students, highlights a contrast with a different scene. Across the mall on the grass, a number of students, mostly from Middle Eastern countries, are lined up side by side. In the midst of the Friday noon rush, they bow, kneel, then prostrate themselves. They are Muslims performing the *jum^{c}a* (Friday) prayer. The canonical prayer performed at noon on that day is the most important prayer ceremonial of the week. *Jum^{c}a* means "congregation," and were they back in their home towns, these Muslims would no doubt join members of their families and neighbors at a nearby mosque, crowded to capacity and overflowing, for the Congregational Prayer.

The actual performance of worship in the Islamic world might also seem strange to us at first. Hymns are not sung, collections are not taken, and children are not baptized. No one equivalent to an ordained priest, rabbi, or pastor serves in a sacral capacity. Having first prepared themselves through ritual cleansing called *wuḍū',* worshippers leave their shoes at the door of the mosque. They enter and stand shoulder to shoulder in rows facing the Qibla, the direction of Mecca. It is the same ritual of prayer that is performed five times each day at home, school, places of business, and nearby mosques. On Fridays a religious leader called the Imam climbs into a pulpit (*minbar*) to deliver a sermon. On this occasion an Imam speaks about theological, political, or moral issues, or matters of common decency and etiquette. All such matters are appropriate in the Friday sermon.

FIGURE 6.1. Muslims in Mali performing midday Salat. (Courtesy of the United Nations.)

Worship in Islam, as in other religions, is performed according to discernible patterns. These patterns exemplify general religious notions that are essential to the Muslim world view. Some of the patterns are common to other religious cultures, and some are distinctive to Islam. At specific stages of life—birth, circumcision, puberty, marriage, and death—rituals sanctify an individual's passage from one stage to the next. These are called "rites of passage" by anthropologists, and such rites are found in one form or another in every culture. We will consider Islamic rites of passage in the next chapter. The lives of Muslims are also religiously ordered by the calendar year. Like Jews and Christians, Muslims celebrate certain appointed holy days, arranged by a calendar that is distinctive to Islam. The notions of "weekdays" and "weekend" are foreign to Islam, although the Islamic week may be said to begin on Saturday or Sunday and to reach its high point on Friday noon. Five times each day normal concerns are interrupted by the muezzin's call to prayer. The attempt to understand these patterns of worship is the purpose of this chapter.

PATTERNS OF WORSHIP IN ISLAM

Another individual's psychological state of mind during worship is difficult to determine accurately. The problem belongs to psychological studies, but some general observations can be made about the matter short of that. Recall from Chapter 3 that as *shākir* a Muslim is "one who is thankful" to God for the goodness of this life and the hope of reward in the Hereafter. The Koran and the

Sunna of the Prophet engender this response. The proper forms of these responses in ritual and worship can be described in terms of what Muslims *appear* to be doing. Each Muslim knows, however, that his or her own private attitudes or intentions are known only to oneself and to God. Therefore before the prayer, pilgrimage, and other times to worship each Muslim privately declares the intention to worship. The public declaration of intention, known as the *niya,* forms a part of the act of worship itself. Worship is both an individual and a corporate act.

On such occasions the inner self is felt to stand in the presence of God. Although in common parlance the term "ritual" often connotes a meaningless repetition of acts, this value judgment would be difficult to maintain in any serious study of religions. Like other religious people, Muslims vary among themselves in the intensity of their devotion. The performance of worship may seem empty or meaningless to any observer who does not look beyond what is immediately apparent. Thus the student of religions must seek to grasp the world view and the nature of the personal commitment within which religious performances take on their culturally determined values and meanings.

Patterns of Space and Time in Muslim Worship

A non-Muslim would not be allowed to enter the vicinity of Mecca, and certainly not to approach the sacred Ka^c^ba. Western visitors to Islamic cities are often only cautiously admitted to mosques, and women in attire regarded immodest are frequently turned away. Why? From the Islamic point of view, such intrusions into these places is forbidden by law and perhaps by a deeply felt sense of taboo. Even a Muslim involved in a serious ritual pollution would not defile a mosque by entering it under these conditions. The comparative study of religions sheds some light on this phenomenon. Insofar as religious traditions create attitudes and conceptions of reality that organize one's sense of sacred and profane geography in definite patterns and structures, some places are given more value than others. Mircea Eliade calls these *sacred spaces.* Churches, temples, shrines, and altars are examples of sacred spaces. Each tradition defines sacred spaces and establishes rules for their consecration. Without rules for the preparatory conditions, these spaces or the persons entering them would be defiled. The Old Testament, for example, speaks about the sacred character of the Yahwist Sanctuary, the rituals appropriate to it, and the rules that govern its sanctity.

The Islamic Shari^c^a also lays down rules governing appointed places of worship. Strictly speaking, however, the distinction between "sacred" and "secular" when applied to the mosque (Arabic, *masjid,* meaning "place of prostration") is not recognized by Muslims. The mosque is the place where Muslims prefer to perform the ritual of the canonical prayer. One may pray only after performing prescribed ablutions (*wuḍū'*). For that matter, the prayer may be performed anywhere. Whether in a mosque, a private home, a place of business, or the mall at State University, the place of prayer is structurally oriented by the Qibla, the direction of Mecca.

The notion of the "sacred" applies more nearly to the territory around Mecca during the pilgrimage. The shrines in and near Mecca are surrounded by boundaries. Within those boundaries is the territory called the *ḥaram,* which is especially sacred during the last 2½ months of the Hijra calendar. Before Muslim pilgrims reach the Haram, they declare to themselves and God the Niya "intention" to make the Greater or Lesser pilgrimage. One thereby becomes a *muḥrim,* that is, "a consecrated pilgrim." When one becomes a Muhrim, special attire called *iḥrām* is donned, and within the Haram special activities derived from the Prophet's Sunna are followed by pilgrims (but not by other Muslims who may happen to be there). Later in this chapter we will describe and analyze the ritual of the pilgrimage in greater detail.

Many Muslims also make visits to shrines or tombs of saints, although such visits are not considered obligatory "Acts of Worship" as these were described in Chapter 1. From crude huts to elaborate mosques and mausoleums, these shrines constitute sacred spaces possessing a special spiritual power or blessing, called *baraka,* from the saint whom each shrine commemorates. Pilgrims visit shrines to receive the Baraka of the saints they esteem.

The act of worship and the rituals this entails are characterized by specially marked-out patterns of time. We used this term earlier to describe the special moment in the sacred history of Islam when the Koran was revealed to the Prophet Muhammad. Following Eliade, we said that a sacred time is a "time out of time." It is a time when believers experience an interruption of the sacred into the profane. The night Muhammad is said to have received the divine message is celebrated on the 27th of Ramadan which is regarded as an especially propitious anniversary. Ramadan is also the month of the Fast, and as well a month in which the unseen evil forces of Iblis and the Satans are said to be diminished by the original sacred event of revelation. Other times are also highly valued. For example, the canonical prayer (*ṣalāt*) is performed within designated periods of time each day, announced by the call of the muezzin. These are significant moments that punctuate each day. The first part of the last month of the year, Dhu al-Hijja, the last portion of the seventy-day period of the annual pilgrimage, is important not only for pilgrims, but also for those who remain at home. In addition, for the Shiᶜites especially, the tenth of the first month, Muharram, is the anniversary of the martyrdom of the fallen Husayn.

The conditions that govern the places and times of Islamic worship are found in the Shariᶜa. A Muslim's life is regulated by patterns established in the Hijra calendar. It will be useful at this point to describe briefly the annual, monthly, weekly and daily patterns followed in the Islamic world.

In Table 6-1 the months of the Hijra calendar are presented with their Islamic names. We learned in Chapter 2 (footnote 1) that Hijra years have about 354 days consisting of twelve lunar months of twenty-nine or thirty days, reckoned by the sighting of the new moon. Until the time of the Prophet, the Arab

TABLE 6-1. HIJRA CALENDAR

	Month	*Major Celebrations Common to Sunni and Shi^cite Islam*
1	Muharram	New Year: Ashura (10th)
2	Safar	
3	Rabi^c al-Awwal	Prophet's Birthday (12th)
4	Rabi^c al-Thani	
5	Jumada al-Ula	
6	Jumada al-Akhira	
7	Rajab	
8	Sha^cban	
9	Ramadan	Month of Fast; Night of Power (27th)
10	Shawwal	Breaking the Fast (1st); Pilgrimage Season
11	Dhu al-Qa^cda	Pilgrimage Season
12	Dhu al-Hijja	Hajj (8th-13th); Festival of Sacrifice (10th)

shrine known as the Ka^cba in Mecca was also governed by a lunar year, but in pagan times (Jahiliyya) an additional month was added every three years to adjust the otherwise shorter year to the full annual cycle of seasons. The Koran had forbidden the addition of this month, perhaps because it interrupted the sacred months set aside for the Arabs to make the pilgrimage to Mecca. The shortened lunar year had the effect of making Islamic festivals occur eleven days earlier each year in relation to the more widely used solar calendars. This had two important results. First, like other religious traditions, such as Judaism and Christianity, Islam had its own distinctive schedule of holy days and festivals. Second, since the lunar calendar does not comport with the annual seasons, Islamic festivals and holy days are not identified with specific seasons of the year such as the agricultural times of planting and harvest.[1] Thus, in each thirty-three-year cycle, rituals such as the pilgrimage and the Ramadan Fast will be observed in all seasons.

Islamic months are cycles in seven-day weeks. The first five days are known as "First Day," "Second Day," "Third Day," and so on. *Jum^ca,* "Day of Congregation," is the day of the common gathering for the noon prayer, corresponding to our Friday. In Islamic cities and villages, shops and offices close at that time.

The five daily prayers also form a pattern that structures each day. Verbally chanted by the muezzin, nowadays over loudspeakers (sometimes from re-

[1] On the Islamic calendar see Marshall G. S. Hodgson, *The Venture of Islam,* 3 volumes (Chicago: University of Chicago Press, 1974), vol. I, pp. 20–22.

TABLE 6-2. DAYS OF THE WEEK

Arabic Name	Corresponding English Name
Yawm al-Ahad (First Day)	Sunday
Yawm al-Ithnayn (Second Day)	Monday
Yawm al-Thalatha (Third Day)	Tuesday
Yawm al-Arba (Fourth Day)	Wednesday
Yawm al-Khamis (Fifth Day)	Thursday
Yawm al-Jum^{c}a (Day of Congregation)	Friday
Yawm al-Sabt (Day of Sabbath)*	Saturday

* "Sabbath" is the literal meaning of *sabt*, although it does not carry that connotation when used in this context.

cordings), the events of prayer are anticipated by a culturally conditioned sense of timing. The first prayer period begins with the muezzin's call to prayer at dawn. Most Muslims perform this prayer in their homes. The second prayer period begins at noon. Many Muslims perform the noon prayer in their school or place of business if not in a mosque. Sometimes the noon repast, followed by a rest from daily activities, separates this prayer from the third, which begins later in the afternoon. Many businesses, shops, and offices stay open until the fourth prayer is called at sunset. Religious instruction and guidance are offered by Imams in mosques in many parts of the Islamic world before or after the sunset Salat. At this hour many will return home for the evening meal with their families. The final prayer of the day is called about two hours after sunset. Some

TABLE 6-3. TIMES OF PRAYER

Arabic Name	Period of Time*
Salat al-Fajr (The Dawn Prayer)	From dawn to sunrise
Salat al-Zuhr (The Noon Prayer)	From noon to early afternoon
Salat al-Asr (The Afternoon Prayer)	From end of noon prayer to sunset
Salat al-Maghrib (The Sunset Prayer)	From after sunset to end of P.M. twilight
Salat al-Isha (The Night Prayer)	From after P.M. twilight to before A.M. twilight

* The call to prayer is given at the beginning of the period and the prayer said and performed at some time before the next call to prayer is given.

Muslims schedule the evening dinner and social intercourse with family and friends after that hour.

Islamic Festivals and Holidays

During many of the twelve months of the Hijra year Islamic festivals, called *ᶜīd* in the singular (pronounced "eed"), are observed. Some festivals are universally observed throughout Islam. Others derive from local traditions, not from the Koran and Sunna. For example, the annual Hindu pilgrimage in Sri Lanka centers on the shrine of a Hindu deity. One scholar reports that "temples, priests, and pilgrims of both Hinduism and Buddhism are found at the site; Muslims and Christians also attend the annual festivities. The atmosphere is one of tolerance and ecumenism."[2] Another scholar has compared two local Muslim saints, one in North Africa and the other in Indonesia, describing both the common Islamic and the distinctively local legends and ceremonials that surround these figures.[3] Although the local colorations that are infused with Islamic worship and ritual are not without significance, we will confine ourselves here to the more universally observed Islamic elements.

MUHARRAM. The first day of this, the first month of the Muslim calendar, marks the beginning of the new year in Islam. It is the anniversary of the Prophet's Hijra from Mecca to Medina. The tenth of Muharram originally began a fast that lasted for twenty-four hours. Called *ᶜāshūrā'*, meaning "tenth," this holy day at the beginning of the Prophet's Mission coincided with Yom Kippur, the Day of Atonement in Judaism. Muslim authorities have also traced the significance of this *ᶜīd* to pre-Islamic origins. The Prophet had felt betrayed by the Jews in Medina. (This is reminiscent of Jesus' conflict with the Pharisees and the Hebrew Prophets' conflict with the priests of Baᶜal.) A Koranic revelation prescribed that the period of fasting should be the month of Ramadan rather than Ashura. Ashura has remained a voluntary day of fasting. According to the Sunna of the Prophet, it is recommended but not obligatory to fast on that day.[4]

Shiᶜite Muslims attach a quite different significance to the tenth of Muharram. It is the traditional anniversary of the martyrdom of Husayn, son of Ali. The ritual and drama of this day for Shiᶜites is extremely important. We have given a brief description of this Passion drama in Chapter 1, and we will analyze its meaning in more detail later in this chapter.

---

[2] Brian Pfaffenberger, "The Kataragamma Pilgrimage: Hindu-Buddhist Interaction and Its Significance in Sri Lanka's Polythenic Social System," *Journal of Asian Studies,* 38, no. 2, (1979), 253.

[3] Clifford Geertz, *Islam Observed* (New Haven, Conn.: Yale University Press, 1968).

[4] See articles entitled "ᶜAshurā'" and "Muharram" in *Shorter Encyclopaedia of Islam,* ed. H. A. R. Gibb and J. H. Kramers (Ithaca, N.Y.: Cornell University Press, 1953).

BIRTHDAY OF THE PROPHET (MAWLID AL-NABĪ). Muhammad's birthday is celebrated on the twelfth day of the third month, Rabi^{c} al-Awwal. During the first two centuries of Islam this festival was not observed. For one thing, the exact date of Muhammad's birth was not exactly known. By the ninth century a set body of traditions about the Sunna of the Prophet had become standardized. One precedent in the Prophet's life that emerged was that many important events had occurred on Mondays (Yawm al-Ithnayn). His Hijra to Medina and his death were thought by many to have occurred on that day of the week. Tradition also formed in favor of Monday, the twelfth day of Rabi^{c} al-Awwal as the anniversary of Muhammad's birth. Even though this anniversary does not necessarily fall on a Monday, many Muslims have regarded Mondays as particularly auspicious days of voluntary fasting.

The twelfth of Rabi^{c} al-Awwal has become a major religious festival for Muslims in many parts of the Islamic world. Not only the Prophet, but other holy men are remembered with religious celebrations on the anniversaries of their birth or death. In addition, Shi^{c}ite Muslims also celebrate the birthday anniversaries that tradition has assigned to Ali and members of his family. The Sufis elaborately honor their saints in the same fashion. Most Muslims observe the ^{c}Id of Mawlid al-Nabi. Some Sunni Muslims (particularly in Saudi Arabia) have refrained because the celebration, in their view, is an innovation. That is, it was not mentioned by the Prophet or his closest companions. More alarming for some is that this holiday has tended to deify the Prophet at the expense of his humanity.[5]

An anthropologist who lived for some time in a small village near Cairo has written an interesting description of the celebration of the Mawlid al-Nabi among the villagers.[6] They begin their actual preparations for the celebration as much as four days prior to the twelfth of Rabi^{c} al-Awwal. Homes are decorated and in many yards tents are set up to provide shelter from the sun for the large number of friends and family that will gather. In the evenings, over loudspeakers, trained reciters from the village chant verses from the Koran and a specially prepared text about the life of the Prophet. Mawlid al-Nabi is a legal holiday throughout Egypt. On that day homes and the tents are filled with friends and relatives, and the mood is one of festivity. In the village of Kafr el-Elow merchants arrive in wagons to sell varieties of candy, including some shaped as knights on horses for boys, and doll brides for girls, Egyptian symbols for Muhammad's birthday.[7]

---

[5] Information on the history of this festival is summarized in the article "Mawlid" in *Shorter Encyclopaedia of Islam.*

[6] Hani Fakhouri, *Kafr el-Elow: An Egyptian Village in Transition* (New York: Holt, Rinehart & Winston, 1972), pp. 85–86. A broader, more historical treatment of the festival in Islam is found in Gustav E. von Grunebaum, *Muhammaden Festivals* (London and New York: Akeland-Schuman, 1958).

[7] See Fakhouri, *Kafr el-Elow,* p. 86. I am indebted to Dr. Muhammad Abdul-Rauf for this and many other details about these celebrations.

FESTIVAL OF BREAKING OFF THE FAST (ᶜĪD AL-FIṬR). This religious holiday, also called the Minor Festival, occurs on the first day of the month of Shawwal immediately after the Ramadan fast.[8] The day stands in sharp contrast to the preceding thirty days of fasting and self-denial. It begins in the morning with a visit, mostly by the men folk, to the mosque for morning prayer. This is followed, according to the Sunna of the Prophet, by a visit to cemeteries. These more solemn religious expressions then change into a happy festival in the homes of heads of families. It is an occasion for dressing up in one's best clothing.

The thematic shift from death to life, from deceased relatives to living children, is expressed in several ways. Gifts and money are given to children and to the homes of newly married daughters. More significant is the joyous return for all to a normal life without the symbolic denial of vital processes of life-giving activities—eating and sexual intercourse. In many places this festival lasts for three days, and in many lands it is also a national holiday. Islamic law requires that *zakāt al-fiṭr* or "alms of breaking off the fast" be given to the poor. This would seem to heighten one meaning of the fast, namely, focusing one's attention on the plight of the poor (who often go hungry) by making their plight easier. It is a personal response to having experienced hunger and denial in ritual form, and an aid to the needy to help them share in the festivities.

FESTIVAL OF THE SACRIFICE (ᶜĪD AL-AḌḤĀ). This religious festival, also called the Major Festival, is celebrated on the tenth of Dhu al-Hijja, the last month of the year. Although Muslims observe this holiday in their home towns all around the world, its most sacred observance is in Mina, a small village four miles East of Mecca. There hundreds of thousands of Muslims (about two million in 1979) observe the sacrifice as part of the pilgrimage to Mecca and to the other sacred sites nearby. The Sunna of the Prophet requires heads of families who are able to do so to purchase a sheep for the sacrifice. The meat of the slaughtered animal must be shared with the poor; the Prophets's Sunna recommends giving one-third to the poor, giving one-third to neighbors and friends, and letting one-third remain in the family. Like the Festival of Breaking off the Fast, the Festival of the Sacrifice lasts three days. For pilgrims camped at Mina near Mecca the day marks a return to normal life. These days are spent in conviviality with other pilgrims from around the world.

Muslims not making the pilgrimage celebrate the Festival of the Sacrifice in their home towns and villages. In the Egyptian village of Kafr el-Elow, the festival is celebrated in much the same fashion as the Breaking off of the Fast. It begins on the first day with morning prayers in the local mosque followed by visits to the graves of deceased family. Then sheep are sacrificed. Sweets and great quantities of food are prepared for family and guests. Again, one's best clothes are worn, and the general mood is one of happiness and hospitality.

[8] See the article on ᶜId al-Fitr in *Shorter Encyclopaedia of Islam.*

PILGRIMAGE TO MECCA

Each year during the last month, Dhu al-Hijja, over a million Muslims make the pilgrimage called the Hajj to Mecca. It is the fifth Pillar of Islam, and both the Koran and the Sunna of the Prophet offer information and guidance to Muslims who decide to make this journey. Many of the Prophet's sayings and many pages in the books of Islamic law describe and regulate one's participation in the Hajj. Although it is an obligatory religious duty, practical considerations exist. Only those who can afford the journey and who are physically able to endure the hardships are required to make the Hajj.

Until recently, Muslims from such faraway places as Spain and India had to begin months in advance, often as much as a year, in order to reach Mecca at the appointed time. Muslims from these and other lands would join regular processions of pilgrims along well-traveled routes leading to Mecca from Syria, Iraq, Egypt, and South Arabia. Those who wrote about their adventures and experiences along the way became important sources of information about Islamic lands and local customs in the Middle Ages.

Nowadays the city of Jidda on the western coast of Saudi Arabia, about fifty miles west of Mecca, is the main port of entry. By chartered plane and ship, pilgrims arrive in great throngs at Jidda in the tenth month, Shawwal. From this swelling port of entry they proceed to Mecca. At some point before reaching the Haram, the sacred territory surrounding the Ka^{c}ba, usually even before arriving in Jidda, they consecrate themselves for the sacred ritual. Buses and cars have replaced the camel as the chief means of transportation to Mecca. Nonetheless, pilgrims on foot or astride camels and donkeys are still to be seen on the road to Mecca.

The person who makes the Hajj is called a Hajji (Hajjiya if female). Both before departing and after returning home, a Hajji is a celebrated person in his or her home town. Many who cannot afford the journey vicariously experience the sacred journey through those who can. Poems and songs about the Hajj are sung with neighbors and friends. Hajjis often paint special symbols on their homes, depicting their experiences. Wealthier Muslims may offer to finance the trip for those who are less fortunate. Throughout the Islamic world newspapers, radio, and television stations cover the many aspects of this mass ritual. Although only a fraction of the Muslim population make the Hajj in any given year, the entire world of Islam participates in this important religious holiday, the fifth Pillar of Islam.

The Pilgrimage Experience

In the following pages we shall follow the footsteps of Muslims making the Hajj. Their repsonses to the symbols and rituals involved have been conditioned by their Islamic environment since childhood. As non-Muslims, our understanding of their experience is determined by our own cultural heritage. Some of the questions we may wish to have answered will be suggested by our own religious notions. Through the encounter between the Hajj experience and our own interest in the study of religious symbols and rituals we hope to illuminate both an internal and an external view of the fifth Pillar of Islam.[9]

As the plane first lands at Jidda on the western coast of Saudi Arabia, one is caught in a bundle of emotions.[10] First, there are immigration checkpoints, clogged with thousands of people of all races. Language and communication appear to be a problem. Confusion seems to prevail at first. Even with family and friends one feels like a small drop in a vast ocean of people. Yet this is not a "lonely crowd." Despite differences of color, language, and socioeconomic status, all are brothers and sisters in Islam. All are dressed alike; all share identical beliefs; and despite language barriers, all can speak common words of greeting. During the events of the next few days, the acquaintance of many people is made along the way. By the end of the Hajj, a common feeling of brotherhood throughout the entire body of pilgrims will have been established.

The difficulties of negotiating one's way during the Hajj are considerable. Therefore, over the centuries Muslims from afar have often employed agents to handle local arrangements for them and to guide them on their journey. More recently, organizations have formed to handle arrangements for entire groups.

Pilgrims normally exchange their street clothes for the sacred white Ihram before arriving in Jidda. For men it consists of two white pieces of cloth, each about the size of a large towel, one draped over the shoulder and knotted on the opposite side, the other fastened around the waist. Most women wear full-length white dresses and a white head covering. By donning the Ihram a Muslim enters a consecrated state. Bodily hair and fingernails may not be cut, colognes and perfumes may not be worn, and sexual activities are to be suspended. Bathing is also suspended during the state of being Muhrim (consecrated) except to remove a pollution, such as menstruation for women and nocturnal emission for men.

The trip from Jidda to Mecca is one of mounting excitement and anticipation. As pilgrims pass through the boundaries that mark the Haram, shouts of *labbayka* pierce the air. It is the traditional exclamation of Muslim pilgrims, and it means, roughly, "Here I am, O Lord," Crossing the border into the Haram, the state of consecration becomes complete. No shedding of blood or fomenting any kind of strife is permitted. Animals may not be hunted, and even plant life must be left undisturbed. Just as there is bodily cessation of bathing and cutting of hair and nails, the land within the Haram is itself consecrated for those in the state of Ihram. Fasting, on the other hand, is not required.

A great welling of emotion comes when pilgrims enter the city of Mecca. They invariably head straight to the Great Mosque within whose giant courtyard

---

[9] The account of the Hajj that follows has been gathered from many sources, several of which will be noted in the next few pages. Conversations with Muslim friends who have made the Hajj have inspired the medium of personal observation injected into the narrative description.

[10] An interesting personal account by a black American Muslim making the Hajj was given by Malcolm X in *Autobiography of Malcolm X* (New York: Grove Press, Inc., 1966), pp. 318–42.

stands the Ka^{c}ba. Several times each day of their lives in their home towns Muslim pilgrims have oriented themselves toward the Ka^{c}ba during the canonical prayer. All of a sudden it looms very large and real, a cubical stone edifice covered by a black cloth embroidered in gold calligraphy. It would be difficult to grasp or describe all the possible feelings Muslims might have at this moment. The famous nineteenth-century British traveler and adventurer, Sir Richard Burton, once posed as a Muslim in order to make the Hajj. His impressions of his first glimpse of the Ka^{c}ba are worth quoting.

> There at last it lay, the bourn of my long and weary pilgrimage, realizing the plans and hopes of many and many a year. The mirage medium of Fancy invested the huge catafalque and its gloomy pall with peculiar charms. There were no giant fragments of hoar[y] antiquity as in Egypt, no remains of graceful and harmonious beauty as in Greece and Italy, no barbarous gorgeousness as in the buildings of India; yet the view was strange, unique—and how few have looked upon the celebrated shrine! . . . It was as if the poetical legends of the Arabs spoke the truth, and that the waving wings of angels, not the sweet breeze of morning, were agitating and swelling the black covering of the shrine.[11]

The Umra or Lesser Pilgrimage

By declaring a Niya (intention), a Muslim may choose to perform the Lesser Pilgrimage prior to the main performance of the Hajj or Greater Pilgrimage. Many other pilgrims will perform the Lesser Pilgrimage later, or even at another time of the year. After the first few moments of awe one may join hundreds of other Muslims circumambulating the Ka^{c}ba.

The Umra is highlighted by seven such counterclockwise circuits. This circling is known as the *ṭawāf.* The Ka^{c}ba, which stands in the center of this activity, is so situated that each of its four corners points in one of the four cardinal points of the compass (see illustration). Set in the east corner of the Ka^{c}ba is a black stone rimmed by a silver casing. The first Tawaf around the Ka^{c}ba begins on the side of the courtyard of the Great Mosque nearest the stone. An attempt to actually touch it—the desire of every pilgrim—may be blocked by the press of the crowd. Many get close enough to actually kiss the stone. An aerial view of the Tawaf shows just how massive yet homogeneous the ritual process is. Thousands of Muslims dressed in the common Ihram attire move in a common gesture around the House of God, the sacred geographical center of Islam.

The Ka^{c}ba is not the only sacred monument within the Great Mosque of Mecca. Out from the northeast wall of the Ka^{c}ba is the Place of Abraham, a smaller, more ornate shrine that commemorates the ancient Patriarch's founding of the first house of worship. Closer to the black stone is the well of Zamzam. Tradition has it that while Hagar searched frantically for water, her infant Isma^{c}il (Ishmael) kicked the ground and water miraculously sprang forth. All

[11] Richard F. Burton, *Personal Narrative of a Pilgrimage to Al-Madinah and Meccah,* 2 volumes, ed. Isabel Burton, (London: G. Bell & Sons, Ltd., 1898), vol. II, pp. 160–61.

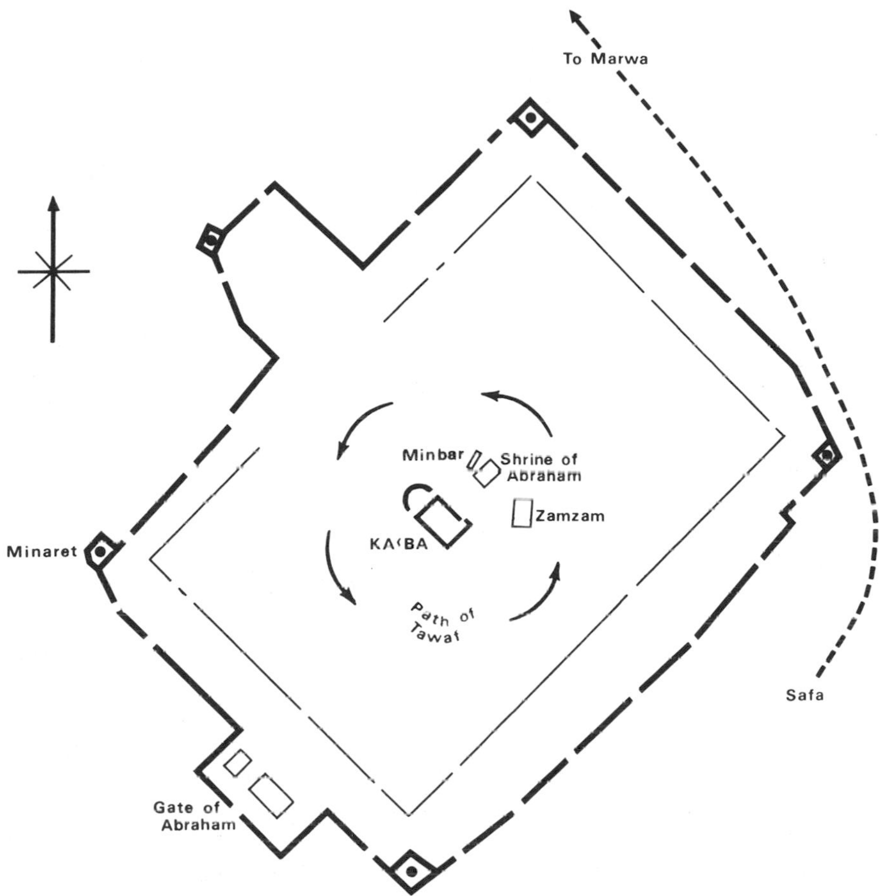

FIGURE 6.2. Plan of Ka^{c}ba and Great Mosque. (Illustration by David Stodola.)

pilgrim visitors to the shrine seek a draught of the sacred refreshment that continues to flow in the well of Zamzam. Adjacent to the Place of Abraham is a decorated pulpit or *minbar* that looks out over the central grounds from atop a flight of stairs. On Fridays prior to the Hajj, pilgrims gather to hear a sermon delivered by a leading Imam. The purpose of the sermon is to prepare pilgrims for the spiritual journey ahead.

After the Tawaf, Muslims making the Lesser Pilgrimage head for the eastern gate of the courtyard of the Great Mosque and pass into a long covered corridor that connects two points known as Safa and Marwa (see "Plan of Ka^{c}ba"). Each pilgrim runs or walks rapidly the distance of a few blocks from one point to the other, seven trips in all. The traditional meaning of this act is a symbolic remembrance of the plight of Hagar, who ran in desperation between these two points in search of water and help against the harsh conditions of the barren desert. Following the "running" between Safa and Marwa, pilgrims have a lock of hair cut, removing themselves from the state of being Muhrim. The duties of the Umra have ceased.

The Hajj or Greater Pilgrimage

DAY OF WATERING (YAWM AL-TARWIYA). On the eighth of Dhu al-Hijja great masses of Muslims set out from Mecca with the Niya (intention) of making the Greater Pilgrimage (unless this was already declared before reaching Jidda). The day is also known as "Going out to Mina," a small town four miles to the east of Mecca. It is reported that during his Farewell Pilgrimage just before he died, Muhammad spent his first night in Mina. The name "Day of Watering" has puzzled Muslim historians. Some have concluded that it was originally a day for watering camels in preparation for the days ahead. It remains a day of spiritual and physical preparation for the rigors of the Hajj. Thousands of tents are tightly arranged along the valley floor at Mina to accommodate the increasing number of pilgrims each year. Many pilgrims, however, move on to Arafat to be at the next day's station ahead of the rush.

DAY AT ARAFAT (YAWM ᶜARAFAT). On the ninth day of Dhu al-Hijja, pilgrims begin to gather at the easternmost distant station of the Hajj, the Plain of Arafat. As they swarm onto the plain, they pass between two markers that designate the boundary of the Haram; Arafat lies just outside of it. At noon both the midday and afternoon prayers are performed together. The afternoon is then spent standing at the foot of a small rocky hill called the Mount of Mercy. From a position on the hill during his Farewell Pilgrimage, Muhammad had delivered a sermon to his followers gathered on the plain. This event has been commemorated since the early days of Islam with a sermon delivered by a respected Imam. The homily repeats the Prophet's farewell call for peace and harmony among his followers. Many Muslims will spend the entire afternoon standing beneath or even on the hill; the more pious hope to locate themselves near where Muhammad had stood. Those unable to take the long hours of heat, especially in years when Dhu al-Hijja occurs during the summer, retire after a while to tents erected on the plain for that purpose. They too will spend the afternoon in prayer and quiet reflection.

At sunset a signal is given for the "Hurrying to Muzdalifa," a small town back on the road to Mecca. As camp in the Plain of Arafat is broken, shouts of *labbayka* pierce the air. The mood of somber reflection disappears with the sun; excitement and anticipation rouse the crowd into frantic activity. Reports from Muslim travelers in the Middle Ages confirm the impressions of Sir Richard Burton.

> The Pilgrims . . . rushed down the hill [of Arafat] with a "Labbayk" sounding like a blast, and took the road to Muna [Mina]. Then I saw the scene which has given this part of the ceremonies the name of . . . the "Hurry from Arafat." Every man

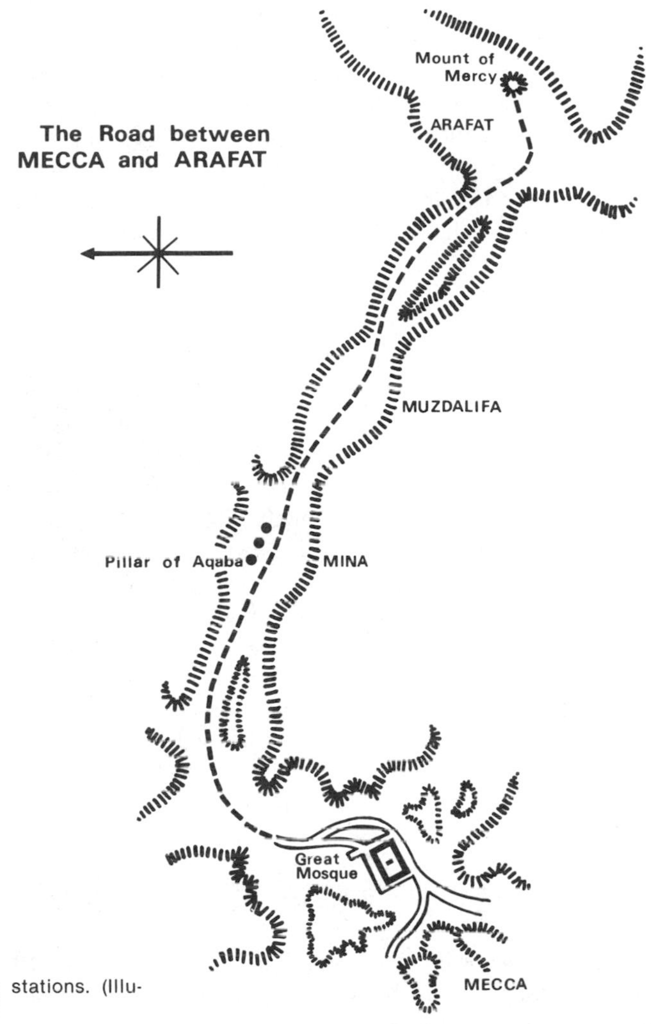

FIGURE 6.3. Plan of Hajj stations. (Illustration by David Stodola.)

> urged his beast with might and main: it was sunset; the plain bristled with tent-pegs, litters were crushed, pedestrians were trampled, camels were overthrown . . . briefly, it was chaotic confusion.[12]

Like other religious ceremonials, the Hajj has quick changes of tempo. The entire experience stands in sharp contrast to everyday life. Following this description we will evaluate some of these contrasts. With so many people presently making the Hajj, some logistic control over the Hurry to Muzdalifa has been ex-

[12] Burton, *Pilgrimage,* vol. II, 199.

erted. Many pilgrims nowadays ride in buses from site to site, but the sense of excitement and anticipation runs high nonetheless.

Arriving in Muzdalifa after dark, pilgrims recite the sunset and late evening prayers together. This is a relaxation that applies during any journey in order to provide for keeping the prayer without interrupting necessary activities. That evening a lighted mosque on a nearby hill draws everyone's attention. Around the camp in Muzdalifa, pilgrims may be seen gathering numerous small stones that will be ritually tossed at symbolic representations of Satan on the following days.

FESTIVAL OF THE SACRIFICE (ᶜĪD AL-ADHĀ). Before daybreak on the morning of the tenth of Dhu al-Hijja a signal again rouses the encamped pilgrims to break camp and move on. Arriving in Mina, they carry the stones gathered the previous evening to a stone pillar called *Aqaba.* Seven stones are thrown by each pilgrim at this symbol of Satan. Islamic sacred history, recorded in the Koran and elaborated in tradition, relates the story that God had required Abraham to sacrifice his son Ismaᶜil. Satan repeatedly sought to tempt Abraham into ignoring the command, and each time Abraham resisted temptation, remaining steadfast in his intention to carry out God's costly command. At the last minute God spared Abraham this painful duty.

The stoning of Aqaba is a ritual repulsion of the Tempter, Satan. After tossing the stones, pilgrims move to the edge of the plain around Mina and begin the sacrifice. Sheep and other animals are purchased and slaughtered on the open plain. We have described this festival as a ritual that takes place throughout the Islamic world, not just at Mina. The sacrifice signifies Abraham's willingness to sacrifice what was most precious to him, his son. The sacrificer symbolically affirms he is willing to give up, for the sake of God, that which is dearest to him. It is a sacred gesture of thanksgiving and measure of charity.

Following the sacrifice, male pilgrims form in line to have their hair cut. In privacy, women will cut a lock of hair, again as a symbolic gesture. Many men will have their heads shaven—a sign of being a Hajji. Others may choose to have only a "trim," which, as a ritual gesture, is considered efficacious. Then pilgrims doff the Ihram and thereby deconsecrate themselves to the extent allowed while still within the Haram around Mecca. Normal street clothes can now be worn. Bathing and grooming then follows as all Muslims return to normal life. Only sexual activity (including kissing and entering into a marriage contract) is forbidden until the "post Arafat" Tawaf is performed. While the pilgrims have been on the Hajj, the Kaᶜba has received a new *kiswa* or black shroud, beautifully embroidered in calligraphy. Those who have not yet made the Lesser Pilgrimage may do so at this time.

DAYS OF SOCIAL GATHERING (AYYĀM AL-TASHRĪQ). The eleventh through the thirteenth days of Dhu al-Hijja provide a happy, convivial climax to the Hajj. Pilgrims remain encamped at Mina, where they enjoy a period of deepening friendships gained along the way. Muslims from around the world have gotten to know each other during the entire pilgrimage. Even if two Hajj acquaintances do not speak a common language, usually someone nearby can interpret for them. Arabic, the liturgical language of the Hajj ritual, is the language heard most often. All Muslims learn to exchange religious greetings in Arabic. On each of the three days pilgrims return to Aqaba and the two other stone pillars in the center of Mina to toss seven stones at each. On the third and final day of social gathering many Muslims return to Mecca to make a final Tawaf around the Ka^{c}ba in the Great Mosque. Afterwards many purchase a few mementos to bring back to friends. Then buses are boarded for the trip to Jidda, and back home.

Many Muslims take this opportunity to make another pilgrimage. Nearby Medina is the second holy city of Islam (Jerusalem is the third). The Prophet's mosque and tomb are visited by thousands of pilgrims each year, particularly at this time. Muslims visit Medina to offer salutations to the Prophet and to seek forgiveness of their sins at the mosque and house from which he directed the establishment of the Islamic Umma during the last ten years of his mission. Muslims believe Muhammad brought the Guidance to humankind, and their reverence and thankfulness are especially keen on this second pilgrimage to Medina.

Understanding the Pilgrimage Experience

Throughout the centuries many travelers have made the Hajj and described their experiences. Interesting as these reports are to readers who are otherwise unfamiliar with this phenomenon, understanding the pilgrimage experience offers the student of religion a considerable challenge. One point to be considered is that the Hajj was an important ritual in pagan Arabia long before the rise of Islam. As a young man Muhammad is said to have made the Hajj while the rite still bore its pre-Islamic meanings. The Muslims from Mecca who immigrated with Muhammad to Medina were denied access to this important ritual until the sixth year after the Hijra. The Prophet himself became a pilgrim in 632, and his performance that year significantly changed certain aspects and much of the meaning of the ancient ritual.

The sacred history of Abraham's journey to Mecca with Hagar and Isma^{c}il is the Islamic understanding of the origin of the Meccan shrine. The story of Abraham's difficult duty to sacrifice his son became the Islamic sacred history of the Festival of the Sacrifice in Mina known as *^{c}Īd al-Aḍḥa.* The Plain of Arafat, which lay just beyond the boundaries of the Haram, was originally the scene of an annual fair held during the pilgrimage season. Muhammad's Farewell Pilgrimage brought his own person directly into the meaning of the several sacred days precisely in the middle of the journey at the extreme geographic outpost beyond the ancient sacred boundaries. The Islamic understanding of the Hajj took its classic form with reference to the Sunna of the

Prophet. It was the work of the legal theorists of the orthodox Shari^{c}a law schools that clarified the duties and options encumbent upon all Hajjis. Tradition, both popular and formal, gave the ancient practice continued life with new meanings. The fine points of duties and options, such as how long one should stand at Arafat, were established by consensus in the schools of Shari^{c}a Law.

The social, cultural, and economic effects of the Hajj in medieval Islam, writes historian Bernard Lewis, are of immense importance.

> Every year, great numbers of Muslims, from all parts of the Islamic world, from many races and from different social strata, left their homes and travelled, often over vast distances, to take part in a common act of worship. . . . The needs of the pilgrimage—the commands of the faith reinforcing the requirements of government and commerce—help to maintain an adequate network of communications between the far-flung Muslim lands; the experience of the pilgrimage gives rise to a rich literature of travel, bringing information about distant places, and a heightened awareness of belonging to a larger whole. This awareness is reinforced by participation in the common ritual and ceremonies of the pilgrimage in Mecca and Medina, and the communion with fellow-Muslims of other lands and peoples. . . . The pilgrimage was not the only factor making for cultural unity and social mobility in the Islamic world [during the Middle Ages]—but it was certainly an important one, perhaps the most important.[13]

The religious significance of those pilgrimages performed in a variety of the religions of humankind has been studied by anthropologists and historians of religions. The writings of Victor Turner in particular have offered vital new insights. Earlier theories about rites of passage in tribal societies showed that a cross-cultural pattern can be discerned in the rites of all peoples, as, for example, in initiation ceremonials. A major shift takes place between the structured society in which one lives his or her everyday life, and the sense of brotherhood or community that is created by the ceremonial. In the society of one's village or city, vertical relations based on social class and economic status are clearly defined. These are dissolved when one enters the community that has been created by ceremonial rites. Society is a secular or "profane" phenomenon; community is sacred.

Turner's studies suggest that pilgrimages performed in the major living religious traditions of the world are manifestations of the same patterns of movement from secular to sacred and back to secular life that is characteristic of many rites of passage. The term used by social scientists for the religious experience of a sacred community is *liminality.* Turner defines liminality as follows:

> The attributes of liminality or of liminal *personae* ("threshold people") are necessarily ambiguous, since this condition and these persons elude or slip through the network of classifications that normally locate states and positions in cultural space. Liminal entities are neither here nor there; they are betwixt and between the positions assigned and arrayed by law, custom, convention, and ceremonial. As such, their ambiguous and indeterminate attributes are ex-

[13] Bernard Lewis on the social aspects of the Hajj in the article "Hadjdj," *Encyclopaedia of Islam,* 2nd ed. H. A. R. Gibb et al (Leiden: E. J. Brill, 1960-).

> pressed by a rich variety of symbols in the many societies that ritualize social and cultural transitions. Thus, liminality is frequently likened to death, to being in the womb, to invisibility, to darkness, to bisexuality, to the wilderness, and to an eclipse of the sun or moon.
>
> Liminal entities . . . may be represented as possessing nothing. They may be disguised as monsters, wear only a strip of clothing, or even go naked, to demonstrate that as liminal beings they have no status, property, insignia, secular clothing indicating rank or role, position in a kinship system—in short, nothing that may distinguish them from their fellow neophytes [i.e., pilgrims].[14]

Turner's illuminating analysis provides some valuable insights into the Hajj experience. The pilgrimage to Mecca is a liminal experience. The Shari^{c}a carefully lays out the structure of relationships and obligations that ought to prevail in Islamic society. The respective roles of men and women, the proper forms of government, even the everyday performance of prayer and other religious duties belong to the domain of "society" in social scientific terms. But within this highly structured mode of living, pressures build up; sin and human failure alienate one from fellow human beings. One then becomes a pilgrim, setting out on a sacred journey to a sacred space within which the binding structures and obligations of society are altered or dissolved. Equality with other human beings is felt as never before, and spiritual renewal is keenly experienced. It is a rich adventure. Pilgrims cross social and political boundaries in order to reach a sacred center. At the sacred center (the Ka^{c}ba in Islam), brotherhood is achieved in a way that is not feasible back in one's normal social setting.

During the state of Ihram or "consecration," Muslims suspend or reverse the usual patterns of both sacred and secular life back at home. As we have seen, the pilgrim alters the normal times of prayer at Arafat. Cutting the hair and nails is suspended. Street clothes, the symbol of one's status in society, are exchanged for a common garb, the Ihram. Sexual activity, the force that perpetuates society, is temporarily ceased. The liminal experience of brotherhood relieves the burden of society, and one's responsibilities within it are lifted, and a true community of believers is experienced. Then this process of inversion ends, and the pilgrim returns to his or her normal social context. It is a process of renewal that each Muslim must decide whether and when to undertake in his or her own personal quest for salvation.

THE MUHARRAM PASSION

The Ta^{c}ziyeh of Qasim

Qasim, son of Hasan, is betrothed to his cousin, Fatima. The marriage had been the wish of Imam Hasan before his death. Qasim also feels compelled to join his family's fight against the troops of the Umayyads, led by the Caliph Yazid. This

[14] Reprinted from Victor Turner: *The Ritual Process.* Copyright © 1969 by Victor W. Turner. Used by permission of the publisher, Cornell University Press.

conflict has already taken the life of his cousin, Ali Akbar. In this particular performance of the Iranian Ta^cziyeh theater, Qasim himself must face a violent end. All of these events form separate episodes of the main tragedy of Shi^cite salvation history, the violent death of Imam Husayn at the hands of the troops of Yazid, who was caliph and commander of the Umayyad troops.

In the Ta^cziyeh of Qasim, Imam Husayn is reluctant to let his nephew march off to war. "How can I send him? He is the living memory of my brother [Hasan], an unwed boy in the flower of his youth who has not yet tasted the pleasures of life."[15] As the family tearfully discusses whether or not Qasim should join the battle, a riderless horse appears. Piercing wails rise up from the grief-stricken family. It is the mount belonging to the martyred Ali Akbar, son of Husayn and cousin of Qasim. Qasim's desire to seek revenge is now overwhelming. He will go to war. But first he must wed the beautiful Fatima, daughter of Husayn and Sister of Ali Akbar.

Thus in the midst of grief for the dead, a traditional Islamic wedding ceremonial is prepared. Qasim will wear the bridegroom costume of his fallen cousin, Ali Akbar. Imam Husayn, the living family Patriarch, sends sweets to his enemies. This symbolic gesture is based on the custom that the family hosts the nuptial celebrations with entertainment and food for the larger community. After the wedding, when they are finally alone, Qasim tells Fatima that he must leave immediately for war. Time and events will not allow them to consummate the marriage. Against Fatima's protests, Qasim offers the consolation that perhaps their union will become beautifully complete in Heaven.

In the battle that is next staged Qasim fights bravely, but he is soon stricken from his mount, ironically by the enemy to whom the ceremonial sweets had been sent announcing his marriage. Qasim begs for a reprieve to see his bride and fulfill his love for her before the death blow is struck. As Qasim is cradled in the arms of the mourning Patriarch, Imam Husayn, his plea is ignored. The enemy delivers the fatal blow. As he breathes his last breaths, Qasim refuses to let Husayn return his mutilated body to Fatima. When Qasim expires on the field of battle, Husayn returns to the family encampment to deliver the tragic news.[16]

THE TA^cZIYEH IN HISTORY. War and marriage, passion and unrequited love, gestures of friendship and cruelties of revenge, heaven and earth—these and other conflicting themes emerge as actors and audience participate together in the Shi^cite rituals of sacred history. As a stage performance the Ta^cziyeh is a

[15] Line from the Ta^cziyeh of Qasim cited by Sadeq Humayuni, "An Analysis of the Ta^cziyeh of Qasem," in *Ta^cziyeh: Ritual and Drama in Iran,* ed. Peter Chelkowski (New York: New York University Press, 1979), p. 13. Copyright © 1979 by New York University.

[16] A fuller account and analysis of this scene is given by Humayuni, "Ta^cziyeh of Qasem," pp. 12–23.

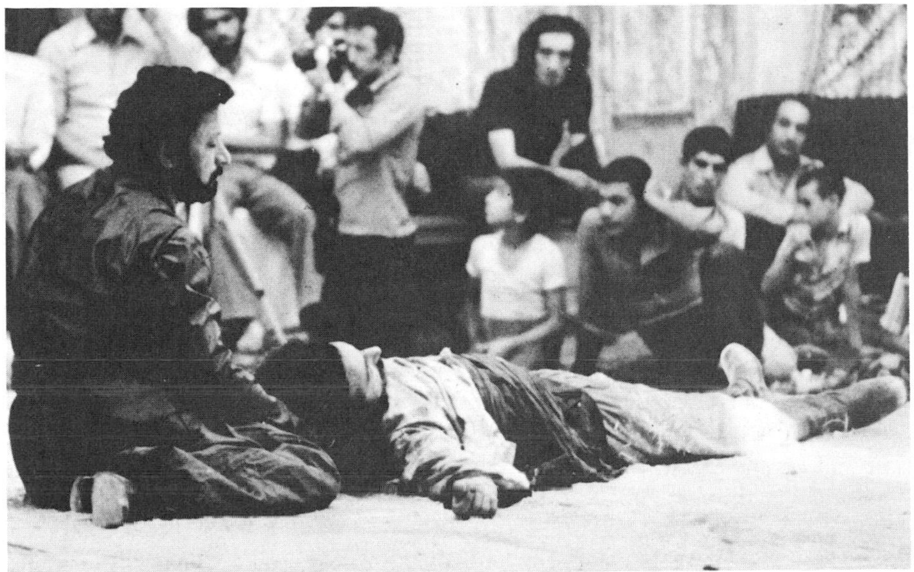

FIGURE 6.4. Ta^{c}ziyeh scene staging Husayn's murder. (Photo by Peter Chelkowski.)

recent form of a classic mode of Shi^{c}ite piety. Karbala, Iraq, was the historic scene of the martyrdom of Husayn on the tenth of Muharram in A.D. 680. This was the seed event that inspired the many episodes of the Ta^{c}ziyeh performance. Until the nineteenth century the main form of piety was the pilgrimages to the shrines of the Shi^{c}ite martyrs, especially to the site at Karbala. In addition, in Persian cities and villages scripts of the scenes of their martyrdom were read before emotion-filled audiences. In time, special performance halls were erected. A stage constructed especially for Ta^{c}ziyeh performances is called a *takiyeh;* it marks out a sacred space, and the events that are performed within its boundaries become moments of sacred time. Peter J. Chelkowski says of the Ta^{c}ziyeh performance:

> The word *ta^{c}ziyeh* literally means expressions of sympathy, mourning and consolation. As a dramatic form it has its origins in the Muharram processions commemorating [Husayn's] martyrdom and throughout its evolution the representation of the siege and carnage at Kerbela has remained the centerpoint. Ta^{c}ziyeh has never lost its religious implications. Because early Shi^{c}ites viewed [Husayn's] death as a sacred redemptive act, the performance of the Muharram ceremonies was believed to be an aid to salvation; later they also believed that participation, both by actors and spectators, in the Ta^{c}ziyeh dramas would gain them [Husayn's] intercession on the day of the Last Judgment.[17]

[17] Peter Chelkowski, "Ta^{c}ziyeh: Indigenous Avant-Garde Theatre of Iran," in *Ta^{c}ziyeh: Ritual and Drama in Iran,* p. 2. Copyright © 1979 by New York University.

Experiencing Sacred Space and Time

Personal salvation is a theme common to monotheistic religious traditions. It is a major theme of the Ta^cziyeh's dramaticized ritual. The sufferings of the Prophet's cousin and son-in-law, Ali, and of Ali's two sons, Hasan and Husayn, are paradigmatic experiences for the Shi^cite minority. The many unfolding episodes involving tragedy, heroism, and loyalty to Ali's branch of the Prophet's family provide Shi^cite Muslims a distinct identity within the Islamic Umma. The historic conflict with governmental oppression is dramatized in the ritual experience of sacred space and time.

SACRED SPACE. The Islamic proscription against the artistic representation of living beings, discussed in Chapter 4, is not observed in the Ta^cziyeh performance. Many paintings of this scene have been made. On the stage and throughout the space occupied by Takiyeh theaters, players boldly represent the main personalities of Shi^cite salvation history. A Takiyeh theater constitutes a sacred space, and Shi^cite pilgrimage to the Takiyeh is a liminal experience.

The design of the Takiyeh indicates the sacral character of the many dramas performed by audience and actors alike. Chelkowski's description is illuminating.

> The design of the *takiyeh* preserved and enhanced the dramatic interplay between actors and spectators which was characteristic of the traditional Muharram rites. The main action took place on a stark, curtainless raised platform in the center of the building. Surrounding it was a narrow circular band of space used by the performers for sub-plots and to indicate journeys, passage of time, and change of scene. At the periphery of this space, extending into the audience-filled pit, small secondary stages were often erected. Scenes of special significance were acted upon them and sometimes players from these auxiliary stages would engage in dialogue or action with those on the central stage.[18]

A Takiyeh may be enclosed by an outer wall, itself a prop used to dramatic effect. Action courses along aisles leading from gateways through the walls to the central stage. Messengers, riders, soldiers, and even directors and managers of the performance busily traverse these passageways. The drama is seldom confined to a single action. The siege of Ali's family is symbolized by the very arrangement of the Takiyeh space, with the audience surrounding the central stage, and actors pushing toward it, often through the crowd.

SACRED TIME. Scholarly studies of the Ta^cziyeh performance indicate an aspect of sacred time. Ta^cziyeh performers are not actors in the usual sense of the word in Western theatrical traditions. The players *represent* scenes and personalities from Shi^cite sacred history that are well known to the audience.

---

[18] Chelkowski, "Ta^cziyeh," p. 5. Copyright © 1979 by New York University.

Costumes and props are more symbolic than actual reproductions of authentic clothing and items from the days of Husayn and the Caliph Yazid. For example, sunglasses may be worn to indicate the player is an enemy. Green worn by a player designates him as a good member of Husayn's party; red identifies the evil members of Yazid's party. A white shroud worn by the player who represents, say, Qasim, signifies that he will be martyred gladly. Even the very form in which the lines are uttered differentiates good from evil players: good characters chant their lines in the pleasing mode of poetry whereas evil characters shout their lines with unpleasant gruffness.[19] Thus the entire performance—and there are literally hundreds of different Ta^c^ziyeh scenarios—is a curious combination of symbolic representations, both traditional and modern. Players do not act their parts; through symbolic and formalized speech, emotions and attire, they represent moments in sacred history. Although there is no element of suspense comparable to that in Western drama, audience involvement in the staged events is vicarious and deeply emotional. The unavoidable result of the Ta^c^ziyeh, Husayn's murder, is well known to everyone present. His martyrdom becomes their salvation. Their collective and individual sufferings in history are resolved in the Ta^c^ziyeh experience even as the historic conflict of Shi^c^ism will be ultimately resolved in the sacred time of Judgment.

[19] William O. Beeman, "Cultural Dimensions of Performance Conventions in Iranian Ta^c^ziyeh," in *Ta^c^ziyeh,* ed. Chelkowski, pp. 24-31.

7 community and society in islam

The Western traveler to the Islamic world is immediately struck by obvious cultural and social differences. In the Middle East, for example, clothing is different, especially the clothing worn by villagers and the urban poor and working classes. Men wear ankle-length beltless robes called *jalabiyas*. It is a practical garb for almost all kinds of work and activity. Many men also wear cloth turbans or brimless caps and hats. Women, too, wear clothing that covers their arms, legs, and hair. For the peasant woman, this often consists of a print dress over which a black outer garment is worn. The veil, still worn by many women, derives from ancient tradition, not from the Koran itself.

Apart from traditional attire, social relations also appear to be differently ordered in Islamic countries. In the Middle East, where Islam has had the most direct effect upon society, several characteristics are readily noticed. Couples, whether married or not, are not usually seen together in public. On the other hand, men are often seen in the company of other men in public—at coffee houses, on the streets, or at places of work. Women, too, keep each other's company while they perform household chores, but the Western visitor is not likely to see women in public as much. Signs of affection between the sexes are seldom noticed, but within groups of men (or women) friendship and affection are more openly displayed. Occasionally these patterns of social relations are punctuated by arguments and loud shouting that seldom go beyond the level of verbal exchange.

Sexual relations between men and women are strictly disapproved outside of marriage. Even within marriage, sex is a very private matter. On the other hand, in households where extended families live under one roof, intimacies between parents must necessarily occur in a crowded social space. In extended families the eldest male is usually the patriarch of the household, although sons are expected to relieve their fathers of the burden of providing for so many people as soon as possible. The wife of the male head of the house usually rules the domestic affairs of the family. Family-run businesses predominate in the marketplace.

Given this kind of social structure, it would be improper to ask a Muslim male, "How's your wife?" It is more appropriate to pay respects by inquiring, "How is your family?" The answer will invariably be *al-ḥamdu li-llāh,* "praise be to God (they are well)." This matter of courtesy is still just as appropriate among the urban middle classes, where the traditional social patterns are changing under the impact of modernization.

On the streets of towns and cities, the Western visitor is quickly engulfed in a fascinating apparent confusion of activity. There is much clamoring and noise, especially in the marketplace, called the *sūq* (Arabic) or *bāzār* (Persian). As one walks through these crowded mazes of booths and shops, the direct relation of craftsman, product, and customer is quite impressive. Jewelry-making and metalworking are done right before your eyes. The noises of hammering and grinding compete with the cries of vendors and merchants in a cacophony of sounds. Less desirable commercial activities, such as the slaughtering of animals and tanning, are usually at some distance from grocers, booksellers, craftsmen, and merchants of sundry items. Food shops usually specialize in particular kinds of consumables, and thus shopping is a complicated art. One shop may specialize in fruits and vegetables. Another may be filled with sacks of grains,

FIGURE 7.1. Iranian woman in traditional attire. (Courtesy of the United Nations.)

rice, and pastas. Individual portions must be weighed under the watchful eyes of both seller and buyer. Price tags are seldom seen; prices are established in the ritual of bargaining—a process that requires seller and buyer to come to mutual agreement about value for each exchange. If the purchase is an involved one, or if a close friend or visitor to the neighborhood is discerned, tea or Turkish coffee will be offered to balance the contest of bargaining with the pleasantries of hospitality.

International trade in the Middle East was known even in the time of the ancient Babylonians and Egyptians. In the time of the Prophet, goods from Byzantium and India passed through Arabia in caravans contracted by the merchants of Mecca. Small businesses in local markets, however, have been run by families that by and large have produced their own goods. This has been the traditional form of commercial activity in Islamic society for centuries. Thus the bazaar is a social experience that lies at the heart of Islamic society. Mosques and madrasas (religious schools) form a part of the social ecology of religion and life within the bazaar. It is a social space enmeshed with the normative requirements of Koran and Sunna.

In the larger cities, supermarkets and department stores are beginning to compete with the more traditional economy of the neighborhood bazaars. The social effects are noticeable but perhaps not yet fully realized. Western clothing is worn by men and women working for corporations, larger businesses, and the government. Many young men and women are leaving traditional family means of support to look for new opportunities in the modernized sectors of cities. The result has been that traditional social and religious values have been challenged

FIGURE 7.2. Traditional marketplace (Suq), Fez, Morocco. (The Bettmann Archive, Inc.)

by the forces of modernization. The Ulema in particular and traditional Muslims in general have sought ways to counter the eroding effects of modernization upon Islamic life.

How is Islamic society structured and organized? What types of social organization are found within the Islamic world? What sorts of problems and aspirations do members of Islamic society attempt to meet through their patterns of behavior? The answers to these questions are as complex as the variety of discrete cultures encompassed within Islam, from North Africa to Southeast Asia. The process of modernization and change must also be factored into the discussion. We now turn to some general observations about the study of Islamic society. This will be followed by descriptions of select social groups and settings within the Islamic world.

RELIGION AND SOCIETY

Definitions of religion often specify beliefs and rituals as essential elements. Religion, however, is also a form of social behavior. Families, schools, occupations, and governments are products of human society; and society itself—along with history, art, beliefs, and rituals—is created by human beings. We have seen that ideally the Shari^{c}a governs the totality of human life. In addition to religious duties, social, economic, and political responsibilities fall within its scope. Beyond the mosque and the sacred precincts of shrines such as the ones at Mecca and Medina, the home, bazaar, and bureau are institutions that assume distinctive forms in Islamic society. Social behavior, then, belongs to the study of Islam. Islamic society is the achievement of Muslims who, throughout history, have responded to the precepts of the Shari^{c}a, under local climatic, geographic, and political conditions, thus producing distinctive forms of behavior.

The Dialectic of Man and Society

The dialectic of man producing society and society producing man is discussed by the sociologist of religion, Peter L. Berger.[1] In agreement with other social scientists and historians of religions, Berger believes that religion is a corporate, social phenomenon. The Friday congregational prayer and commerce are social activities. The mosque and bazaar are social spaces. The study of how individuals actually perform in these settings is different from but related to the study of what the Shari^{c}a stipulates they *ought* to do. Beyond these questions are others relating to stages of life, attitudes toward the opposite sex, and types of social groupings.

Berger's title, *The Sacred Canopy,* indicates his point that reality as seen

---

[1] Peter L. Berger, *The Sacred Canopy: Elements of a Sociological Theory of Religion* (New York: Anchor Books, 1969).

within a religious tradition is itself a social product. Middle Eastern (and other) traditions have viewed the cosmos in three levels of reality corresponding to Heaven, Earth, and the underworld. Supernatural forces are thought to operate within and upon the natural ones. In some traditions there is no clear distinction between the natural and the supernatural. Religious expressions of the interconnections between divine forces, revealed laws, myths, and rituals are the data with which students of religions must reconstruct the reality that was or is experienced within a given tradition. These data are found to be closely associated with patterns of behavior at home, in the marketplace, and in other social and political institutions.

The process of becoming a social being is related to the process of learning the native language of one's culture. It begins in infancy and develops through each stage of life. Our native language is learned from and within the society into which we are born, and through language we interact with society. With additional languages such as gestures, art, music, and rituals we creatively express our individual participation through idioms we learn to share with others.

Like other traditions, Islam presents a world view that is learned from society and that forms a basis for being in society. Shared beliefs and myths make possible common attitudes toward good and evil, individual and collective goals, and other shared concerns. The Hajj, Salat (prayer), and other rituals are shared idioms that mediate between the ideals of belief and the realities of life. Languages and religions alike respond to historical changes—not rapidly, but change there is. Elizabethan English and contemporary American English are modes of expression appropriate to much different historical and social circumstances, despite the obvious fact that they are both dialects of the same language. Islam has adapted to many historical changes. From conquering and incorporating many ethnic and religious groups in the seventh century, to being conquered by Turkish, Persian, and Mongol warlords in the Middle Ages, to experiencing the impact of westernization and modernization in the nineteenth and twentieth centuries, Islam has persisted as a social reality. It has done so within a structure suggested by Koran and Sunna and perpetuated by individuals and social groups that have interpreted and applied this world view to each new situation more, or less, successfully.

Great Tradition and Little Tradition

The Western study of Islam began in a serious way in the mid-nineteenth century. Much of that study has concentrated on the texts of Islamic history and religions, and very little has been devoted to the study of the lives of Muslim peoples. The strong literary tradition in Islam since the eighth century drew European and American scholarly interest to the important initial task of locating and learning to read, translate, and interpret the texts and documents of religion and history. This type of scholarly activity is not yet complete. More and more manuscripts—some quite old—in Arabic and other Islamic languages are being discovered in ancient mosques and libraries. In addition to the textual studies of historians and humanists, anthropologists and sociologists are beginning to show increased interest in the social organization of Islamic tribes, villages, and cities. Political scientists and economists are also interested in Islamic social phenomena. Often the published writings of these social scientists read much differently than the older historical studies. For one thing, social scientists pay less attention to official statements about religion and more attention to its actual practice. The official teachings of the more distinguished personalities and writers of the Ulema and the intelligentsia are often found to differ from the expression of religion at the popular level. For example, historians have usually explained Islamic religion by consulting theological manuals. Social scientists often ignore these and describe instead their observations of rituals and practices in the everyday life of a Muslim village.

Robert Redfield, an anthropologist, has offered a solution to this diversity of scholarship (which admittedly can be very confusing to the newcomer to Islamic studies). Redfield makes a distinction between great and little traditions. He describes the humanist-historian as one whose "studies are *textual:* he studies not only written texts but art and architecture as part of his textual corpus. Ours [social scientists'] are *contextual:* we relate some element of the great tradition—sacred book, story-element, ceremony or supernatural being—to the life of the ordinary people, in the *context* of daily life as in the village we see it happen."[2] The *great tradition* is reflected in the more readily accessible literary products of theologians, judges, and lawyers of the Islamic academies of learning. The *little tradition* exists in the tribes, villages, and groups within cities where, in the process of social organization, people must attempt to apply Koran and Sunna to everyday life, in varying contexts and under diverse circumstances.

Later in this chapter we will take a closer look at different social contexts in Islam—the medieval Islamic city, a village in Egypt, the urban bazaar in Iran, and a Sufi cloister in North Africa. Each of these contexts stands in strong, but quite different, relation to the great tradition of normative Islamic teaching.

ELEMENTS OF SOCIAL STRUCTURE IN ISLAM

Umma and Caliphate

The model for all subsequent societies in Islam was the one that formed around the figure of the Prophet in Medina after the Hijra from Mecca in 622. In the Koran, "Umma" appears frequently in reference to ethnic and religious groups (or nations) that are part of the divine plan of salvation. The people of Abraham, Lot, Noah, Moses, and Jesus were Ummas. An Umma is usually identified as a

---

[2] Robert Redfield, "The Social Organization of Tradition," *The Far Eastern Quarterly* 15 (1955), 17 (Italics added).

nation to which God has sent a messenger or prophet. The Koran states that past Ummas rejected their messengers, for which they suffered divine acts of retribution. Muhammad's first appearance as a Messenger/Warner in Mecca also met with rejection by all but a very few close followers. The sacred history of past Ummas was preached as a warning. In Medina, however, an Umma was formed which was more receptive to the Prophet. The Medinan Umma included Jews and other non-Muslims and, although not all members of the Islamic Umma were loyal to the Prophet, the concept of inclusiveness within the community of Islam was to have far-reaching consequences for the subsequent development of Islamic society.

During the reign of the rightly guided caliphs from 632 to 661, the Arabian conquests of Middle Eastern lands resulted in a religious empire that sought to implement the notion of the Koranic Umma on a much grander scale than the Medinan community. The Abode of Islam was now much more than Arabia, Arabs, and even Islam. It was a multiethnic empire comprising several religious traditions. For six centuries the empire was ruled by caliphs.

The term "caliph" (*khalīfa,* successor, viceregent) designates the rulers who assumed Muhammad's function as head of the Umma, but not his function as Messenger of Allah. Also called "Commanders of the Faithful," the caliphs became, as a result of the Conquests, imperial rulers over vast territories and diverse peoples. This political order lasted until the thirteenth century, when Mongol warlords destroyed the caliphate and themselves assumed political rule over much of the Islamic world. Many of the Mongol conquerors converted to Islam. The political symbol of unity, however, at least in theory if not always in fact, was the caliphate. By the sixteenth century the Islamic world had become divided into smaller empires, the most powerful of which were in Turkey, Persia, India, and Egypt. Ruled by sultans and shahs, these regional empires attained great heights in cultural achievement. In modern times the regional empires have broken up into national states, in some cases after periods of colonial rule by European powers.

For more than thirteen centuries of history, the basic concept of Islamic society has been the Prophet's Umma. In the Middle Ages the Umma contained numerous ethnic and religious groups—social groups with individual social characteristics. In matters of religion and civil affairs each group or minority was allowed to maintain its own traditionally conceived order. The Islamic city, as we have seen, preserved this arrangement by forming separate quarters for each religious group and ethnic minority. Rabbis, bishops, and other leaders replaced some of the roles of the Ulema within non-Muslim groups. In modern times and without the caliphate, the Islamic Umma may find itself to be the predominant religious group, as it is in Egypt, or a minority group among many others, as it is in India. In all settings throughout history the Umma has attempted to heed the Koranic warning of what had happened to past Ummas that rejected God and His Messengers. The Koran and Sunna of the Prophet are the central symbols and sources of guidance for the Islamic Umma. Local historical and political circumstances have determined the specific forms the Umma has taken as expressions of human society.

Ulema

By now the term "Ulema" is quite familiar in our discussion of Islam. A few observations about this class of religious leaders within Islamic society should be reiterated at this point. First, the term is a plural of the Arabic, *^{c}ālim,* which means "one who is knowledgeable (that is, about the Shari^{c}a)." Thus the Ulema are the custodians of traditional learning about the Koran, the Sunna of the Prophet, and the legal theory and application of sacred law to all aspects of life. The Ulema serve in the functional occupations of trained Koran reciters, teachers in madrasas and schools, Imams (prayer leaders) and Khatibs (preachers) of local mosques, and professors of sacred law and theology on university faculties.

Second, in Sunni Islam, the Ulema is but loosely organized in an institutional sense. They are implicitly recognized to be purveyors of guidance to each community by virtue of their training and learning. Their authority is effective to the extent that they are able to reach a consensus among themselves and to articulate relevantly the idiom of consensus of past tradition to the exigencies of present circumstances. In Shi^{c}ite Islam, the Ulema carry on the special interpretation of the Shari^{c}a derived from Ali, the fourth caliph and cousin of the Prophet, and from the eleven Imams who succeeded Ali as spiritual leaders of the Shi^{c}ite community. Today, the highest ranking members of the Twelver Shi^{c}ite Ulema known as *ayatollahs* lead the Shi^{c}ite community in the temporary absence of the twelfth Imam, who went into occultation in the ninth century. The Shi^{c}ite Ulema serve the same basic functional occupations as in Sunni Islam, but with a greater degree of hierarchical authority. The requirement of consensus is implicitly there, but the theoretical basis of their interpretations of Koran and Sunna is also channeled through the received teaching of the twelve Imams about Koran and Sunna.

Third, the Ulema perform no sacral functions. This is the reason behind the often stated observation that in Islam there is no priesthood and thus no institution comparable to the church. The Ulema perform duties as a body of learned ones of Islam; no ordination, sacral office, or priestly function is involved. Virtually any Muslim can perform most of the duties of the Ulema, such as leading the Friday congregational prayer.

Popular resentment against the leadership of the Ulema in various historical periods has differed from lay anti-clericalism in the history of Christianity. The main function of the Ulema has been to remain in touch with the pulse of Islamic society in order to guide it in its real concerns, and to maintain lines of communication and understanding between central political authorities and the people. In periods when the Ulema have become excessively preoccupied with scholastic dogmatism, popular religious sentiment has openly defied their leadership. Often in those periods the popular alternative to the leadership of the Ulema has been the spiritual appeal of Sufi masters, centered in convents and the shrines of famous saints.

Waqf

Without a church or corporate religious entity to effect religiously inspired humanitarianism, how has the religious establishment in Islam been able to provide tangible benefits to Islamic society? The answer lies in legal provisions in the Shari^ca for the establishment of pious foundations. The term for such foundations is *waqf.*

Tradition teaches that when the Prophet once sought to purchase land on which to build a mosque, he was refused; instead the tribal leaders who owned the land gave it to him "for the sake of God." Precedent for religious endowments has been traced to such early incidents recorded in the Sunna of the Prophet and his Companions. Another form of Waqf is the income from a piece of land or property that is specifically assigned by its owner to religious (mosques, madrasas) or charitable (hospitals, orphanages) institutions. During the course of Islamic history, more and more land has been given or committed to Waqf endowments. The growth of endowment lands has reduced available taxable lands.

Waqf endowments, then, have provided the Ulema with the means to run religious and charitable institutions within Islamic society. With the rise of national states within the Islamic world, however, government ministries of education, welfare, health, and culture have also assumed the state's interests and responsibilities in these areas. In addition, modern states have instituted civil and criminal courts and legal systems that have functioned independently of the Shari^ca courts of the Ulema. The effect of parallel sacred and secular systems within Islamic society is more pronounced in cities, especially political capitals, than in villages and nomadic regions. The general observation that Islam does not separate the domains of church and state must be qualified when one is speaking about these trends of Islamic society in modern times.

An interesting aspect of this growth of parallel functions by the Ulema and the national governments has been the resurgent vital appeal of religion and religious leadership. Popular movements in both predominantly Sunni and predominantly Shi^cite countries have sought to bring the authority of the Shari^ca more directly into the structure of modern society and into national constitutions and governmental processes. This has led to various levels of contact and conflict between Islamic and non-Islamic cultures, chiefly through international economic and political involvements in Islamic national states. For this reason it has become all the more important to appreciate the cultural heritage to which more and more Muslims are turning to articulate their identity within the world of nations. Beneath the more salient manifestations of confrontation and political unrest is a process not unlike the reassertion of cultural pride expressed by native American Indians, blacks, and other subcultures within Western society.

CONTEXTS OF ISLAMIC SOCIETY

To illustrate the point that religion can be studied as a form of social behavior, the following pages focus on different specific social contexts in the Islamic world. In each case specific examples drawn from the textual studies of Islamists and the contextual field work of social scientists will serve as fixed points from which to make some general remarks.

The Islamic City

In our discussion in Chapter 2 of the building of the city of Baghdad, several general characteristics of Islamic towns and cities were given briefly. Baghdad is usually considered a good example of a truly Islamic city because it was deliberately planned and developed with Islamic principles in mind. Many other cities that were conquered or built by the Muslims sooner or later exhibited similar characteristics. In an important essay entitled "Structure of the Muslim Town," Gustav E. von Grunebaum made the following observation: "To the Muslim, a town was a settlement in which his religious duties and his social ideals could be completely fulfilled."[3] The validity of this remark is not difficult to see. Although such religious duties of Islam as the canonical prayer can be fulfilled anywhere, even in the desert, the important Friday congregational prayer requires a mosque, which is to say, a city. Moreover, throughout the ages the city has attracted rural and pastoral nomadic elements in search of spiritual, intellectual, and economic opportunities. By naturally forming in quarters and neighborhoods of ethnic and sectarian groups, the cities preserved the social ideals of Middle Eastern peoples.

THE CATHEDRAL MOSQUE. Like Baghdad, most Islamic cities and towns had an identifiable orientation with certain fixed points. At the center stood the *Jāmiᶜ*, the cathedral mosque. If the city was the seat of the caliph, a provincial governor, or other high appointed official, state buildings were in the near vicinity of the cathedral mosque. Also at the center was a *hamām,* "public fountain," which provided a place of social gathering as well as a place for worshippers to perform ritual ablutions before their prayers. Thus the central crossroads of the two main thoroughfares of the city was a hub which combined social, religious, and political activities.

The cathedral mosque served several other important functions. Politically

[3] Gustav E. von Grunebaum, *Islam: Essays in the Nature and Growth of a Cultural Tradition* (Totowa, N.J.: Barnes & Noble Books, 1961), p. 142.

FIGURE 7.3. Cathedral mosque courtyard, Baghdad. (Courtesy of the United Nations.)

it was the main public platform for governmental communications to the people. From the pulpit (*minbar*) of the mosque the caliph's name was mentioned each Friday during the sermon of the congregational prayer. Often the ruling official of the city would deliver the sermon at these weekly gatherings of the general population, and the message could be just as appropriately political as religious in nature.

The cathedral mosque also served as an intellectual center for the town and neighboring villages. Before the rise of separate schools and universities in the eleventh century, teachers of the religious sciences, who were usually members of the Ulema, attracted circles of students in the courtyards and hallways of the mosque. Their pupils might come from the surrounding city or nearby villages. If the teacher was particularly famous, students from distant lands would find their way to hear his lectures. Such lectures were carefully dictated and copied. If the circle of students was particularly large, more advanced students or "assistants" would stand midway and relay each phrase to the back of the audience. A professor's signature in a student's notebook was the traditional form of credential that marked a scholar's preparation to gather his own students.

The major schools of Shari^{c}a law in Sunni and Shi^{c}ite Islam sat in the cathedral mosque to deliberate on points of interpretation within their schools. Scholars and judges delivered opinions and judgments on specific cases brought before them. For this reason, other functionaries were required in the service of the mosque, such as notaries and witnesses. The chief judge within each principality, who was called a *Qāḍī,* was a political appointee of the governor of the province. The professors of law who deliberated on more theoretical issues and the lawyers who dealt with specific cases were members of the Ulema. They were independent of the political seat of power, although in Sunni Islam the Ulema has tended to support the government in most matters. This has been less true in Shi^{c}ite Islam.

THE MARKETPLACE. The Koran is replete with allusions to commercial concepts. Mecca and Medina had thriving markets in the time of the Prophet. Islam teaches that a man should provide for his family, and it encourages worldly success and prosperity while cautioning just and fair practices in commerce. Thus a second fixed point of the Muslim city was the *sūq* or *bāzār.* Like the Qadis in legal matters, the Suq had its officially appointed functionary, known as the *muḥtasib.* The Muhtasib was in charge of maintaining order and fair practice in the market. It was his business to resolve matters of violations, quarrels, and thievery.

We have already established some sense of the physical arrangement of the Suq within the city. Closest to the cathedral mosque in the center of town were the booths selling materials necessary to the religious, educational, and professional activities of the mosque. Books, candles, paper, ink, and the like could be

FIGURE 7.4. Village market in India. (Courtesy of the United Nations.)

purchased from the nearest merchants. Next came the textile district, where booths were gathered under a large roof to protect the goods from bad weather. Beyond the textile quarter were craftsmen who fashioned pots, wooden objects, and jewelry right in their shops. Then came the sellers of foodstuffs. At the far end of the Suq were located the least desirable enterprises: potters, tanners, and dyers.

THE QUARTER. The makeup of the residential sections within each city and town has exhibited strong separatist tendencies. Tribal, ethnic, and sectarian groups preserve cultural affinities brought to the city from village and nomadic environments. During the Middle Ages the Arabs who moved to towns and cities settled in districts composed of tribal groups. Dialects and familiar lines of clan leadership no doubt provided part of the rationale for maintaining separate quarters. Jews, Christians, and other non-Muslim groups also held to their separate quarters, as did Shi^{c}ites and other specific religious minorities within Islam.

In modern times this pattern has begun to dissolve, but very slowly. Surrounding villages rather than tribes feed into counterpart quarters or neighborhoods in nearby cities. Young men, with or without their families, move to the city bringing a trade or skill (or looking for a new one) from the local village. Under such circumstances immigrants to towns and cities naturally gravitate to the districts where relatives from their home town have settled. Finding jobs and places to live is thereby simplified. Local village politics and gossip form natural topics of social intercourse for neighborhood gatherings. A fair amount of commuting between village and urban neighborhoods continues, and portions of wages earned in the city are sent back home, where economic opportunities are less promising.

ULEMA, THE UNIFYING FACTOR. The foregoing description of Muslim cities as collections of separate social entities raises interesting questions. In what sense, if any, was the Muslim city a unified social phenomenon? Was it a geographical implosion of scattered social groups that, once gathered under a common urban administration, failed to achieve anything greater than the sum of its parts? Had the Prophet's replacement of tribal loyalties with a higher loyalty to the religion of Islam failed after all?

An Islamic historian who has studied the Muslim city in great depth, Ira M. Lapidus, has argued that Islam *was* able to transcend persisting social and political boundaries within the cities—at least those boundaries that traditionally existed between Muslim groups. The Ulema formed the religious intellectual elite. Local concerns and views within quarters were transcended by the more universal ideals of Islam. Islam provided a common idiom of expression outside indigenous quarters. The Ulema could write and speak in the highly valued classical Arabic (as opposed to village or tribal dialects). The Koran and Sunna of the Prophet were sources of guidance in everyday matters that were shared by

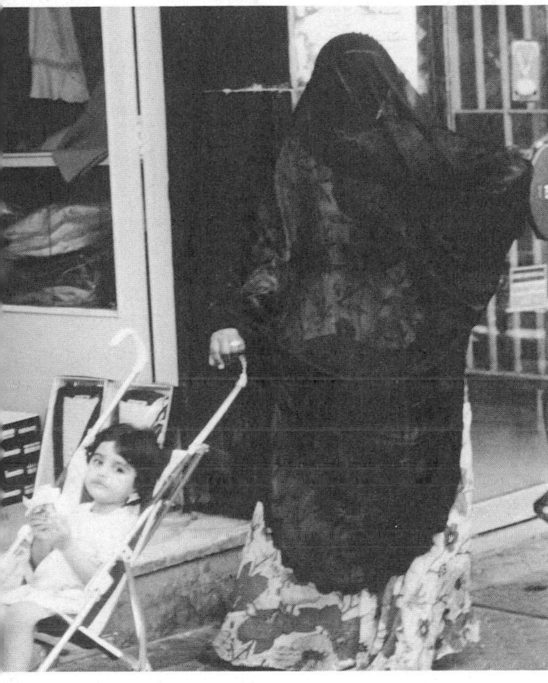

FIGURE 7.5. The Islamic city combines traditional and modern scenes. (Photo by B. Cirone. Courtesy of the United Nations.)

all Muslims. The Ulema articulated a world view that cut across persisting social divisions.[4]

An Egyptian Village

Today, as in the past, the majority of Muslims dwell in village settlements, living mainly by agriculture. Less accessible to the Western media than the city, and less romantic for novels and movies than the world of the Bedouin, the village has remained nearly eclipsed from outside view. Even Islamists have preferred to focus upon the more visible intellectual and cultural achievements of Islamic urban civilization. Lacking cathedral mosques and other aspects of high culture, villages do not normally produce literary texts and other cultural products in high demand in distant scholars' studies. Village life has been available for analysis only to those willing to go to the villages themselves. It is thus to the field work of anthropologists and sociologists that we now must turn.

The late President Gamal Abd al-Nasser once startled the press, both in Egypt and abroad, by remarking that the media gave "too much space to sensational trivialities." Nasser "pointed to a village near Alexandria, Kafr el Bat-

[4] See Ira M. Lapidus, "Muslim Cities and Islamic Societies," in *Middle Eastern Cities,* ed. Ira M. Lapidus (Berkeley: University of California Press, 1969), pp. 47–79.

tikh, as the place where the 'true' Egypt might be found."[5] Nasser knew what the West and even many among the urban sophisticated of Cairo did not, namely, that cities in the Middle East draw their population largely from the countryside. Traditional cultural patterns are transformed under the constant urban trend toward modernization. It is in the village, then, that we must seek to discover ways of life that have survived for centuries. The movable Bedouin camp has resisted the winds of change more successfully than the village, but the village has been more hospitable to such Islamic institutions as the mosque and the leadership of the Ulema than Bedouin life could or would sustain.[6]

KAFR EL-ELOW. Located eighteen miles south of Cairo and five miles southwest of Helwan, Kafr el-Elow covers a land area of about four square kilometers along the east side of the Nile River. In 1960 its population was 6,608.[7] The village is actually comprised of four distinct settlements which, for cultural and administrative reasons, are considered a single entity. A single mosque provides the religious focal point of all four settlements, and all four are governed by a single *omda* or mayor. The subdivision of the village into settlements reflects a common feature of peasant populations in the Arab world. Villages, like cities, have been formed by Bedouins and other migrants in search of new opportunities. Family, tribal, and former geographic roots are maintained in the social structure of village life.

Historical knowledge and cultural expression are kept alive chiefly through oral tradition and popular folk religion in Islamic (and in all) peasant societies. The traditional role of the Ulema as the educators and spiritual leaders of Islamic society ties local societies into the universals of Islamic culture. Tradition has it that six families founded Kafr el-Elow in the mid-eighteenth century. Noble ancestry is traced to these families and to the settlements from which they originated. The main occupation for two hundred years has been agriculture. The *fallāḥīn* (plural of *fallāḥ,* the Arabic term for peasant) constitute the vast majority of the population of Egypt and of many Islamic countries. The image of the ageless character of traditional peasant ways of life in Kafr el-Elow is heightened by the ancient pyramids of Giza, which dominate the distant landscape.

Like other villages in the Islamic world, Kafr el-Elow has not been unresponsive to the changes going on in the modern world. Village workers

---

[5] Morroe Berger, *The Arab World Today* (Garden City, N.Y.: Anchor Books, 1962), p. 75, referring to *New York Times*, June 4, 1961, p. 4.

[6] For a discussion of the differences among the pastoral nomadic communities, villages, and cities in the Arab world, see M. Berger, *Arab World,* pp. 42–97. On Iran these same three types of societies are discussed by Brian Spooner, "Religion and Society Today: An Anthropological Perspective," in *Iran Faces the Seventies,* ed. Ehsan Yar-Shater (New York: Praeger Publishers, Inc., 1971), pp. 166–88.

[7] Hani Fakhouri, *Kafr el-Elow: An Egyptian Village in Transition* (New York: Holt, Rinehart and Winston, 1972), p. 13. Fakhouri's useful descriptive study of the village has been a source of the following remarks on Muslim villages.

commute to nearby Cairo and Helwan, and, in turn, schoolteachers, health officials, and other professionals bring something of the modern world into Kafr el-Elow. Radio broadcasts from Cairo are received in the village, and the growing literacy rate, which is due to modern mandatory curricula, makes newspapers another source of knowledge. Thus regional Arab-world politics and international events are now subjects of local conversations. A century ago peasant world views were limited to their own immediate concerns. Studies have shown that the gap between the levels of political sophistication in cities such as Cairo and villages such as Kafr el-Elow is not so great as one might suspect.[8]

Villages do not have clearly defined social classes. The most obvious distinction has been between those who own the land and those who work the land. Land reform in Egypt and elsewhere has altered somewhat the abuses of absentee landlordism and the terrible gap between the rich and the poor, offering greater stability among tenant farming, ownership of small parcels of land, and other kinds of relationships between Fallah and the land. But life remains extremely simple in the village. Social distinctions are made on the basis of degrees of piety and levels of education as much as wealth. Most villages are headed by a mayor (Omda) who is advised by a council of elders. These leaders usually serve without pay, although they receive certain privileges and enjoy a certain prestige within their communities. A small police force is maintained, but crime is not a major problem in village societies.[9] Services in education, health, and other areas of public works connected with the national government bring trained personnel from the cities into the villages. Jurisdiction in these matters belongs to the national, not the local government.

As modernization increases in the Islamic world, traditional values are maintained in villages more than cities. For example, hospitality is still regarded a solemn duty, and the ability to honor guests lavishly is a mark of one's status within the community. A village mayor is often chosen from among those who have the means to entertain political and other kinds of guests. Respect for age and the elderly is another noticeable social value. Social and moral qualities are extolled and inculcated through Koranic verses and folk proverbs that are often quoted in everyday discourse.

Houses in Kafr el-Elow are made of unbaked mud bricks. This has been true of peasant homes in Egypt since the time of the Pharaohs, and only recently have a few buildings of modern construction begun to appear outside the cities. In the traditional house a single door leads into the square or rectangular edifice and out into a small courtyard. The courtyard is the scene of many household activities of a practical nature. There cooking is done during the warmer months. Washing may be done there, or in nearby canals that flow through the village. An outdoor privy usually stands enclosed in one corner of the yard.

Most villagers are too poor to own much furniture and household or-

---

[8] M. Berger, *Arab World,* pp. 68–69.

[9] M. Berger, pp. 61–62.

naments. Various rooms in the enclosed structure around the courtyard are the dwelling quarters of the many members of the extended family that share the house. Next to the main entrance most houses have guest rooms where male visitors are ushered and entertained by heads of the house. On such occasions, the women disappear from sight until the guests are seated and the door is closed.[10]

Food and diet vary considerably throughout the Islamic world, but Kafr el-Elow is typical of Egypt. The main item in every villager's diet is bread, usually called *khubs* or *ᶜaysh.* It is made of wheat or corn flour and baked in small, flat loaves. Twice each week women prepare the dough in their own homes; then groups of several women gather in the home of one woman who has agreed to play hostess that day. While the bread is baking, children play together and the women socialize, gossip, and joke with one another. It is an important and regular social ritual of village life.

Villagers' diets may include some meat, usually beef or lamb, but in small quantities. As noted in Chapter 1, the eating of pork is forbidden by the Koran. A large portion of the diet is vegetables and fruits, especially melons and cucumbers. The main spices are garlic and peppers. A plentiful source of protein is the fava bean, known as *fūl* in Egypt. *Ta'miya* is a dish made with fava beans ground together with parsley and spices then deep-fried in small patties. It is found all over Egypt and much of the Middle East. The visitor to Cairo will find Tamiya vendors along the streets, and vendors of many other favorite dishes as well. A sandwich made of Tamiya placed in flatbread with chopped vegetables is known as *fallafel;* now an international delicatessen item, peasants in Egypt have been eating it for centuries. A type of meatless chili called *fūl mudāmas* is prepared by boiling and mashing the fava beans and simmering them in spices. Coffee is not often served in villages because it is too expensive. Guests and friends usually socialize over a dark, thickly brewed tea that is heavily sweetened with sugar.[11]

RITES OF PASSAGE. Villagers in Kafr el-Elow, and around the world of Islam, are governed in ritual and worship by the Five Pillars and Shariᶜa. In the last chapter the distinctively Islamic occasions of worship were discussed at length. Special sets of occasions in the lives of Muslims which have both social and religious significance are life crises identified by anthropologists as *rites of passage.* These ritualized occasions are cross-cultural phenomena, that is, similar in most cultures; each culture understands and experiences these transitional moments, however, according to its own myths, rituals, and laws. For Muslims, major religious events in life include birth, circumcision (males), memorization of the Koran, pilgrimage, marriage, and death. In addition to their obvious

---

[10] Fakhouri, *Kafr el-Elow,* pp. 17–18.

[11] Fakhouri discusses food, clothing, education, economy, and several other aspects of the culture of Kafr el-Elow.

religious overtones, these events are also important social rites for the family, the larger clan of relatives, and the entire village (or urban neighborhood). The social group as a whole helps individuals and their families to celebrate these important passages from one stage of life to the next. Thus in the study of rites of passage, Koran and Sunna may blend with folk and popular religion. The following descriptions are of villages in Egypt. Many of the specific details vary from one region or ethnic group to the next, but overall the pattern is much the same in traditional Islamic social groups.

Birth. The birth of a child is a very happy occasion for the entire village. Throughout pregnancy, the mother is carefully protected by her family from any activity that might endanger a healthy delivery. At the end of the first week after birth, a ceremony called *usbū*ᶜ (week) is held for the naming of the child, particularly for the first son. Generally, sons are preferred to daughters. Sons will one day relieve their fathers from the burden of family support. Yet daughters are a great help to their mothers around the house. Traditional families harbor fears that their daughters might bring them shame through sexual indiscretions. However, fathers love their daughters too, and it is believed that girls will be more compassionate when their parents are older.[12]

Circumcision. Male Muslim children are circumcised between the ages of three and seven. In the province of Aswan, Egypt, the event calls for a village celebration. At the invitation of the parents, the men and women of the village gather on the eve of the event to dine and celebrate with the family. The boy to be circumcised, with his playmates, issues another invitation the following day by running through the village. At the family home the people of the village gather once again. This day may also be celebrated with a meal, followed by prayers, Koran recitations, and readings from the story of the Prophet's birthday (Mawlid al-Nabī). The actual circumcision is performed by the village barber. When weather permits, the men gather outside, where the operation is to take place, and the women inside. In one region it is the custom for the young boy to wear a girl's headcloth around his neck. First his head is shaved a little at a time as each gift brought to the father from relatives and well-wishers is announced. Then the girl's headcloth is removed and a special white shirt is put on, over the top of which a green covering garment is worn. During the operation (for which Egyptian barbers nowadays are supplied surgical instruments and training by the Ministry of Health) the boy is encouraged to be brave and to ignore the pain. Following the operation, the entire gathering of men, women, and children heads toward the village mosque for prayers. Then sweets are distributed. A week or so later the newly circumcised boy again goes through the village with his friends asking for gifts of food. These are brought home to his

---

[12] Hamed Ammar, *Growing Up in an Egyptian Village* (New York: Octagon Books, 1966), pp. 91–95.

mother, who prepares a sumptuous meal for his friends. The entire ceremony marks the bringing of a child out into village society. Circumcision brings honor and gifts to the father and the entire family. Also it symbolically, if not physically, prepares the boy for marriage.[13]

Marriage. In traditional Arabic society, marriage is usually within the clan, often between paternal first cousins. It is assumed that marriages will take place inside this pattern; if a marriage is outside this pattern, special arrangements and mediations are required. Once a match has been arranged, an engagement ceremony is held at the home of the prospective bride. The groom's family sends gifts prior to arrival at the home of the bride's parents for the celebration. At the home of the bride, after an exchange of greetings (and more recently, of rings) the groom or his father advances a portion of the marriage payment to the bride's father. The rest of the marriage payment is held until such time as the marriage may end in the death of the husband, or in divorce. The payment serves both to discourage easy divorce and to assist the bride's father if he should have to resume her care. The amount of the marriage payment is negotiated on the basis of the social status of the families. Such payments are warranted in the Shari^c^a.

Next a day is set for the signing of the marriage contract. On the appointed day the couple and their families again gather at the home of the bride. The opening chapter (Fatiha) of the Koran is recited by all assembled. The recitation of the Fatiha is the essence of the nuptial ceremony. Now the couple is legally married, although it is customary for the couple to wait until after yet another ceremony to consummate the marriage. A few days before the final ceremony, in much the same fashion as with the circumcision rite, the groom and his friends (usually mostly cousins) go through the village inviting guests. On the eve of the wedding, the bride and groom entertain friends at their respective homes.

As in the rituals of circumcision and pilgrimage, the nuptial rite of passage calls for ceremonial grooming. On the day of the wedding in the home of a friend or cousin of the groom, the village barber cuts the groom's hair and bathes him. At her own home, the bride is also bathed and beautified by female family members and friends. Once prepared, the groom leads a procession of his friends through the village to his parents' home, where guests are gathering along with musicians and perhaps a Koran reciter.

At the groom's home often a tent is set up to accommodate the many guests. Again gifts are brought, and the barber receives and records the names of donors. Later the bride and her family arrive, and the bride is seated in a con-

---

[13] Ammar, *Egyptian Village,* pp. 116–24. See Fakhouri, *Kafr el-Elow,* pp. 86–87. Both anthropologists discuss a similar ceremony and operation for young girls, the clitoridechtomy, although this has been outlawed in modern times and is slowly disappearing. See Fakhouri, pp. 86–87.

spicuous place for all to see. Sweets, soft drinks, and food are served. Water pipes may be smoked by the men. The celebration lasts into the evening, at which time the groom finally retires to his wife's room, which she now takes in the house of the groom's father.

The ritual of marriage, like other rites of passage, establishes bonds and relationships between and within village families. Thus it provides occasions for social cohesion throughout the village.[14]

Death. The death of a Muslim is also an occasion to express family and clan solidarity. The focus seems to be upon the women of the family, who gather at the home of the deceased and join in mournful wailing of his or her name. The corpse is then placed on a bench, where it is ritually cleansed, perfumed, and blessed with sacred water (if available) from the Zamzam well in Mecca. The body is then wrapped in a white shroud and covered with a green cloth that is embroidered with verses from the Koran. During these procedures a Koran reciter chants appropriate passages. Islamic tradition urges burial as soon as possible. The prepared corpse is brought to the village cemetery and placed in a grave, so positioned on its side as to face the Qibla, the direction of Mecca.

Following burial, the family of the decedent observes a week of mourning. At this time, in a clan guest home or perhaps in a tent near the decedent's home, condolences are brought to the survivers by relatives and friends. During these days of bereavement the male head of the house and the village religious leader receive guests and exchange with them the appropriate religious greetings. A Koran reciter chants verses from the sacred scriptures, and with the advent of loudspeakers these may be heard throughout the village. In a few days the female relatives visit the fresh grave once again, after which they distribute cookies and sweets to others who have followed them there.[15]

At the funeral ceremonial and other rites of passage, it is not uncommon for villagers who can afford it to sacrifice an animal, usually a lamb. Ammar reports that in the district of Aswan in Egypt it is common for the "flowing of blood" ritual to take place at such ceremonies as the naming of the child, the honoring of a youth who has memorized the Koran, and the honoring of a Hajji's return from the pilgrimage.[16] The sacred history of Abraham's duty to sacrifice his son Isma^{c}il (in which at the last minute a heavenly sent ram was sacrificed instead), gives meaning derived from sacred history to several important stages of a Muslim's life. It seems to be appropriate to celebrate the blood sacrifice on those occasions when one has acquired something new. It is a thanksgiving offering that is deeply rooted in the sacred history that Islam shares with other Middle Eastern religious traditions.

---

[14] Fakhouri, pp. 63–70; Ammar, pp. 193–201; see M. Berger, *Arab World,* pp. 106–9.

[15] Fakhouri, pp. 87–90.

[16] Ammar, pp. 91–92.

The Iranian Bazaar

In Sunni Islam, the village exemplified Redfield's notion of the little tradition. The village stands at some geographical and intellectual distance from the great tradition of law and theology that is dominated by the leaders of the Ulema in the cathedral mosques and universities of the cities. In Shi^{c}ite Islam, the urban bazaar is the chief social context within which the Ulema wield their most effective influence. The bazaar is more than the mercantile district of each town and city. It is a socio-religious community with its own internal structure. The normative guidance of Koran, Sunna, and the teachings of the Imams prevail over national and local political directives. Even in modern times the bazaar communities of Iran have remained the chief Shi^{c}ite expressions of Islam as a total way of life. At the same time the national trend toward modernization in Iran has made the bazaar an interesting case study of the dynamic conflict between the norms of traditional religion and the pressures for social change.

THE ROLE OF THE ULEMA. The Shi^{c}ite Ulema are in many ways similar to the Ulema in Sunni Islam. In both branches of Islam the Ulema derive their authority from popular acclamation of their competent knowledge of Koran, Sunna, and the application of the Shari^{c}a to all aspects of life. The Shi^{c}ite Ulema, in addition, represent the teachings of the twelve Imams. Like the Sunni Ulema, Shi^{c}ite religious leaders serve as teachers, Shari^{c}a lawyers, and mosque functionaries. But whereas the Sunni Ulema have traditionally supported the government (whether caliph or modern secular state), Shi^{c}ite religious leaders have often led the Shi^{c}ite community in opposition to governments felt to be oppressive toward Shi^{c}ite Islam. The Shi^{c}ite Ulema in Iran are organized in a more definite hierarchy. Representing the twelfth (hidden) Imam are several *Grand Ayatollahs,* whose honorific title means "sign of God." Beneath them are other ayatollahs. Another class of distinguished religious leaders bears the title *Hojjat al-Islam,* which means "argument" or "proof of Islam." Throughout the many towns, villages, and urban neighborhoods in which there are Shi^{c}ite communities, local religious leaders are called *mullas.* They have usually received their training from one of the renowned ayatollahs or a famous teacher, but their occupation as a teacher or mosque functionary in a local neighborhood places them in constant contact with the everyday lives and needs of the people.

THE MERCHANT. Gustav Thaiss has studied the bazaar communities in Tehran, Iran. In his words,

> A Persian bazaar, from one point of view, can be considered just a marketplace where goods of all types and sizes can be bought and sold. In reality, however, it is much more than this. It is a total social phenomenon, a social and cultural world nearly complete in itself. The bazaar is a multi-faceted entity comprising religious, commercial, political, and broadly social elements. Such diversity

governs its complexity and importance, since it is able to adapt to various situations by emphasizing one or several of its many facets at any particular time. Thus, it is far from being just a marketplace.[17]

The chief occupation of the *bazaari* (one who lives within the bazaar community) is that of merchant. Since the time of the Prophet, marketplaces have been important social spaces within the Islamic world. While the bazaar community has directed much criticism and reform toward governments, the military, and other sectors of Islamic society, it has been hospitable to the normative religious values and teachings of Koran and Sunna. Mosques and schools form a more natural part of the ecology of the bazaar than they do in modernized parts of the city. Commercial exchange requires a degree of literacy, and thus the religious and the practical curricula of commerce have been taught to Bazaari children by the Ulema. Also, the traditional attire of Persian Muslims, including the veil for women, is more likely to be seen in the bazaar than elsewhere in the city.

Kinship ties have remained strong in bazaar communities even in modern times. Traditional marriages between paternal first cousins are still assumed, although, as in Sunni villages, there are provisions for other arrangements through the negotiations of the families involved. The practice of Islam is facilitated by the strong influence the Ulema have within the bazaar. If there is anything like the tension between great tradition and little tradition described above, it would be in the Bazaaris' popular celebrations of the Tenth of Muharram ceremonies commemorating the martyrdom of Husayn. The great tradition, represented by the educated Ulema, has frowned upon the excessive emotionalism the Bazaaris often exhibit in the Ta^{c}ziyeh dramas. At times, however, the Ulema have also capitalized upon this annual display of intense unity within the little tradition in order to foment opposition to unpopular governmental policies.

The Sufi Order

Cities, villages, and marketplaces are environments conducive to the Islamic way of life. Into these social environments, which themselves are typical of most civilizations, Koran and Sunna are woven to produce distinctively Islamic cultural patterns. The term *society* refers to such structured collectives as tribes, towns, cities, and neighborhoods. Society is structured by layers of social strata, ethnic and sectarian boundaries, and other demarcations that serve to organize and regulate human behavior.

Brotherhoods and religious orders comprise social contexts of a different type than those described earlier in this chapter. The term *community* is more appropriately applied to these religious orders. In Islam, the concept of Umma,

[17] Gustav Thaiss, "The Bazaar as a Case Study of Religion and Social Change," in *Iran Faces the Seventies*, ed. Ehsan Yar-Shater (New York: Praeger Publishers, Inc., 1971), p. 193.

defined as the community of believers living by the teachings of Koran and Sunna, has been an ideal that has stood in tension with the realities of everyday life. Community is created annually by Hajjis on the road to Mecca. But the pilgrim's common state of consecration (Ihram) is temporary; each Hajji must return to his or her home town, where society is more structured, less egalitarian. Therefore, like other religious traditions, Islam has witnessed the departure of some individuals and groups who were dissatisfied with society. Many wandered from town to village, wanting no earthly home for themselves. Others formed brotherhoods or communities on faraway frontier outposts or in compounds built within or near towns and cities. They were Sufis. The social significance of Sufi orders also derives from Koran and Sunna, but the impetus for Sufis has been to live in *community,* not society.

The institution of the Sufi order is a combined spiritual and social response to several developments in Islamic history. First, from the earliest days of conquest and empire, many Muslims felt that the acquisition of wealth and worldly gain had destroyed the possibility of one's living according to Koran and Sunna. These Muslims preferred a life of asceticism, that is, a life of poverty for the sake of God. Second, the formal structure of Islam, as defined and implemented by the Ulema, has seemed to some Muslims a much too static environment within which to experience religion. Especially among simpler folk, religious needs for a more personal *experience* of the divine have been felt. Thus many Muslims have chosen to live in a community under the spiritual guidance of a respected Shaykh or holy man, a saint who in the eyes of his followers displays signs of his nearness to God.[18] Third, as Islam expanded into such regions as Africa and India, where other religious traditions were quite alien to Koran and Sunna, the exclusivist claims of Sunni and Shiᶜite Islam, requiring absolute conversion, have set Islam over and against other traditions. The more universalistic, inclusive, and encompassing qualities of Sufism have proved to be more successful in bringing non-Muslims and the uneducated into contact with the literary demands of Koran and Sunna.

The Sufis' search for union (Tawhid) with God through living in community rather than society has created certain tensions with the more orthodox Ulema establishment. For one thing, the Sufis have developed their own interpretations of Koran and Sunna, and as a result charges of heresy have often been leveled against them by the Ulema, especially, as we saw in Chapter 5, during the late Middle Ages. Another problem has been the broad, popular appeal that many Sufi saints and Shaykhs have enjoyed, often at the expense of popular respect for the Ulema. Still another problem, again of interpretation, can be found in Sufi forms of worship. Music, dancing, poetry, and even prayers—either forbidden or carefully regulated in the interpretations of Koran and Sunna by the Ulema—are emotionally exploited in the communal and private rituals of mystical Islam. Although especially in more recent times Sufi orders have

[18] The term for "saint" is *wālī,* which has the connotation of "friend of God."

become more like voluntary associations, and thus less like separate institutions apart from Islamic society, Sufism remains an important area of study for the student who wishes to grasp the variety of expressions within Islamic culture.

THE TARIQA. The Arabic term *ṭarīqa* can mean both "path" and "method." In Sufism a Tariqa is both a way of life and a set of religious practices that focus on God through distinct interpretations of Koran and Sunna. Like the Shiᶜites, who derive their special teachings from the traditional lore of the twelve Imams, Sufis preserve the sacred biographies of revered saints, whose near miraculous lives form models of behavior for the Sufi Tariqa.

By the eleventh century, Tariqa acquired a social significance as well. It designated a common life (community) of several disciples living under the spiritual supervision of the Shaykh. Thus the social concept of Umma became for Sufis the Tariqa, and the functions of the Ulema were performed by the saint or Shaykh. From the eleventh century until the present day hundreds of Tariqas have formed, in most lands where Islam has spread. Most of these Tariqas belong to one of a dozen main lines that trace their spiritual heritage back to famous saints in the Middle Ages. Each saint in turn possessed a spiritual heritage which could be traced to the Prophet Muhammad, and thus to God. This treelike structure with a single source and a diffusion of branches forms the background of the world view and sacred history that characterize mystical Islam.[19]

The impact of the religious and social notions of Tariqa upon Islam has been considerable, with effects felt beyond Sufi organizations themselves. In a geographic sense, the numerous shrines and mausolea of Sufi saints that dot the landscape in many Muslim countries have become focal points of local pilgrimages. The shrines, through the blessings or Baraka of their founding saints, attract the common folk of nearby villages. Although the common folk making pilgrimages to Sufi shrines do not normally strike out on the Sufi path as a constant way of life, the shrines encourage social gatherings that have the significance of creating a temporary experience of community for people in local regions. Observers report that Christian, Hindu, and other religious peoples also visit the shrines of Sufi saints. Thus Sufism, more than Shiᶜite and Sunni Islam, has an ecumenical spirit about it that has avoided interfaith polemics while at the same time attracting conversions to Islam.

The Sufi Tariqas have also played important social and educational roles in local villages and within neighborhoods of cities. Ammar reports that in the village of Silwa, Egypt, the Nakshabandi Sufi order is present to the extent that a Shaykh of that Tariqa maintains a headquarters in a room adjacent to the village mosque. Young men gather for the evening prayers, led by the Nakshabandi

[19] A useful historical survey of the Sufi orders in Islam is J. Spencer Trimingham, *The Sufi Orders in Islam* (New York: Oxford University Press, 1971). Among other things, Trimingham discusses the main Tariqa lines, how the orders were organized socially, and the rituals and forms of worship followed by different orders.

Shaykh. The disciples thus live with their families and work or perhaps attend the village school during the day. At night in a room of the mosque, young disciples stand around the Shaykh to perform the Sufi form of prayer known as the *dhikr. Dhikr* means "remembrance," and for Sufis, who believe the world causes one to forget God, prayer consists of repeating the name of God hundreds, perhaps thousands of times. As the chanting proceeds, the circle of young men begins to sway back and forth, the tempo increasing as the Shaykh, standing in the center, claps his hands or himself dances. This part of the Dhikr is punctuated every quarter of an hour or so by cessation of dancing and chanting while the Shaykh recites a religious poem attributed to a saint from the sacred history of the Tariqa.[20]

In villages like Silwa, the youths who are sent to Sufi schools and Dhikrs are known as young men of "the Path" (Tariqa). They are often from families that cannot afford the expense of sending their children to schools in the cities, or from families who wish their children to have a more religious education than can be had in the state-run village schools. Combining education by oral tradition (in the poems and teachings of the Shaykh) with the social solidarity experienced in the Dhikr, the Tariqa performs important social and religious functions in Islamic society, especially among the poorer, less educated village people.

The village is not the entire extent or only social place occupied by Sufism, today or in the past. The mystical dimension of Islam has been felt and experienced at all levels of Islamic society. Sufi Shaykhs and intellectuals have also ranked among the higher echelons of the Ulema. The study of Islam is not complete without a consideration of Sufism, and Sufism cannot be understood apart from the cultural and religious context of Islam.[21]

---

[20] Ammar, *Egyptian Village,* p. 187.

[21] Two works are highly recommended to those who wish to learn more about Sufism. Annemarie Schimmel, *The Mystical Dimension of Islam* (Chapel Hill: University of North Carolina Press, 1975), brings together a massive amount of material by Muslim and non-Muslim scholars who have studied Sufism in depth, and the author's own insights are extremely valuable. Martin Lings, *A Sufi Saint of the Twentieth Century* (Berkeley and Los Angeles: University of California Press, 1973) is a sensitive biographical study of a North African saint, Shaykh Ahmad al-Alawi, and of his social and religious impact on his disciples and the people of the surrounding area.

8

tradition and change in islam

Allāhu akbar, the Islamic declaration of divine majesty which has summoned the faithful to prayer for more than thirteen centuries, opened the pages of this book. We now come to the final pages, again with reference to the unifying theme of the people and faith we have studied: God is the Greatest! Of course, the history of Islam is far from over. As Wilfred Cantwell Smith has said, "a Muslim might presumably look forward to . . . another thirteen centuries still to come."[1] Whatever the future may be for Islam, it will draw from past structures and symbols essential to its tradition, and as in the past, it will confront the forces of history, and there will be change. As long as there is history, religious traditions will change. Islam changed during the period of the rightly guided caliphs from a local cult in Arabia to a world religion. Forms of leadership and government have changed in every major period since the beginning. The ethnic and linguistic composition of the Islamic world has changed. The bulk of the population of the world of Islam now lies far to the east of Arabia and the central lands of the once great caliphate; yet, the twentieth-century strategic position of much of the Middle East with respect to oil and international politics will continue to bring about changes for Muslim peoples in that region. In the future as well as in the present and the past, "God is the Greatest" expresses an underlying foundation upon which the edifice of Islam is built and presumably will con-

[1] From Wilfred Cantwell Smith, *Islam in Modern History* (copyright © 1957 by Wilfred Cantwell Smith; Princeton Paperback, 1977), published by Princeton University Press, p. 11. Reprinted by permission of Princeton University Press.

FIGURE 8.1. Sun setting over mosque in Cairo. (Photo by B. P. Wolff. Courtesy of the United Nations.)

tinue to stand. Within that structure the religious kaleidoscope of images expressed in myth, ritual, symbol, art, social groupings, and historic events blend together to form variegated but changing patterns that join at one point: *Allāhu akbar!*

SACRED PARADIGMS IN HISTORY

Robert N. Bellah, in an interesting essay on the modernization process in Islam, has said that "the early community under the prophet and the rightly guided caliphs is a paradigm to which [Muslims] return again and again and from which they draw an understanding of their own times. *Qur'an* and Sunna are the glasses through which many Muslims view the world, and it is essential that we discern the shapes they see."[2] Islam has always and everywhere existed in real communities of ordinary human beings involved in meeting the necessities of physical and spiritual life. In this respect Islam differs little from other societies. But the cultural patterns and structures distinctive to Islam are the result of the power and effect of lives lived in response to symbols that stand outside of human experience *except in the Islamic context.* These symbols interact within the context of history in the way of life called "Islamic."

[2] Robert N. Bellah, "Islamic Tradition and the Problems of Modernization," in *Beyond Belief: Essays on Religion in a Post-Traditional World* (New York: Harper and Row, Publishers, Inc., 1970), p. 149.

According to Bellah, among the structural elements and paradigms that emerged in early Islam and continued to act in history were four that are familiar in these pages. In Bellah's words,

> First was a conception of a transcendent monotheistic God standing outside the natural universe and related to it as creator and judge. Second was the call to selfhood and decision from such a God through the preaching of his prophet to every individual human being. Third was the radical devaluation . . . of all existing social structures in the face of this central God-man relationship. This meant the removal of kinship, which had been the chief locus of the sacred in pre-Islamic Arabia, from its central significance. And finally, there was a new conception of political order based on the participation of all those who accepted the divine revelation and thus constituted themselves in a new community, *umma*.[3]

There are, of course, many other paradigms and symbols in Islam. But these four—transcendent God (*Allāhu Akbar!*), personal salvation, new social structures, and a new polity—were viewed in decisive ways through the lenses of Koran and Sunna.

We have seen in earlier chapters, for example, that kinship patterns have varied throughout Islamic history, and they have differed in nomadic, rural, and urban environments. But the Islamic context in all of these cases has emerged in one way or another, such as through tribal heads or Sufi Shaykhs tracing biological or spiritual pedigrees back to the Prophet and his companions, or through attempts to live in confessional rather than kinship communities. Similarly, an Islamic polity based upon the Islamic concept of Umma traces its origins to the sacred time of the Prophet in Medina. As further implemented under the rightly guided caliphs, the Umma was both an ideal and a historic reality. It was an ideal in the sense that the sacred history of the Prophet and the Patriarchal period of his rightly guided successors as heads of the Umma established norms by which succeeding generations have judged themselves. It was a historical reality in the sense that the community in those early years developed different sectarian paths and responses to Koran and Sunna that subsequently gave the totality of Islam its rich variety. Under first the Umayyads then the Abbasids, the paradigm of "caliphate" played itself out and finally collapsed as a historical reality, even though as an ideal it has continued to occupy the minds of some Muslims. Yet, without the caliphate, Islamic polities have continued to form with or in spite of the Ulema, with varying degrees of control or submission to the sultans and secular rulers of later regional empires and national states. In the second half of the twentieth century we continue to see Islamic responses to secular forces with different attempts to reinstate the early paradigms.

---

[3] Bellah, *Beyond Belief*, p. 151.

THE OLD AND THE NEW IN THE YET-TO-COME

Terms such as "secularization," "modernization," and "westernization" often come into the discussion of what is happening to religion in the present day. All three terms denote a process of change, and often the connotation is that religion or the religious dimension of life for modern humankind is eroding because of secular elements. In the Islamic world many religious leaders have made the distinction that Islam must modernize but not westernize. By this they usually mean that using technology in such areas as education, social welfare, and management of the economy is permissible and desirable, but that Western values should not be allowed to transform the Islamic base of society. For example, in Iran and elsewhere the struggle over values has been expressed in public debates about traditional versus Western modes of attire, and about the traditional role of women versus feminist reforms. Here again we see broadly human issues that, in the Islamic context, can be understood only with reference to symbols and paradigms that have long shaped Muslim ways of life.

It is tempting, but probably myopic, to understand the process of secularization as most acute in our own time. We need only recall that in Islam the Umayyad caliphate (661–750) was viewed by many Muslim religious leaders and historians as being terribly secular and unresponsive to the scriptural mandates of the Shari^{c}a. Yet by the end of the Umayyad Age, Islamic developments in the establishment of a religious literary tradition in Arabic were gaining serious momentum. This affected both the new Abbasid caliphate and Islamic society as a whole.

Although there can be no doubt that Western political and economic interests in the Middle East have done much toward effecting changes in traditional Islamic ways of life, the relation of these changes to the Islamic tradition itself must not be overlooked. As Bellah has said, modernization

> . . . does not create [forces of destruction and rebellion in traditional societies such as in Islam]. Rather, they emerge from patterns of motivation and relationship already existing in the traditional society. That is why modernization cannot be treated as a simple unitary process. Everywhere it takes effect only in relation to the tensions and forces, the historical bent, of particular societies.[4]

It would be wrong, then, for Muslims or non-Muslims to hang the future of Islam entirely on the peg of the struggle between tradition versus outside, secular forces. For thirteen centuries Islam has been carried across mountains, deserts and oceans to new lands and peoples, and even when Islamic lands were being conquered by outside powers the Islamic faith survived by responding to the new conditions. Presumably, the symbols and paradigms that have made responses successful in the past still contain power. Bellah's point is that Koran, Sunna and

[4] Bellah, p. 159.

their productive interpretation are the property and responsibility of Muslims. Modernization in Islam—and this will mean different things in different places—will involve change in relation to tradition.

The question of women's rights, to take the previous example, arises in the Islamic context only in part because it also arises in other societies that impinge upon the Islamic world. It is also an inherent Islamic question, however, because the Prophet Muhammad brought social and legal reforms that improved the status of women, children, and the family generally in seventh-century Arabia. The actual status of women in the Islamic world is the result of tradition in the making over the centuries; that is, it is the result of how succeeding generations have chosen to interpret and implement the Shari^ca with respect to local custom and practice. What changes are yet to come in regard to the rights of women and family life generally will be seen by Muslims through the lenses of Koran and Sunna, especially the symbols and paradigms therein that bear upon this question.

The "Islamic revival," talked about so much by modern scholars and in the public media as well, is also related to both modernization and tradition. In Chapter 5 we discussed the reforms sought by such late nineteenth- and early twentieth-century thinkers as Muhammad Abduh and Jamal al-Din al-Afghani. They were Muslims who saw both the advantages and disadvantages of Western science and technology from a Muslim perspective, and they urged reforms in education and social programs so that Islam could become a vital force in the *modern* era. Their approach to resolving the tension between tradition and modernism has led to a solution that is generally called "Islamic modernism." Islamic modernists urge better systems of education in both traditional and modern curricula, and they usually argue for modern forms of government (as opposed to a revival of the caliphate or promoting the Ulema to positions of statecraft) run by Muslims educated in the Koran and other roots of their tradition.

Islamic revival, however, has seen another, more "conservative" development in the twentieth century, and most Western historians did not recognize this phenomenon until the late 1970's. The reason is that the intellectual and spiritual vision that has powered the Islamic revival in recent times came not from westernized or Western-educated Muslims (accessible to Western scholars), but rather from Muslims who have bypassed modern reforms in favor of a revival of a purely Islamic principle of government, economics, social structures, and public morality. Such revivalists did not turn up in Western universities, and their activities were either unknown or considered irrelevant until recently. The revivalists have usually called for a more active role for the Ulema in government and public life, and for a revival of models from the time of the Prophet, the Age of the Rashidun, and the Golden Age of the Abbasids. Such revivalist movements have sprung up in both Sunni Muslim lands such as Pakistan, and Shi^cite lands such as Iran; however, they are quite active and vocal throughout the world of Islam. The revivalists have found new power in traditional Muslim symbols, and they have usually sought to champion those symbols not by assimilation or accommodation to modernist reforms or through Western alliances, but by reviving their vision of traditional Islam to the exclusion of the values and systems of the West.

Although many of the revivalist solutions may appear to be extremist and too archaic to succeed, there can be no doubt that many Muslims have chosen to throw their lot with attempts at reform and revival. Intellectual respectability is once more returning to Muslims in public life who have knowledge of the Koran, Sunna, and other traditional repositories of Islamic symbols and spiritual guidance. Muslims are writing more frequently on such subjects as "Islamic economics," "Islamic government," and other vital issues to which Islamic interpretations can be given. A new consensus of Muslim intellectuals, businessmen, and political and religious leaders is emerging.

The solutions offered by modernists, revivalists, leftists, and pro-Western secularists will probably achieve a consensus that accommodates modernism to tradition in various ways depending upon local circumstances. We must be prepared to discover that the process of change now occurring in the world of Islam marks yet another exciting and promising stage of Islamic history. These will not be the still-life studies of the classical Islamic past, however; now *we* are contemporaries of what is happening in the world of Islam today. Muslims and non-Muslims alike must negotiate between the rich heritage of the past and the challenges and opportunities of the present and future. Perhaps in a curious way we may learn something about the dimensions of our own predicament by witnessing the various attempts of others to preserve the integrities of their own tradition in viable modes for the present. Their solutions may not be ours, and ours may not be theirs, but the search for solutions is a striking common ground for humankind caught, as it always is, between the past and future.

We cannot try to discern the present, much less guess about the future, without learning about the past. A cultural perspective on Islam encompases all aspects of human life. We have tried here to confront the problem of learning how to interpret and explain the process of symbolization and of arriving at meanings in the Islamic world. There can never be a final word on this subject. Muslims repeat a symbol from the Koran that very aptly must be the last word here: *Allāhu aᶜlam aḥkam*—God is the most knowing, the most wise!

Glossary

This glossary includes most of the terms which may be unfamiliar to newcomers to the study of Islam. Names of ideas and concepts that are not found in this glossary as well as names of places and personalities can be found in the book by using the index. Each item in the glossary presents the term as it is spelled in the book followed by a set of parentheses that give technical spellings. The spelling in italics indicates the common form of the Arabic word in transliteration; the unitalicized form indicates the spelling of the title of the relevant article in the *Encyclopaedia of Islam* (1st or 2nd editions) and the *Shorter Encyclopaedia of Islam* if the spelling in these sources is other than the italicized spelling.

Abode of Islam (*dār al-islām*) a religio-political term for land under Muslim rule.

Abode of War (*dār al-ḥarb*) a religio-political term for land that is not under Muslim rule or under treaty with Muslim rulers.

Adab (*adab*) knowledge and learning in poetry and literature, particularly of an urbane, witty, and secular nature. Hence Adab came to be distinguished from religious knowledge on the one hand and scientific knowledge on the other. Today Adab means the study of literature.

Alid a term for a Shiᶜite who has descended from the family of Ali, the Prophet's cousin snd son-in-law.

Ashura (*ᶜāshūrā'*) the "tenth" of Muharram, originally an important day of fasting, now also a Shiᶜite sacred anniversary commemorating the martyrdom of the third Imam, Husayn.

Aya (*āya*) a verse of the Koran. Aya has another related meaning of "sign," "miracle," or "mark." Thus the honorific title of *Ayatollah* means "mark of Allah" and designates a higher member of the Shiᶜite Ulema.

Baraka (*baraka*) a spiritual blessing derived from the power of holiness associated with a Sufi saint, the saint's tomb, or other auspicious manifestation of God's power.

Bazaar (*bāzār*) marketplace (see *Suq*).

Bedouin (*Badw*) a pastoral nomad of Arabian blood and/or linguistic and cultural stock found chiefly in Syria, Arabia, and North Africa.

Caliph (*khalīfa*) the "successor" or "viceregent" of the Prophet who was elected (appointed or otherwise designated) to head the Muslim state. The office of caliph or *Caliphate* was subsumed under three periods, the latter two of which were dynastic: the Rashidun (632–661); The Umayyads (661–750); and the Abbasids (750–1258). The caliph was also known as "Imam (leader) and "Commander of the Faithful."

Dhikr (*dhikr*) "remembrance" (with the mind) or "mentioning" (with the tongue) Allah or the many names of Allah. Dhikr is a Sufi term for spiritual exercises that focus the consciousness upon God.

Dhimmi (*dhimmī;* Dhimma) a tolerated religious people of the Book (that is, primarily Jews and Christians) living within lands under the caliphate and with the right of retaining their non-Muslim religious status in exchange for payment of a poll tax and observing certain other obligations to the Muslim body politic.

Hadith (*ḥadīth*) a tradition or saying traced back to the Prophet through a chain of trusted human transmitters. The orthodox collections of Hadith comprise the literary record of the Prophet's Sunna or customary practice.

Hajj (*ḥajj;* Ḥadjdj) pilgrimage to Mecca, the fifth Pillar of Islam. It is a duty for every Muslim to make the Hajj once in his or her lifetime if they are physically, mentally and financially able to do so; women must make the journey under the protection of male members of their families.

Haram (*ḥaram*) the sacred space or territory associated with the cities of Mecca, Medina, and Jerusalem. The Shari^{c}a prohibits certain activities within the Haram and enjoins others (see *Muhrim*).

Hijra (*ḥijra,* Lat. Hegira; Ḥidjra) the migration of the Prophet and his followers from Mecca to Yathrib (henceforth called Medina) in A.D. 622 (= A.H. 1).

Ibadat (^{c}*ibādāt*) the ordinances of Muslim worship and rituals explained and interpreted in the Shari^{c}a by the Ulema. The Ibadat generally include rules governing ritual purity, prayer, alms, fasting, and pilgrimage.

Ihram see *Muhrim.*

Imam (*imām;* Imām, Imāma) a term for spiritual leaders in Islam; hence in the most general form the leader of the prayer (Salat). In Shi^{c}ite Islam "Imam" designates the specially revered descendants of Ali (Alids) who led the Shi^{c}ite community during the early centuries and whose teachings Shi^{c}ites preserve as special sources of insight into Koran and Sunna.

Ja^{c}fari The orthodox school of interpreting the Shari^{c}a to which most Shi^{c}ites adhere. The name is derived from the sixth Imam, Ja^{c}far al-Sadiq.

Jahiliyya (*jāhiliyya;* Djāhilīya) the Muslim designation for the cultural and religious state of affairs in Arabia prior to the rise of Islam. Jahiliyya is often translated "Time of Ignorance" or "Time of Paganism."

Jihad (*jihād;* Djihād) "striving" for moral and religious perfection within the Muslim community and in response to the specific needs of the community, including bearing arms in defense of Islam. One who so strives for moral and religious perfection is a *Mujtahid,* a patriot or citizen of Islam. Jihad as "holy war" must be seen in this broader context; martyrdom in the context of Jihad promises certain rewards in Paradise.

Ka^{c}ba (*ka^{c}ba*) the cube-shaped stone building in the center of the courtyard of the Great Mosque in Mecca; in the eastern corner is set the famous black stone. The Ka^{c}ba is the most important shrine in Islam. It serves as the focal point of the prayer (Salat) and the destination of the pilgrimage (Hajj).

Kafir (*kāfir*) one who is "ungrateful" and unresponsive to God's blessings; hence a general term for an unbeliever.

Koran (*qur'ān;* Ḳur'ān) the "recitation(s)" that comprise the sacred scripture of Islam. The Koran was revealed by Allah through His angel Gabriel to Muhammad and hence to the Arabs in Mecca and Medina. The Koran is a perfect Arabic revelation in both its literary and oral forms.

Madrasa (*madrasa*) a school, often associated with mosques, in which the religious subjects of Islam are studied in the traditional manner.

Mawla (*mawlā,* pl. *mawālī*) a slave or other non-Muslim captured under Islamic conquest then freed by virtue, usually, of becoming Muslim. Mawalis are often referred to as "clients" because in early Islam they were required to associate with a sponsoring tribe.

Mihrab (*miḥrāb*) a "niche" within the mosque wall that is closest to Mecca. The Mihrab serves to orient Muslim worshippers toward Mecca during the prayer (Salat).

Minbar, Mimbar (*minbar*) an ornate flight of stairs atop which is a seat from which a sermon is delivered to worshippers in a mosque, especially during the Friday midday prayer. The Minbar or "pulpit" is a podium for political and social as well as religious messages.

Mosque (*masjid, jāmi^{c};* Masdjid) literally, the "place of prostration" for Muslim prayers. The larger central mosques in Muslim cities are known as Jami^{c}s because they are the places of "gathering" or "assembly" for the Friday prayer.

Muharram (*al-muḥarram*) the first month of the Muslim calendar. The first of Muharram is celebrated as New Years for all Muslims; the tenth of Muharram (Ashura) is an especially sacred holiday for Shi^{c}ite Muslims.

Muhrim (*muḥrim*) a Muslim who has entered the state of consecration (Ihram, *iḥrām*) appropriate to entering the sacred precincts of Mecca for the purpose of pilgrimage (Hajj). A Muhrim is distinguished by the special attire of simple white garments (also called *Ihram*).

Mu^c^tazilites (*mu^c^tazilī,* Mu^c^tazila) a theological school or movement in the classical period of early Islam that accepted reason as a primary criterion for establishing the validity of the content of Muslim beliefs.

Qibla (*qibla,* Ḳibla) the direction of Mecca (more precisely, the Ka^c^ba in Mecca) toward which Muslims orient themselves for the prayer (Salat).

Salat (*ṣalāt*) canonical prayer, the second Pillar of Islam. The Salat is performed facing the Ka^c^ba (in Mecca) during five periods throughout the day and evening. The times of the Salat are called out from the minarets of mosques by a muezzin, "one who calls the prayer times."

Sawm (*ṣawm* or *ṣiyām*) fasting, the fourth Pillar of Islam. Sawm is meritorious at any time, but it is a duty during the daylight hours of the ninth month, Ramadan.

Shakir (*shākir*) a term for a Muslim in the sense of "one who is grateful" to God for His blessings.

Shari^c^a (*sharī^c^a*) the term for sacred law which is derived from revelation (the Koran) and the example of the Prophet (Sunna, Hadith) through the activities of the Ulema.

Shaykh (*shaykh,* Shaikh) a term for "maturity" and hence "wisdom" and "authority" in Muslim religious leaders. A Shaykh is often a teacher, a Sufi master, or other respected member of the Ulema.

Shaytan (*shayṭān,* S̲haiṭān) Satan, or a satanlike unseen being or spirit that operates within the Muslim cosmology (the realms of Heaven and Earth).

Shi^c^i, Shi^c^ite (*shī^c^ī,* S̲hī^c^a) a designation of a minority of Muslims (about 10%, living primarily in Iran and Iraq today) who trace their spiritual heritage to the Prophet through his cousin Ali. Shi^c^ites assert Ali's special knowledge of the meaning of the Shari^c^a, gained directly from the Prophet, and passed down through 5, 7, or 12 Imams who descended from Ali.

Shirk (*shirk*) a term for polytheism or "associating" other deities with Allah. Shirk was and is a particularly repugnant form of heresy in Islam.

Sufi (*ṣufī,* Taṣawwuf) an Islamic ascetic or, more recently, mystic who belongs to a spiritual brotherhood and who practices a specific life of discipline.

Sunna (*sunna*) The customary practice of the Prophet as reported by his Companions, concerning Muhammad's deeds, utterances and unspoken approval. The Sunna is a source of authority in Islam second only to the Koran.

Sunni (*sunnī*) a designation of the vast majority of orthodox Muslims (about 90%). Sunnis acknowledge the authority of the Koran and Sunna as interpreted by the Ulema, but not the authority of the Alid Imams.

Suq (*sūq,* Suḳ) the marketplace which, in Islam, has traditionally been governed by provisions in the Shari^c^a. Hence the Suq (or *Bazaar* in Persian) has religious and social as well as economic significance.

Sura (*sūra*) the name of the chapters of the Koran. There are 114 suras; these were revealed to Muhammad at Mecca and Medina.

Tariqa (*ṭarīqa,* Tarīḳa) a term meaning "method," "way" which designates both a Sufi brotherhood as an institution and the special teaching and practice associated with each brotherhood.

Tawhid (*tawḥīd*) "making one" or "asserting the oneness" of God. The "science of Tawhid" is a term for Islamic theology. Experiencing oneness or Tawhid with Allah is a spiritual aspiration of Sufis.

Traditions see *Hadith.*

Ulema (*ᶜulamā'*) a plural form of *ᶜalīm,* "one who possesses knowledge" in the sciences of Islam. The Ulema study and apply the religious sciences such as the disciplined study of Koran, Hadith, and law. As a class of nonordained religious functionaries, the Ulema play important socio-political roles as a buffer between the commonality and the government.

Umma (*umma*) a Koranic term for a community that is part of God's plan of salvation, that is, a people to whom prophets have been sent with a scriptural message. The Islamic Umma is constituted by the Koran and Sunna.

Waqf (*waqf,* Waḳf) a pious disposal of land and other kinds of property which provides for endowment income to be administered by the Ulema for religious and charitable purposes.

Wudu' (*wuḍū'*) an act of ritual ablution (purification) performed prior to the prayer (Salat).

Zakat (*zakāt*) "alms" or a pious tax to provide for the poor, the third Pillar of Islam. Calculated on the basis of certain kinds of property (including personal income), today the Zakat is usually given at the end of the Hijra year on a voluntary basis to individuals in need and to charitable institutions as prescribed by the Shariᶜa.

Zawiya (*zāwiya*) a gathering place for Sufis, whether a room in a mosque, a saint's shrine, or an entire compound of buildings around a mosque.

Zindiq (*zindīq,* Zindīḳ) a term originally for the Mazdakite heresy of ancient Persia. "Zindiq" came to designate a heretic whose teaching was regarded as a danger to the state.

Bibliography

REFERENCES

Bacharach, Jere L. *A Near Eastern Studies Handbook, 570–1974.* Rev. ed. Seattle: University of Washington Press, 1977.

Encyclopaedia of Islam. 2nd ed. Ed. H. A. R. Gibb et al. Leiden: E. J. Brill, 1960–.

Holt, P. M., Ann K. S. Lambton, and **Bernard Lewis,** eds. *The Cambridge History of Islam.* 2 vols. Cambridge, England: Cambridge University Press, 1970 (with additional volumes and parts).

Pearson, James Douglas, compiler. *Index Islamicus, 1906–1955: A Catalogue of Articles on Islamic Subjects in Periodicals and Other Collective Publications.* Cambridge, England: W. Heffner & Sons, Ltd., 1958 (with supplemental volumes).

Roolvink, Roelof. *Historical Atlas of the Muslim Peoples.* Amsterdam: Djambatan, 1957.

Sauvaget, Jean. *Introduction to the History of the Muslim East: A Bibliographical Guide.* Based on second French edition; Berkeley: University of California Press, 1965.

Shorter Encyclopaedia of Islam. Ed. H. A. R. Gibb and J. H. Kramers. Ithaca, N.Y.: Cornell University Press, 1953.

Weekes, Richard V., ed. *Muslim Peoples: A World Ethnographic Survey.* Westport, Conn.: Greenwood Press, 1978.

ISLAMIC SOCIAL AND POLITICAL HISTORY

Ahmad, Aziz. *Studies in Islamic Culture in the Indian Environment.* Oxford: Clarendon Press, 1964.

Berger, Morroe. *The Arab World Today.* Garden City, N.Y.: Doubleday & Co., Inc., 1962.

Gibb, Hamilton Alexander Rosskeen. *Studies on the Civilization of Islam.* Ed. Stanford J. Shaw and William R. Polk. Boston: Beacon Press, 1962.

Hitti, Philip Khuri. *History of the Arabs from the Earliest Times to the Present.* 10th ed. New York: St. Martin's Press, 1970.

Hodgson, Marshall G. *The Venture of Islam: Conscience and History in a World Civilization.* 3 vols. Chicago: University of Chicago Press, 1974.

Keddie, Nikkie R., ed. *Scholars, Saints, and Sufis: Muslim Religious Institutions in the Middle East Since 1500.* Berkeley: University of California Press, 1972.

Lewis, Bernard. *The Arabs in History.* 2nd rev. ed. New York: Harper and Row, Publishers, Inc., 1967.

———. *The Assassins: A Radical Sect in Islam.* New York: Basic Books, Inc., Publishers, 1968.

———. *Islam in History: Ideas, Men and Events in the Middle East.* London: Alcove Press, 1973.

Peters, Francis E. *Allah's Commonwealth: A History of Islam in the Near East, 600–1100 A.D. New York: Simon and Schuster, Inc., 1973.*

Smith, Wilfred Cantwell. *Islam in Modern History.* Princeton, N.J.: Princeton University Press, 1957.

Trimingham, John Spencer. *The Influence of Islam Upon Africa.* New York: Praeger Publishers, Inc., 1968.

Watt, William Montgomery. *A History of Islam in Spain,* with additional sections on literature by P. Cachia. Edinburgh: Edinburgh University Press, 1965.

———. *The Influence of Islam on Medieval Europe.* Edinburgh: Edinburgh University Press, 1972.

SURVEYS OF ISLAMIC ART, CULTURE, AND CIVILIZATION

Grabar, Oleg. *The Formation of Islamic Art.* New Haven: Yale University Press, 1973.

Kühnel, Ernst. *Islamic Art and Architecture.* Trans. Katherine Watson. London: G. Bell & Sons, Ltd., 1966.

———. *The Minor Arts of Islam.* Trans. Katherine Watson. Ithaca, N.Y.: Cornell University Press, 1970.

Lewis, Bernard, ed. *Islam and the Arab World.* New York: Alfred A. Knopf, Inc., 1976.

Nicholson, Reynold Alleyne. *A Literary History of the Arabs.* 2nd ed. Cambridge, England: Cambridge University Press, 1930.

Rice, David Talbot. *Islamic Art.* London: Thames and Hudson, 1965.

Savory, R. M., ed. *Introduction to Islamic Civilization.* New York: Cambridge University Press, 1976.

ISLAMIC RELIGION

Arberry, Arthur John. *The Koran Interpreted: A Translation.* New York: Macmillan, Inc., 1955.

———, ed. *Religion in the Middle East: Three Religions in Concord and Conflict.* 2 vols. London: Cambridge University Press, 1969.

———. *Sufism: An Account of the Mystics of Islam.* London: George Allen & Unwin, 1950.

Chelkowski, Peter J., ed. *Ta^{c}ziyeh: Ritual and Drama in Iran.* New York: New York University Press, 1979.

Cragg, Kenneth. *The Call of the Minaret.* New York: Oxford University Press, 1956.

———. *The Event of the Qur'ān: Islam in Its Scripture.* London: George Allen & Unwin, 1971.

———. *The Mind of the Quran: Chapters in Reflection.* London: George Allen & Unwin, 1973.

Cätje, Helmut. *The Qur'ān and Its Exegesis: Selected Texts with Classical and Modern Muslim Interpretation.* Trans. Alford T. Welch. Berkeley: University of California Press, 1977.

Gibb, Hamilton Alexander Rosskeen. *Mohammedanism: An Historical Survey.* 2nd ed. London: Oxford University Press, 1961.

Kamal, Ahmed. *The Sacred Journey Being Pilgrimage to Makkah.* New York: Duell, Sloan and Pearce, 1961.

Nasr, Sayyed Hossein. *Ideals and Realities of Islam.* Boston: Beacon Press, 1972.

Pickthall, Marmaduke William. *The Meaning of The Glorious Koran: A Bi-lingual Edition with English Translation, Introduction and Notes.* Albany: State University of New York Press, 1976.

Rahman, Fazlur. *Islam.* 2nd ed. Chicago: University of Chicago Press, 1979.

______. *Major Themes of the Qur'ān.* Chicago: Bibliotheca Islamica, 1980.

Schimmel, Annemarie. *Mystical Dimensions of Islam.* Chapel Hill: University of North Carolina Press, 1975.

Trimingham, John Spencer. *The Sufi Orders in Islam.* Oxford: Clarendon Press, 1971.

Watt, William Montgomery. *Bell's Introduction to the Qur'ān.* Edinburgh: Edinburgh University Press, 1970.

———. *Muhammad, Prophet and Statesman.* London: Oxford University Press, 1964.

ISLAMIC THOUGHT AND LEARNING

Fakhry, Majid. *A History of Islamic Philosophy.* New York: Columbia University Press, 1970.

Hourani, Albert Habib. *Arabic Thought in the Liberal Age.* London, New York: Oxford University Press, 1962.

Nasr, Sayyed Hossein. *Science and Civilization in Islam.* Cambridge, Mass.: Harvard University Press, 1968.

———. *Three Muslim Sages: Avicenna, Suhrawardī, Ibn ᶜArabī.* Cambridge, Mass.: Harvard University Press, 1964.

Rahman, Fazlur. *The Philosophy of Mulla Sadra.* Albany: State University of New York Press, 1975.

———. *Prophecy in Islam: Philosophy and Orthodoxy.* London: George Allen & Unwin, 1958.

Sharif, Mian Muhammad, ed. *A History of Muslim Philosophy.* 2 vols. Wiesbaden: Otto Harrassowitz, 1963–1966.

Watt, William Montgomery. *The Faith and Practice of al-Ghazali.* London: George Allen and Unwin, 1953.

———. *The Formative Period of Islamic Thought.* Edinburgh: Edinburgh University Press, 1973.

———. *Islamic Philosophy and Theology.* Edinburgh: Edinburgh University Press, 1962.

———. *Islamic Political Thought: The Basic Concepts.* Edinburgh: Edinburgh University Press, 1968.

Index